KNOWLEDGE-BASED INTELLIGENT TECHNIQUES in INDUSTRY

D1420463

The CRC Press

International Series on Computational Intelligence

Series Editor
L.C. Jain, Ph.D.

L.C. Jain, R.P. Johnson, Y. Takefuji, and L.A. Zadeh
Knowledge-Based Intelligent Techniques in Industry

L.C. Jain and C.W. de Silva
Intelligent Adaptive Control: Industrial Applications

L.C. Jain and N.M. Martin
Fusion of Neural Networks, Fuzzy Systems, and Genetic Algorithms: Industrial Applications

H.N. Teodorescu, A. Kandel, and L.C. Jain
Fuzzy and Neuro-Fuzzy Systems in Medicine

C.L. Karr and L.M. Freeman
Industrial Applications of Genetic Algorithms

L.C. Jain and Beatrice Lazzerini
Knowledge-Based Intelligent Techniques in Character Recognition

L.C. Jain and V. Vemuri
Industrial Applications of Neural Networks

KNOWLEDGE-BASED
INTELLIGENT
TECHNIQUES
in INDUSTRY

Edited by
L.C. Jain
R.P. Johnson
Y. Takefuji
L.A. Zadeh

CRC Press
Boca Raton   London   New York   Washington, D.C.

Library of Congress Cataloging-in-Publication Data

Catalog record is available from the Library of Congress.

No claim to original U.S. Government works
International Standard Book Number 0-8493-9803-7
Printed in the United States of America 1 2 3 4 5 6 7 8 9 0
Printed on acid-free paper

PREFACE

The purpose of this book is to gather together research results from some of the more recent applications of knowledge-based signal processing. The emphasis in compiling the chapters has been to focus on those applications where the technology presents new ways to overcome difficult or previously intractable problems in industries where the payoff can be significant. The areas of industry covered include power distribution, transportation, medical and communications. The more general industry topics of scheduling and routing are also covered.

In general, the problems described are those of large, complex, distributed systems and the techniques that have been developed to deal with them are oriented to obtaining results rather than developing elegant new concepts in signal processing. This has resulted in an extremely interesting collection of papers that expose some of the practical problems that can be encountered in making a large signal processing system work in the real world. Two of the key practical factors addressed in these chapters are methods for extracting salient data from the vast amount of information presented by complex systems and methods for managing the complexity of models so that mechanisms can be developed to produce effective solutions in realistic time-scales. These two factors can be identified in almost any real-world signal processing problem and the solutions presented here may provide insight into practical approaches to deal with them.

The chapters of this collection are more likely to appeal to the applications researcher rather than the signal processing purist, since the techniques that have been used would appear to be already well understood in theory. However, one of the primary novelties of the collection is that it represents efforts to apply advanced signal processing techniques to real problems, in some cases where the risk of failure is not of minor academic significance, but could be catastrophic. Exposing signal processing techniques to the cold light of reality has a remarkable focusing effect and forces the researcher to choose those techniques that really do the job, rather than those that are the current "in thing". In a sense, this type of collection provides a much needed reality check on the more esoteric end of the spectrum of signal processing research and should provide a useful guide to direct future research into topics that are of real and practical significance.

The techniques that are reported on in these chapters are remarkable for their diversity. In general, the primary task has been to make automated systems more "human-like"; so, the primary technique employed has been fuzzy logic. The researchers have also been willing to use a variety of other methods, including biologically inspired techniques such as neural networks and genetic algorithms, as well as more conventional approaches such as predictive filtering and rule based techniques. In addition, there is an apparent trend to use combinations of these techniques to achieve specific capabilities that cannot be obtained from individual techniques. In a sense, this trend to selectively choose and combine the best of existing techniques mimics the evolutionary approach of the genetic algorithm, so there is a sound biological basis for the approach taken. The editors suggest that combinations of techniques, as shown in these chapters, may be the best approach to the solution of a wider variety of practical problems.

The editors are grateful to the authors for preparing such interesting and diverse chapters. The collection is commended to the reader as a summary of some of the more significant current applications of modern signal processing techniques. We would like to express our sincere thanks to Berend Jan van der Zwaag, Ashlesha Jain, Ajita Jain and Sandhya Jain for their excellent help in the preparation of the manuscript. Thanks are due to Gerald T. Papke, Josephine Gilmore, Jane Stark, Dawn Mesa, Mimi Williams, Lourdes Franco and Suzanne Lassandro for their editorial assistance

L.C. Jain
R.P. Johnson
Y. Takefuji
L.A. Zadeh

Contents

Chapter 1:

An Intelligent Driver
Warning System

AN INTELLIGENT DRIVER WARNING SYSTEM

Chris J. Harris
Dept. of Electronics & Computer Science
Southampton University, Southampton, U.K.

Jonathan M. Roberts
CRC for Mining Technology & Equipment
CSIRO Div. Manufacturing Technology
Kenmore, Australia

P. Edgar An
Dept. of Ocean Engineering
Florida Atlantic University, Boca Raton, Florida 33431, U.S.A.

This chapter is focused on the research and development of an intelligent driver warning system (IDWS) as a means to improve road safety and driving comfort. Two independent IDWS case studies are presented. The first study examines the methodology and implementation for attentive visual tracking and trajectory estimation for dynamic scene segmentation problems. In the second case study, the concept of driver modelling is evaluated which can be used to provide useful feedback to drivers. In both case studies, the quality of IDWS is largely determined by the modelling capability for estimating multiple vehicle trajectories and modelling driving behaviour. A class of modelling techniques based on neural-fuzzy systems, which exhibits provable learning and modelling capability, is proposed. For complex modelling problems where the curse of dimensionality becomes an issue, a network construction algorithm based on Adaptive Spline Modelling of Observation Data (ASMOD) is also proposed.

1   Introduction

Imagine commuting on a congested motorway during rush hour. You are agitated with the slow moving traffic and exhausted from a long day of hard work. Half way through your journey, an accident on the break-down lane catches your eyes and your attention is diverted. During this brief inattentive moment, unexpected road construction ahead causes the traffic to slow down suddenly. As soon as

Portions of driver modelling materials were reprinted with permission from IEEE Transactions on Systems, Man and Cybernetics, Vol.26, No.2, pp.254-261, March, 1996.

you realise what has happened it is too late to brake and you become a victim of another accident.

Unfortunately this is not an unusual incident. Statistically speaking, human error causes 90% of all road accidents [52]. In 1991, the death rate from road accidents in the UK was 5,000 per year, and in the EU as a whole, 50,000 per year [64]. In 1995, the death rate from road accidents in the U.S. was more than 40,000 per year (averaged to more than 100 persons die each day), among which 41% were related to alcohol influence. For every age from 5 to 27, road accidents are the leading cause of death, and its economic cost alone in the U.S. in 1994 was more than \$150 billion dollars [59]. Although the fatality rate has improved over the past decade through the use of seat belts and education on alcohol influence, road accidents remain a significant social and economic issue to be addressed nationally and internationally.

Humans often react too slowly to complex situations that can overwhelm their senses while driving. It is primarily this slowness to react and their inability to process information fast enough which causes most accidents to occur. For an alert driver, the braking response time is typically 1 second given that the front vehicle has functional brake lights, and can be longer than 2 seconds otherwise [32]. Reaction time can be even longer for any driver who is not fully alert, such as a drunk, tired or bored driver. A long reaction time generally requires a large distance between vehicles for safe driving and hence the density of road traffic is limited. With the additional constraints of increasing number of road vehicles and decreasing new road construction, there is an emerging need to engage in research and development which optimises the traffic flow throughput without compromising road safety.

To improve the road safety and increase the efficiency of the existing road infrastructure, the degree of autonomy of road vehicles must be increased. Programs such as the Intelligent Vehicle Highway Systems (IVHS) in the U.S. and Japan, as well as Road Transport Informatics (RTI) in Europe, were primarily developed to address the issues of road safety and traffic management by improving the vehicle intelligence and existing road infrastructures [16, 31]. By receiving information from multiple sensors located around the vehicle and/or from other vehicles/central computer via radio communication, these systems can perform the following functions:

- **Driver Information System (DIS)** - With onboard GPS-based navigation, the DIS plans the most efficient route based on maps stored onboard or obtained remotely via radio links, and advises the driver when to turn and which road to follow. DIS are currently available and have been used successfully in Japan for a number of years [16, 64].

- **Driver Warning System (DWS)** - These include scenario processing, obstacle detection and localisation [65], lane-keeping, parking aids, and blind spot motion detector warnings. Although the driver retains complete vehicle control at all times, the additional processed sensory information through an efficient human computer interface can provide the driver shorter reaction time and better alertness. A few DWS have been implemented on a commercial basis (e.g., parking aids), and other systems are likely to become commercially available in coming years.

- **Intelligent Co-pilot System (ICPS)** - In addition to the basic functions of the DWS, an onboard computer also controls basic driving functions, such as steering, braking and acceleration. Implementating collision avoidance for road driving is a complex task because it requires not only an accurate perception of the road environment but also prompt execution of control actions which can satisfy the kinematics constraints of the controlled vehicle. In this system, drivers do not play a direct role in low-level control loops, and most of their effort can be redirected to high-level decision making, such as navigation and planning [12, 16, 18, 19, 21, 46, 51, 52, 56, 57]. The ICPS includes autonomous intelligent cruise control (AICC) and autonomous intelligent maneuvering control (AMC). Given a specified speed, the AICC executes longitudinal control tasks through braking and acceleration actions provided that the road ahead is clear. Otherwise, it automatically readjusts the vehicle speed in order to keep a safe distance from the front vehicle. The AMC provides lane keeping or changing capabilities through steering and speed actions in order to execute lateral control tasks. It has been shown through simulations [10] that when 40% of vehicles are equipped with an ICPS, traffic density is increased by 10% and traffic flow throughput by 15% based on a 1 second time gap between vehicles.

- **Traffic Management System (TMS)** - This system maximises the efficiency of the road infrastructure by providing supports such as adaptive traffic light timing, electronic warning signs, automated toll collection, and smart convoy. Smart convoying can lead to a reduction in fuel consumption from the reduced drag due to slip streaming [64].

While these four functions are each critical to achieving the overall goal of the IVHS program, this chapter is focused on the research and development of an intelligent driver warning system (IDWS) as a means to facilitate indirect obstacle avoidance. The nature of obstacle avoidance is indirect because the driver retains direct control of the vehicle, and the system only issues warning messages when collision is likely to occur as a result of unexpected movement of nearby obstacles, or when there is a significant change in the driver's behaviour. The critical sensing tasks for the IDWS are obstacle detection, obstacle range estimation and overall scene interpretation. These issues must be addressed before the benefits of reduced inter-vehicle distance can be achieved.

To ensure an effective system for collision avoidance, the representation and evaluation of a range of driving situations can be highly critical. In the IDWS, the situation assessment is comprised of both short-term evaluation of the vehicle maneuvering, and a long-term consistency check on the driver's behaviour [4, 6, 44]. The former output is an objective measure which is based on the physical vehicle constraints and its interaction with the road environment. The latter output is a subjective measure based on the degree of deviation of the driver's behaviour from his/her typical driving style. The deviation can be caused by factors, such as fatigue, agitation or excessive alcohol intake. In general, the range of observed driving styles can vary significantly from one driver to another because of different bases of risk assessment. Thus the use of a *fixed* driver model is inappropriate and can desensitize driver's reactions to the warning signal. Thus, the level of *intelligence* in our IDWS is in part measured by its ability to model accurately the interaction between the individual driver's behaviour and the road environment.

In this chapter, two independent IDWS case studies are presented. The first study examines the methodology and implementation for attentive visual tracking and trajectory estimation for dynamic scene segmentation problems. These problems require visual detection and tracking of moving vehicles from a moving observer, and from which time-to-collision can be estimated (short-term evaluation of potential collision threat). The second case study evaluates the concept of driver modelling which in turn can be used to evaluate the consistency of driving behaviour over time, and thus can provide a useful feedback to regulate the driver's state of alertness (long-term evaluation of driver-vehicle interaction). In both case studies, the quality of the IDWS is largely determined by the modelling capability for estimating multiple vehicle trajectories and modelling driving behaviour.

It is well known in modelling literature [11, 24, 39] that nonlinear approximation techniques, such as artificial neural networks, can generally provide an adequate representation for any multi-dimensional surface with an unknown degree of nonlinearity. Among these networks, the Multi-Layered Perceptron (MLP) network has been the most widely used because of its universal approximator property [17, 48]. By generalising with a hidden layer of squashing functions, the MLP can be applied efficiently to high-dimensional matching problems even with limited training samples. However, the learning process is generally sluggish because of the nonlinear optimisation operations on parameters in the hidden layer [11].

In contrast to the MLPs, neurofuzzy systems have emerged in recent years as researchers [11, 29, 61] have tried to combine the natural linguistic/symbolic transparency of fuzzy systems with the provable learning and representation capability of "linear in the weights" artificial neural networks (ANN) which have fast adaptation and local replanning capabilities. However, these systems are not generally well suited to high dimensional problems, especially with limited training samples, because the model complexity as well as training experience grow exponentially with the input dimension. A network construction algorithm based on Adaptive Spline Modeling of Observation Data (ASMOD) is thus proposed to address the curse of dimensionality issue. To provide a basic understanding of how these neurofuzzy algorithms can be applied to the case studies, relevant learning theory and network structures are briefly reviewed.

2 Neurofuzzy System for Modelling

A neurofuzzy algorithm can be both initialised and verified using a fuzzy algorithm; equally, it can be trained via a variable rule confidence or weight vector [11]. The combination of qualitative based reasoning via fuzzy logic and quantitative adaptive numeric/data processing via ANNs is a potentially powerful concept, since it allows intelligent qualitative and quantitative reasoning (IQ^2) to be achieved within a single framework. Truly intelligent systems must make use of all available knowledge: numerical (e.g., sensory derived data), expert or heuristic rules (including safety jacket rules to constrain network learning or adaptability), and known functional relationships such as physical laws (so called mechanistic knowledge). Neurofuzzy systems allow all these knowledge sources to be incorporated in a single information framework. Fuzziness is introduced through the need for effective, interpretable knowledge representation (in terms of vagueness, data compression, interpretation/transparency). The architecture or topology of the class of neurofuzzy algorithms enables them to be readily assessed in terms of their modelling capability, structure, learning, construction and numerical stability, since the results of linear optimisation and algebra are directly applicable [25].

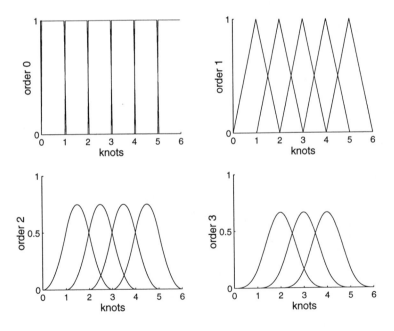

Figure 1: B-splines of order $\rho = 0, 1, 2, 3$

Fuzzy logic generalises the concept of a characteristic function in Boolean logic, whereby a fuzzy membership function $\mu_A(x) \in [0,1]$ is used to represent vague statements such as x *is negative small*. Overlapping fuzzy sets (see Figure 1) across the domain (universe of discourse) of x give specific meaning to vague linguistic concepts; additionally this overlap is necessary for both learning and interpolation through generalisation. A standard fuzzy logic system utilises the logic functions of AND, OR, IF(.) and THEN(.). If the *algebraic* operators of *product* and *sum*, rather than the more useful truncation operators *min* and *max*, are applied then the resultant system produces: (i) smoother interpolation, (ii) an equivalence between ANNs and fuzzy logic if $\mu_A(x)$ are radial basis functions or B-splines and (iii) a fuzzy system that can be readily analysed [11, 29, 61]. The following result is significant in this context:

Theorem 1 *When B-splines are used to implement fuzzy sets, the real valued inputs are represented via singleton fuzzy sets, and algebraic operators are used to implement fuzzy logic function, a centre of defuzzification method is used and the rule confidences are normalised. Then the neurofuzzy output is given by:*

$$\hat{y}(\mathbf{x}) = \frac{\sum_{i=1}^{p} \mu_{A^i}(\mathbf{x})w_i}{\sum_{i=1}^{p} \mu_{A^i}(\mathbf{x})} = \sum_{i=1}^{p} \mu_{A^i}(\mathbf{x})w_i, \quad \mathbf{x} \in R^n \qquad (1)$$

where $\mu_{A^i}(\mathbf{x})$ is output of the ith $(i = 1, 2, \ldots, p)$ fuzzy membership function given a multivariate input $\mathbf{x}$, w_i is the ith weight, and p is the total number of multivariate fuzzy sets. ∎

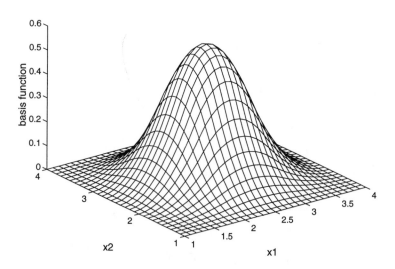

Figure 2: A two-dimensional quadratic multivariate B-spline basis function

The equivalence (1) is based on the constraint of a partition of unity on the input membership functions; whilst a restriction, this aids generalisation and regularisation of the network. B-spline functions are local, compact, piecewise polynomials of order ρ, for which simple recurrence relationships exist [11, 49]. To have a modular placement of univariate basis functions (e.g., see Figure 1), each of the input axes (ith) is quantised into a pre-defined number of non-overlapping intervals (S_i). Support of each of the univariate basis functions is defined over ρ intervals, and neighbouring basis functions are overlapping across $\rho - 1$ intervals. Multivariate basis functions are then formed from a tensor product of the univariate basis functions (see Figure 2). That is, the kth multivariate B-spline basis function, $B_k(\mathbf{x})$, is generated by multiplying n univariate basis functions $B_i^{k_i}(\mathbf{x})$ so

$$B_k(\mathbf{x}) = \prod_{i=1}^{n} B_i^{k_i}(x_i)$$

where $k = 1, 2, \ldots, p$, and p is the total number of multivariate basis functions. Also, define p_i as the number of univariate basis functions on the ith axis, $p = p_1, p_2 \ldots p_n$, and an index $k_i = 1, 2, \ldots, p_i$. ρ is an important *fixed* parameter (also known as the generalisation parameter) which affects the approximation capability and convergence rate performance. If ρ is set too large, the network will exhibit *slow* learning, especially for any desired input-output mapping which contains high spatial *Fourier* components. In contrast, the network is *unable* to generalise between neighbouring input samples if ρ is set too small. A multivariate function $\hat{y}(\mathbf{x})$ can be expressed as

$$\hat{y}(\mathbf{x}) = \sum_{k=1}^{p} B_k(\mathbf{x}) w_k = \sum_{k=1}^{p} \prod_{i=1}^{n} B_i^{k_i}(\mathbf{x}) w_k \qquad (2)$$

The neurofuzzy structure described in Figure 3 also represents a wider class of lattice based associative memory systems including Cerebellar Model Articulation Controller (CMAC), Radial Basis Functions (RBF), Karneva distributed memory and Takagi-Sugeno networks. Note that these networks do not naturally have a partition of unity which implies that the network response to any input is not uniform. Gaussian RBF's are very popular due to their localised spatial and frequency content and inherent flexibility in that they can readily cluster data to make it sparse, and are infinitely differentiable and integrable. However, they do not have compact support, a partition of unity, lack transparency and are not naturally formulated for pruning redundant submodels or rules.

The placement of multivariate basis functions can be geometrically decomposed into K sets of overlays. An overlay is defined as a union of basis functions with non-overlapping rectangular supports which exactly covers the input lattice. The overlay arrangement forces any input to only lie in one support, and thus there are always K non-zero basis function outputs. Although p is generally much greater than K, the computational costs associated with addressing the active basis functions and computing $\hat{y}$ are insignificant and predictable because of the modular placement property. To increase the network resolution, the

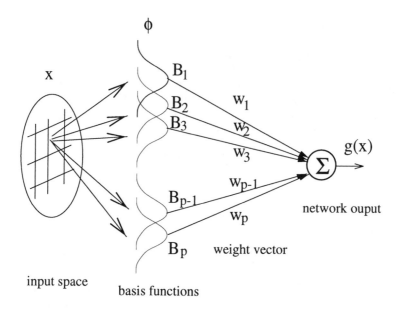

Figure 3: A lattice-based associative memory system

overlays are partitioned with a relative offset so that a given input is mapped onto different parts of a support (or different supports) in different overlays (see Figure 4).

Among the lattice associated memory networks, the arrangement of overlays and offsets can be significantly different which in turn affect how these networks generalise. In standard B-Splines, $K = \rho^n$ whereas in the standard CMAC, $K = \rho$ can be set independently of the input dimension, and the partitioning of supports is relatively offset along the diagonal of the input lattice, thereby providing a uniform projection of supports onto each axis [2, 3]. An example of the CMAC overlay structure for a two-dimensional input is given in Figure 4 where ρ is set to 4. The diagonal placement, however, forces the distribution of basis functions to be less uniform within a support of side ρ, and this can reduce the approximation capability if the basis functions are input-dependent. Alternative placement schemes for improving the uniformity of the basis function distribution have been proposed [3, 45]. As compared to the B-Splines, the CMAC has sparse distribution of multivariate basis functions, and this leads to an important trade-off between computational cost and modelling performance.

A neurofuzzy network must be able to learn inherent relationships contained in input/output data sets $\{\mathbf{x}(t), y(t)\}_{t=1}^{L}$ where $y(t)$ is the desired output. The networks (1) and (2) can be expressed as

$$\hat{y}(t) = B^T(\mathbf{x}(t))W(t-1) \qquad (3)$$

where $B^T(\cdot)$ is the p-dimensional input basis(fuzzy) functions; $\mathbf{x}(\in R^n) \rightarrow B(\in$

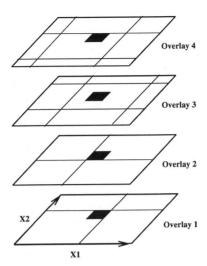

Figure 4: An example of a two dimensional CMAC overlay architecture with input x_1 and x_2. These overlays illustrate how the partitionings are offset along the diagonal of the input space, and the offset resolution is defined by the number of quantisation intervals not shown in the Figure.

$R^p, p >> n$). As these networks are linear with respect to their weights, $\{w_i\}$ are generally adjusted by a feedback learning law such as the *instantaneous* normalised least mean squares algorithm (NLMS):

$$\Delta W(t-1) = \delta \frac{\varepsilon_y(t) B(\mathbf{x}(t))}{\|B(\mathbf{x}(t))\|_2^2} \tag{4}$$

This algorithm estimates the normalised mean squared performance surface at every time step with a normalised squared output error generated by a single sample, and the weights are adapted in the direction of steepest descent down this highly singular surface thereby minimising the normalised squared error. δ is a user-defined step size for the weight update ($0 \leq \delta \leq 2$ for stability), and $\epsilon_y(t)$ is the output error at time step t, which is defined as $y(t) - \hat{y}(t)$. It is well known that, for a poorly conditioned network, small output errors do not imply small weight errors [11]. This is significant since the network's ability to generalise locally depends on the parameter error, ε_W. The neurofuzzy systems are generally well-conditioned, and their convergence performances are generally adequate for a variety of real-time low-dimensional applications.

Given important properties such as qualitative/quantitative reasoning, low computation cost, fast convergence and flexible modelling, the neurofuzzy systems, like other rule base systems, suffer from the curse of dimensionality, which has implications on the number of basis functions stored (or equivalent fuzzy rules), the training times, the network's ability to generalise and the overall resolution of the network. This in turn has serious implications for resultant neurofuzzy controller and estimation design.

3   Network Construction

The curse of dimensionality occurs in neurofuzzy systems as a complete rule base is exponentially dependent on the input dimension, n. For example, for $n = 5$, with single output and with 7 basis (fuzzy sets) functions on each variable, 16,800 weights or rules are required! Neurofuzzy construction algorithms [9] attempt to select models that minimise three criteria simultaneously: (i) MSE, (ii) complexity (through number of model parameters or degrees of freedom) and (iii) network smoothness to give good regularisation by constraining the network curvature or weight values. Considerable use is made here of conventional statistical metrics such as Akaikes' Information Criterion, Structural Risk Minimisation, or Minimum Description Length[9]. Whatever criteria are used the construction algorithm should embody the principles of:

- *Data Reduction:* the smallest number of input variable are used to explain the maximum amount of information.

- *Network Parsimony:* the best models obtained using the simplest possible structures that contain the smallest number of adjustable parameters.

A convenient framework for generating parsimonious neurofuzzy models is the generalisation of the Gabor-Kolmogrov input/output Analysis of Variance (ANOVA) representation [8]:

$$y = f(\mathbf{x}) = f_0 + \sum_{i=1}^{n} f_i(x_i) + \sum_{i=1}^{n-1} \sum_{j=i+1}^{n} f_{ij}(x_i, x_j) + \cdots + f_{1,2,\ldots,n}(\mathbf{x}), \qquad (5)$$

where $f_j(.)$ etc. represent *additive* univariate, bivariate, ... components of $f(.)$ in which each component is represented by a separate neurofuzzy system with reduced dimension (and rule set). So for $n = 5$, if 7 basis functions are used for each variable, and if it is known or can be determined $f(\mathbf{x}) \simeq f_{12}(x_1, x_2) + f_{23}(x_2, x_3) + f_{45}(x_4, x_5)$, then the number of rules required collapses from 16,800 to 100 for a complete rule base. Parsimonious neurofuzzy models are critical in both control and estimation problems, since the complexity and state dimension of the resultant controller or estimator is directly related to the process model complexity. Ideally we seek a canonical model structure and parameterisation, utilising only input/output data. Recent research [9] had concentrated on the automatic iterative construction of B-spline algorithms, e.g., the Adaptive Spline Modelling of Observational Data (ASMOD) procedure, that constructs models by a one-step-ahead error minimisation process where a number of possible rule-base refinements such as the addition of univariate or bivariate functions are evaluated, retaining those which minimise the residual error. Regularisation can be used to constrain the network weights in those input regions where there is little or no data as well as improving the network generalisation as utilising local regularisation techniques. ASMOD [30] also allows refinement through the introduction (or deletion) of basis functions, and removal of redundant inputs and submodels. ASMOD in its commercial variants NeuFrame and NeuFuzz [43] has been applied to a wide variety of industrial applications including modelling of gas turbines, satellite and submersible vehicles, metal fatigue, and pharmaceuticals [9]. The network structure allows *linear* learning algorithms such as conjugate gradient or singular value decomposition to be used to adapt weights or rule confidences, and to simultaneously extract the *internal* structure of the network,

- which *inputs* are important (including model orders),
- number and input vector for each subnetwork, and
- the number, position, and shape of the fuzzy input sets in each subnetwork.

directly from the training data, which can be formulated as a one-step-ahead growing/pruning procedure. These algorithms repeatedly evaluate different network structures (including extended additive models to accommodate multiplicative or product based processes). The resultant models are not only parsimonious in parameters (i.e., number of weights or rules), but also provide improved generalisation and statistical significance, by *not* modelling the *inherent* noise in the data. This is significant to control and estimation design, since the models used in their design are *almost* canonical.

There are other techniques for implementing construction algorithms, including hierarchical networks of subnet experts [42]. Other approaches include: product/additive networks [9] and input space partitioning strategies such as K-tree and quad trees to produce axis orthogonal splits (see Figure 5). Unfortunately almost all these methods lose the transparency of interpretation that additive models such as ANOVA offer, since they remove the online adaptability of *linear in the weights* structure.

4   Neurofuzzy State Estimation

Given that a minimal parameter input/output process model can be generated, can a state space realisation be generated and its associated state be estimated? Without imposing some structure on the model which is then amenable to state space analysis, the answer is no. A general approach for performing state estimation is shown in Figure 6 [41].

In this approach, the fuzzy mappings $f_1 : u \rightarrow \mathbf{x}, f_2 : \mathbf{x} \rightarrow y$ form an input-output transfer function $R = f_1 \circ f_2$ which can be identified by input/output data via a neurofuzzy construction algorithm such as ASMOD. $f_1(.)$ is found from the relationship $f_1 = f_2^{-1} \circ R$ where $f_2(.)$ is assumed known and invertible since it defines the state vector. (Note that a fuzzy relation always has an inverse, albeit non-unique.) The estimation problem is now to find the fuzzy

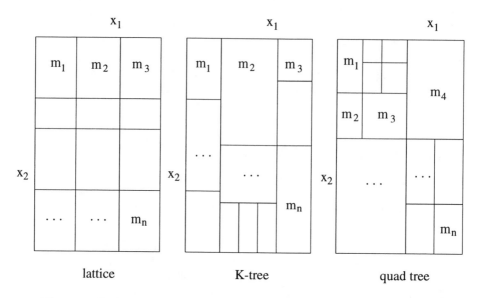

lattice   K-tree   quad tree

Figure 5: Different state (overlapping envelope) space decompositions

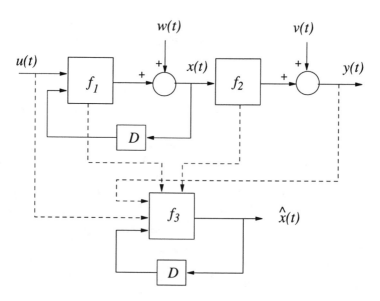

Figure 6: A general estimation approach

correlational mapping $f_3(.)$ such that $(\mathbf{x}(t) - \hat{\mathbf{x}}(t)) \to 0$. The resultant estimator is

$$\hat{\mathbf{x}}(k) = f_3 \left[f_1 \left[\begin{array}{c} \hat{\mathbf{x}}(t-1) \\ u(t-1) \\ f_2^{-1}(y(t)) \end{array} \right] \right] \tag{6}$$

A variety of techniques have been used for ensuring convergence, including nonlinear optimisation methods such as genetic algorithms, or stability methods such as Lyapunov. A natural extension of linear state space theory is to form global models using multiple *local* ARMA type models [42, 62]. The local models can be parameterised by an operating point, O_k, non-state observable (e.g., Mach number and attitude for an aircraft) or by a state region $\{m_i\}$ for which each model is applicable (see Figure 5). In the latter case ASMOD type construction algorithms can be used to determine the minimum number and average of models in the state space. Note that non-orthogonal split techniques (e.g., quad trees) will lead to fewer models (and consequently estimators/controllers), and interpolation between models (regions) in the state space is achieved by imposing fuzzy overlaps for each region [24].

Take a general SISO stochastic nonlinear system given by

$$y(t) = f(y(t-1), \ldots, y(t-n_y), u(t-d-1), \ldots, u(t-d-m_u)) + \varepsilon(t) \tag{7}$$

where $f(.)$ is assumed unknown, the system orders, (m_u, n_y), and delay, d, are assumed known. Define an observational vector $\mathbf{x} = [x_1, \ldots, x_n] = [y(t-1), y(t-2), \ldots, y(t-n_y), u(t-d-1), \ldots, u(t-d-m_u)]^T$, where $n = m_u + n_y$. Consider a fuzzy rule representation of the above, with input $\mathbf{x} \in R^n$ and output $y \in R$. A functional fuzzy rule base for (7) is:

$$k^{th} \text{ Rule}: \text{ if } x_1 \text{ is } B_1^{k_1} \text{ and } \cdots x_n \text{ is } B_n^{k_n} \text{ then } y \text{ is } y_k(\mathbf{x}), \quad (k = 1, 2, \ldots, p) \tag{8}$$

where $i = 1, 2, \ldots, n$ and $k_i = 1, 2, \ldots, p_i$. $y_k(\mathbf{x}) \in Y, B_i^{k_i}$ are linguistic values for x_i, and p is the total number of rules $\prod_i^n p_i$. If we select

$$y_k(\mathbf{x}) = a_1^k x_1 + a_2^k x_2 + \cdots + a_n^k x_n \tag{9}$$

then (8) and (9) is a locally linear fuzzy model of (7). If in addition we choose algebraic product/sum fuzzy operators and B-spline membership (basis) functions $B_k(\mathbf{x}) = \prod_{i=1}^n B_i^{k_i}(x_i)$, then it can be shown [66] that

$$\hat{y} = \sum_{k=1}^p \prod_{i=1}^n B_i^{k_i}(x_i) y_k(\mathbf{x}) = \sum_{k=1}^p B_k(\mathbf{x}) y_k(\mathbf{x}) \tag{10}$$

Substituting $y_k(\mathbf{x})$ from (9) gives

$$y \approx \sum_{k=1}^p B_k(\mathbf{x})(a_1^k x_1 + a_2^k x_2 + \cdots + a_n^k x_n)$$

$$
\begin{aligned}
&= \left(\sum_{k=1}^{p} B_k(\mathbf{x})a_1^k\right)x_1 + \left(\sum_{k=1}^{p} B_k(\mathbf{x})a_2^k\right)x_2 + \cdots + \left(\sum_{k=1}^{p} B_k(\mathbf{x})a_n^k\right)x_n + e(t) \\
&= a_1(\mathbf{x})y(t-1) + \cdots a_{n_y}(\mathbf{x})y(t-n_y) + \\
&\quad a_{n_y+1}(\mathbf{x})u(t-1) + \cdots a_n(\mathbf{x})u(t-d-m_u) + e(t)
\end{aligned}
\tag{11}
$$

where $a_i(\mathbf{x}) = \sum_{k=1}^{p} B_k(\mathbf{x})a_i^k$, $(i = 1, 2, \ldots, n)$, and $e(k)$ is the modelling mismatch error.

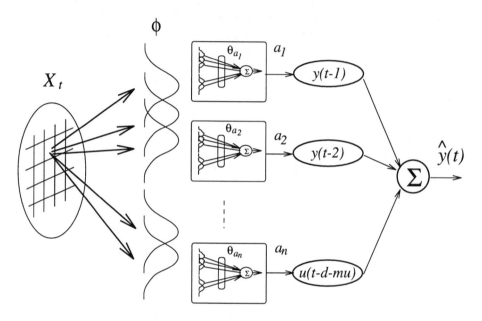

Figure 7: Neurofuzzy modelling network

Equation (11) is an ARMA type model, whose autoregressive parameters $\{a_i(\mathbf{x})\}$ are nonlinear functions of the state $\mathbf{x}$, each of which can be identified via an ASMOD type neurofuzzy algorithm. Define $\phi = [B_1(\mathbf{x}), B_2(\mathbf{x}), \ldots, B_p(\mathbf{x})]^T$, $\theta_{a_i} = [a_i^1, a_i^2, \ldots, a_i^p]^T, (i = 1, 2, \ldots, n)$. Figure 7 represents the system model (11) as a two layer neurofuzzy feedforward network. This local model construction can be used to produce state estimates either by the *indirect method* in which system identification is used to parameterise a Kalman filter, which is in turn used to generate states (see Figure 8), or the *direct method* in which the identification and estimation processes are combined in a boot-strap scheme to generate state estimates directly (see Figure 9).

Both approaches use a Kalman filter for the model (11). Assume that $m_u = n_y = m$ (or $n = 2m$) and denote

$$
\tilde{u}(t) = a_{m+1}(\mathbf{x})u(t-d-1) + \cdots a_{2m}(\mathbf{x})u(t-d-m)
\tag{12}
$$

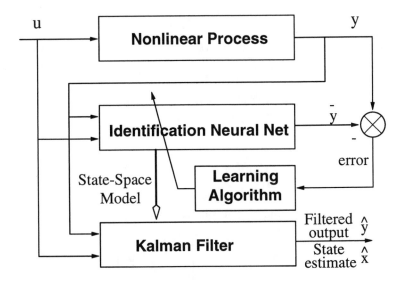

Figure 8: Indirect state estimation scheme

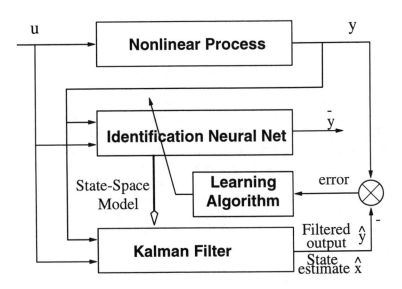

Figure 9: Direct state estimation scheme

then model (11) becomes

$$y(t) = a_1(\mathbf{x})y(t-1) + \cdots a_m(\mathbf{x})y(t-m) + \tilde{u}(t) + e(t) \qquad (13)$$

Define

$$z_1(t) = y(t-m),$$
$$z_2(t) = y(t-m+1),$$
$$\vdots$$
$$z_{m-1}(t) = y(t-2),$$
$$z_m(t) = y(t-1),$$

then (13) can be rewritten in canonical controllable state form:

$$z(t+1) = \begin{bmatrix} 0 & 1 & & & \\ 0 & 0 & 1 & & \\ \vdots & \vdots & & \ddots & \\ 0 & \cdots & \cdots & & 1 \\ a_m(\mathbf{x}) & \cdots & & a_2(\mathbf{x}) & a_1(\mathbf{x}) \end{bmatrix} z(t) + \begin{bmatrix} 0 \\ 0 \\ \vdots \\ 0 \\ 1 \end{bmatrix} \tilde{u}(t) + v(t), (14)$$

$$y(t) = [\; a_m(t) \quad \cdots \quad a_2(t) \quad a_1(t) \;]z(t) + \tilde{u}(t) + \omega(t) \qquad (15)$$

This is a nonlinear system for which extended Kalman filters [15] can be applied, assuming that the noise characteristics of $\{\omega(t), v(t)\}$ are known or can be estimated.

4.1 Training of Neurofuzzy Kalman Estimators

The modelling network shown in Figure 7 can be viewed as a two-layered neural network. The first layer is composed of standard neurofuzzy (B-spline) subnetworks (see Figure 3), and the second (output) layer is simply the regression calculation of equation (11). The free parameters are the weights of the B-spline subnetworks in the first layer, while the "weights" of the second layer are viewed as fixed in every iteration of the back-propagation training. The network can be trained by many traditional learning algorithms for feed-forward neural networks. In the rest of this section, we present a method of training the networks by the Normalised Least Mean Squares (NLMS) algorithm.

At time t input

$$\mathbf{x}(t) = [x_1(t), x_2(t), \ldots, x_n(t)],$$
$$= [y(t-1), \ldots, y(t-n_y), u(t-d-1), \ldots, u(t-d-m_u)]^T \in R^n$$

is presented to the neural network of Figure 7. In the forward pass, the network calculates its output, $\bar{y}(t)$, by (11). Let

$$\varepsilon(t) = y(t) - \bar{y}(t) \qquad (16)$$

be the error between the system's and the network's output. Because no free parameters in the second layer are to be trained, the error ε is propagated back through the second layer to the output of the first layer. Therefore, the errors in a_i, normalised by $\mathbf{x}(t)^T\mathbf{x}(t)$, are given by:

$$\varepsilon_{a_i} = \frac{x_i(t)\varepsilon(t)}{\mathbf{x}(t)^T\mathbf{x}(t)}, \qquad i = 1, 2, \ldots, n \qquad (17)$$

Then the errors ε_{a_i} are used to update the weights of the network's first layer. The NLMS algorithm for the network is therefore:

$$\theta_{a_i}(t) = \theta_{a_i}(t-1) + \delta \frac{\phi(t-1)x_i(t)\varepsilon(t)}{c + \phi(t-1)^T\phi(t-1)\mathbf{x}(t)^T\mathbf{x}(t)}, \qquad (i = 1, 2, \ldots, n) \quad (18)$$

with $\theta_{a_i}(0)$ given, where $0 < \delta < 2$ is the learning rate, and $c > 0$ is an arbitrarily small positive number which has been added to avoid division by zero.

5   Case Study 1: NF/ASMOD Application to Motion Estimation

The main aim in this case study is to design and implement a sensible feature detection and tracking strategy that is capable of tracking image features independently, in parallel, and in real-time. Features are clustered /segmented by utilising the inherent temporal information contained within the feature trajectories. For estimating the feature motion, the Multiple Model Adaptive Estimator (MMAE) algorithm is extended to cope with constituent Extended Kalman filters with different states in an attempt to accurately estimate the time-to-collision of a feature which in turn provides a reliable measure for potential collision threat. To further improve the motion estimation performance, it is proposed the state estimates of the Extended Kalman filters in the MMAE be initialised using ASMOD-based modelling techniques.

5.1   Feature Detection and Tracking

Images contain far too much information to be processed by higher-level understanding processes in real-time. The information density of an image must therefore be reduced significantly before being passed on to higher-level processes. Feature detection and tracking produces *feature trajectories* that can be used by higher-level processes to interpret the scene. The strategy outlined here uses *corners* as feature tokens; these are two-dimensional in nature and are therefore easier to track than one-dimensional edges. Tracking is achieved using a region-of-interest tracker that looks for corners in a small area around the predicted position of the corner being tracked.

A number of corner detection algorithms have been reported, including the Harris[22] and SUSAN[53] corner detectors. The crucial requirement for tracking is that, having found corners in one frame, the same corners should be found and matched in successive frames, so building a time history of the corners and allowing their motion to be analysed. The ability to consistently find and match corners in this way relies on the corners being *temporally stable* and *well localised*:

- **Good temporal stability** - corners should appear in every frame of a sequence (from the time they are first detected) and should not *flicker* (turn on and off) between frames.

- **Accurate localisation** - the calculated image-plane position of a corner, given by the detector, should be as close to the *actual* position of the corner as possible.

Both the *Harris* and *Smith* corner detectors have been used for tracking in the past. The *Harris* detector was originally developed as part of the DROID 3D vision algorithm[13, 14, 23] and was designed to be temporally stable. The *Smith* detector was used in ASSET[54]. ASSET used the 2D image-plane flow of corners to segment a scene into independently moving objects. Both corner detectors performed well as part of their respective motion algorithms (DROID and ASSET).

One of the vital problems in motion analysis is how to match (or track) a set of features between successive frames and/or over an entire image sequence. This feature tracking problem is known as the *correspondence problem*[60], and has been the subject of a great deal of research in recent years[13, 50, 55]. The problem may be considered in two separate parts. Firstly, having found a feature (a corner in this case) in frame t, where in the image is the same feature in frame $t + 1$? This is considered a *motion prediction* problem. Secondly, having decided where to look for the feature, how do we decide which feature (if there is more than one) in that area of the image is the *correct* feature? This second problem is therefore a *feature matching* problem.

Methods to predict the motion of image features for tracking may be divided into two classes based on whether 2-dimensional or 3-dimensional positional information is used. DROID[13] performed so-called 3D to 2D matching/tracking by projecting uncertainty regions around the predicted position of 3D features into the 2D image-plane. These regions, known as *validation gates*, were then searched for candidate corners. The 3D to 2D approach has a number of significant drawbacks[47] and hence a number of researchers have proposed working entirely in two dimensions when tracking features from independently or deformable (non-rigid) objects. Shapiro *et al.*[50] proposed a simple constant image-plane velocity predictor for their video-phony application. They showed that a simple motion predictor was adequate when image-plane motions were small. Smith[54] used a constant position predictor for his ASSET system, and simply searched for candidate corners in a rectangular region around the last known position of each corner to be matched.

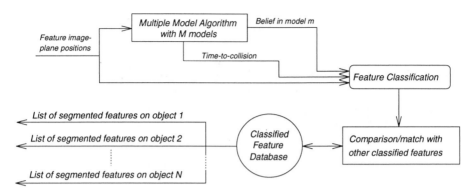

Figure 10: A feature based model for motion segmentation based on feature classification. Feature classification should use all the information available to classify and cluster features such as image-plane positions, time-to-collision, and the type of motion observed (in the form of a belief in a particular model).

5.2   Feature Clustering using Trajectory Analysis

One of the requirements of the vision system is the separation of independently moving objects from the background scene. This operation, commonly called *segmentation*, can be performed by using either similarities or the dissimilarities of certain properties or information pieces of features tracked over an image sequence. Feature trajectory analysis is required to obtain these information pieces before being passed on to the segmentation process.

It is proposed that features may be segmented or clustered into independently moving objects using a combination of three measures:

1. Image-plane position of the feature.

2. Time-to-collision of the feature with the image-plane (a temporal depth measure).

3. The *type* of motion.

Features should be individually *classified* and compared/matched with previously classified features from a database with *similar* features being attributed to the same object (Figure 10). In this way, features belonging to the same independently moving object would be grouped together. The second and third measures (proposed above) provide the motivation for investigations into state estimation and multiple model filtering described below.

It has been popular in the past to use Kalman filters (KFs) and extended Kalman filters (EKFs) to track visual features[28, 58, 63]. Kalman filtering requires *a priori* knowledge about the expected motion of a feature in the form of a motion model. It was shown in [47] that Kalman filtering based on a single

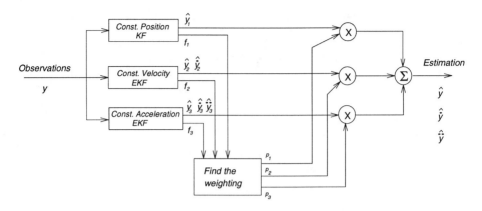

Figure 11: Three component filter MMAE used to test motion model identification accuracy

motion model is unable to accurately or reliably estimate the motion of a feature point for this particular application area - that of a vehicle operating at normal speeds on ordinary roads and in normal traffic.

The Multiple Model Adaptive Estimator[36] (MMAE) has been widely used [28, 34, 36, 37, 38, 58, 63] for situations where a single motion model is unable to achieve the desired estimation accuracy. Iu and Wohn[28] used the MMAE specifically for the recovery of the three-dimensional motion of a single visually tracked particle. Their results suggest that the MMAE algorithm, which uses a number of filters based on different motion models, is ideally suited to the problem considered here. This algorithm produces belief measures generated by the individual constituent filters which can be used to classify a feature's type of motion.

To determine the ability of the MMAE to accurately identify types of motion an MMAE was constructed using three filters based on different motion models. The three models used were a constant position (in the motion plane), the constant velocity model, and the constant acceleration model. The constant position model was implemented as a standard Kalman filter as the motion model was linear. The other two models were implemented as EKFs. The configuration of the MMAE is shown in Figure 11.

The MMAE was presented with 250 randomly generated trajectories of each type of motion (constant position, velocity and acceleration). Figure 12 shows how well the MMAE performed with respect to model identification. At a given time, the model with the highest probability was assumed the dominant or matched model. If this model was the correct model, a successful model match was declared; if not, a failure was declared. The identification accuracy for each type of motion was defined as the number of successes over each 250 trajectory run divided by the total number of successes and failures over the same time period. Figure 12 therefore shows how well the MMAE identified particular

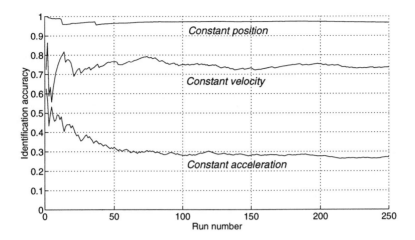

Figure 12: Identification accuracy versus run number for three types of motion tested

types of motion, and clearly shows that both constant velocity and particularly constant position type motion were identified correctly the majority of the time. Unfortunately, constant acceleration motion could not be identified reliably (only a third of the time).

The reasons for the poor performance of the MMAE at identifying constant acceleration motion can be traced to the poor performance of the component constant acceleration EKF. This EKF performed badly for two reasons. Firstly, its estimates were slow to converge to the correct values. Secondly, the filter was prone to fail and its estimates often *diverged*. Slow convergence is due to incorrect initialisation (assuming that the filter's state model correctly describes the actual observed motion). A Kalman filter's performance is extremely sensitive to initialisation. Good initial state estimates will ensure fast convergence, with poor estimates giving rise to slow convergence or even filter divergence. In this implementation the states were initialised using the first available observations.

Both Kalman filters and Extended Kalman filters are prone to divergence. That is, although it is an optimal filter, there are practical limitations to Kalman filters that may lead to its divergence[1, 20]. Three types of divergence exist:

1. True divergence - due to unbounded system modelling errors which lead to some elements of the state covariance matrix increasing without limit. This is the most severe divergence since errors become unbounded very quickly.

2. Apparent divergence - due to the mismodelling of plant excitation, measurement noise variances, and the effects of system biases. Here, a steady state is reached but the associated errors are too large to allow the esti-

mates to be useful.

3. Numerical divergence - due to filter computation round-off errors and finite precision arithmetic.

Both true and apparent divergence were observed during simulation. Apparent divergence tends to manifest itself as a constant bias in the estimates. The phenomenon of apparent divergence is critical to the operation of the MMAE. It is this effect that provides the MMAE the mechanism with which to *choose* the most appropriate filter from its component filters. Apparent divergence shows itself when the residuals have a non-zero mean (a correctly converged filter will have zero-mean residuals). It is therefore true divergence that adversely effects MMAE performance.

True divergence leads to error magnitudes that become unbounded very quickly. It is therefore important to detect the occurrence of true divergence as quickly as possible. In this implementation true divergence is detected by analysing the values of the leading diagonal of the state covariance matrix. When the value of any one of these elements exceeds a pre-set threshold the filter is said to have truly diverged and it is re-started and re-initialised at that time. If the divergent filter is the *correct* filter, there will be a significant time delay before its estimates converge again and hence a lag before it is *recognised* as the correct filter. The problem of poor initialisation is hence an issue after true divergence.

5.3 Improved Kalman Filter Initialisation using Neuro-fuzzy Estimation

It is traditional to initialise Kalman filters and extended Kalman filters with estimates of the states calculated directly from the observed (raw) noisy inputs[28, 40]. As mentioned above, a Kalman filter's performance is extremely sensitive to state initialisation accuracy (Figure 13). Good initial state estimates will ensure fast convergence, while poor estimates may give rise to slow convergence or even filter divergence. True divergence leads to error magnitudes that quickly become unbounded and are generally due to unbounded modelling errors caused by excessive noise[1, 20]. When a filter truly diverges, it must be re-initialised. States re-initialised at this time will have poor estimates because the observations are extremely poor (which is why the filter diverged).

It is proposed that if neurofuzzy estimators (trained on noisy input data and the corresponding noiseless, *true* output data) produce more accurate state estimates than those calculated directly from the observed noisy inputs (using the known state model), then neurofuzzy estimates could be used to initialise the states of Kalman and extended Kalman filters. Filters whose states have been initialised with neurofuzzy estimates should give improved performance by way of faster convergence when the filter is first started, and when a filter is re-started after true divergence.

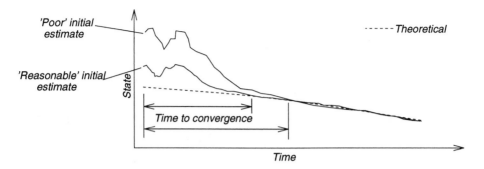

Figure 13: More accurate initial state estimates result in shorter convergence times

5.3.1   Image-plane Velocity Estimation using ASMOD

The ultimate aim of the work presented here was to increase the accuracy of KFs and EKFs by means of improving initialisation (or re-initialisation) accuracy and hence reduce filter convergence times. It is proposed that it is possible to improve the accuracy of KF state initialisation by using a neurofuzzy estimator such as ASMOD. Kalman filter performance will only be improved if ASMOD can produce more accurate estimates than those achieved using the known state and measurement equations and the noisy observation data.

We show here by example that ASMOD is capable of learning a system model in such a way as to reduce the effects of observation noise. The aim is to let ASMOD model the motion (which we think we know) plus the measurement noise (which we do not know) and use these estimates to initialise the KFs and EKFs. The ability of ASMOD to learn a noise filtering system model will be shown by considering the estimation of image-plane velocity of a tracked feature which was moving with constant velocity in the real-world.

Constant velocity motion (with respect to the real world) was simulated using the following equation:

$$y(t) = \frac{-fh}{\lambda + v_z t} \tag{19}$$

where h was the height of the feature below the optical axis, λ was the initial distance of the feature from the focal point (O), and v_z was the velocity of the feature along the z-axis (Figure 14). Note that h, λ and v_z were all in the intervals $h[-2.5, 2.5]$, $\lambda[1, 30]$ and $v_z[-10, 10]$, and were all randomly generated. Training and test data were artificially generated using MATLAB[2]. Output values, $u(t)$, were generated as follows:

$$u(t) = \dot{y}(t) = \frac{y(t) - y(t-1)}{\Delta t} \tag{20}$$

---

[2] The MATHWORKS Inc, USA

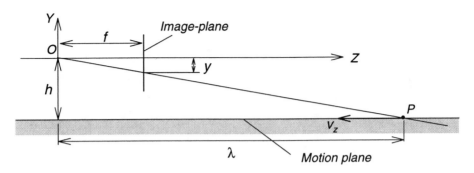

Figure 14: Imaging geometry used to generate simulated training and test data

where Δt was the sampling interval ($\Delta t = 40$ms). Zero mean Gaussian noise with a standard deviation σ was added to the input $y(t)$ to simulate real noisy observations.

It can be seen from equation 20 that a minimum of two inputs are required ($y(t)$ and $y(t-1)$) to estimate the output ($\dot{y}(t)$). Training and test sets were generated consisting of 18750 and 6250 randomly generated training and test pairs respectively, where a training or test pair is defined as the input $y(t)$, $y(t-1)$, and output $\dot{y}(t)$. A value of $\sigma = 0.004$ was used, which corresponds to a standard deviation of 0.5 pixels in a 256x256 pixel image. Figures 15 and 16 show the scatter plots of the two inputs for both the training and test sets. It is clear from these plots that most input data were clustered around the $y(t) = y(t-1)$ line. This distribution of data resulted from the physical constraints of the system being simulated, as described by the dynamics of the motion (equation 19). The *empty* or non-populated regions of the input space were therefore physically unrealisable.

A large proportion of the training data was found to be clustered around the centre of the input-output space. This is clearly shown in Figure 17, which shows the output plotted against one of the inputs. The majority of data were densely packed about the $u(t) = 0$ line. This distribution of training data in the input-output space was due to the imaging model (equation 20), which performs a perspective transform resulting in input values ($y(t)$) that are inversely proportional to the distance of a feature from the camera.

Because uncorrelated training data produce faster learning and, more importantly, produce a model that is not biased (artificially) in any regions of the input-output space where a large amount of training data exist [5], it was necessary to filter the training data. Filtering involves scaling the input data set so that it lies in the interval $[-1, 1]$, randomising their order and applying a Euclidean norm (with threshold ϵ) as a distance measure to remove some of the redundant data that adds a little knowledge about the process being modelled, but would otherwise bias the learning. Figure 18 shows the effect of filtering the training data. Note that the overall shape of the plots remained the same and

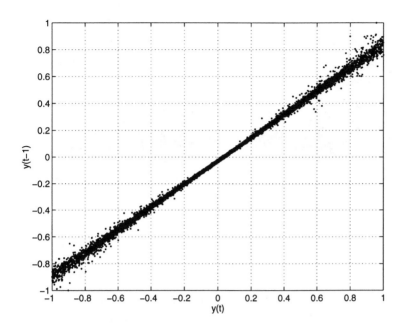

Figure 15: Training input data (two input case, $\sigma = 0.004$).

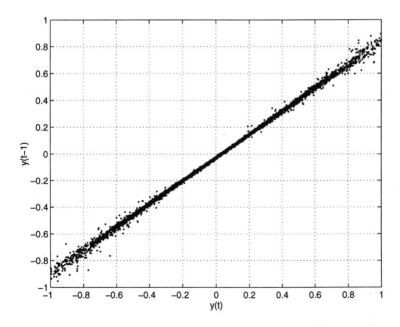

Figure 16: Test input data (two input case).

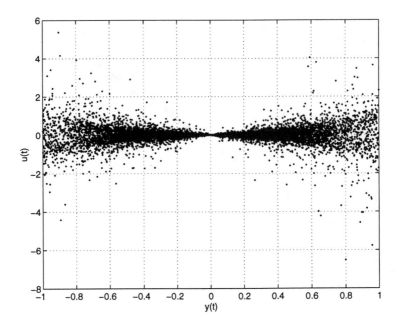

Figure 17: Unfiltered training sets (two input case).

that the more widely spaced data were not affected by filtering.

It is clear from Figures 15 and 16 that the input data (both training and test) were clustered around the $y(t) = y(t - 1)$ line in the two input case. Similarly, input data were clustered around the $y(t) = y(t - 1) = y(t - 2)$ line in the three input case, and so on. This distribution of input data was governed by the physical constraints of the system being modelled. The distribution of data in this example leaves two large areas of the input space completely empty. This is not necessarily undesirable, but a more globally populated input space may result in better ASMOD approximations. Rotation of the input data so that the major axis of the data's distribution (*i.e.*, the $y(t) = y(t-1) = \ldots = y(t-N+1)$ in this example) is parallel to an input axis results in a more globally populated input space, and may reduce the number of dimensions required to model the data (the principle of data reduction). Figures 19 and 20 show the two input training data used previously and the result of input data rotation. Data rotation was performed using *Principal Components Analysis* (PCA)[26]. A rotation matrix U was calculated from the eigenvectors of the *correlation matrix*:

$$R = E[y_0 y_0^T] \tag{21}$$

where y_0 was the input vector y minus its mean (*i.e.*, y_0 has zero mean). The corresponding rotated input space was given by:

$$a = U^T y_0 \tag{22}$$

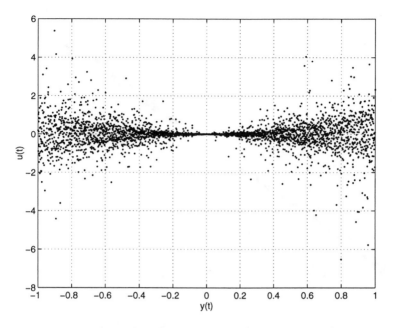

Figure 18: Filtered training sets (two input case)

The rotated input data shown in Figure 20 was scaled and filtered as before and resulted in a more evenly populated input space distribution. ASMOD could then be trained using the rotated data. Input dimensions were not discarded on the basis of their having small eigenvalues, rather it was left to the ASMOD algorithm to *choose* which dimensions were redundant.

ASMOD was trained using the filtered and rotated data described above and to measure its performance when presented with the test, two performance metrics were evaluated:

- Mean Square output Error (MSE):

$$MSE = \frac{1}{T} \sum_{t=1}^{T} (\hat{u}(t) - u(t))^2 \tag{23}$$

where $\hat{u}(t)$ was the estimated output of either the ASMOD or raw estimators ($\hat{u}_a(t)$ and $\hat{u}_r(t)$ respectively), $u(t)$ was the *true* output, and T was the number of test pairs in the test set.

- Relative Performance (R_a):

$$R_a(\%) = 100 \times \frac{1}{T} \sum_{t=1}^{T} b(\hat{u}_a(t), \hat{u}_r(t), u(t)),$$

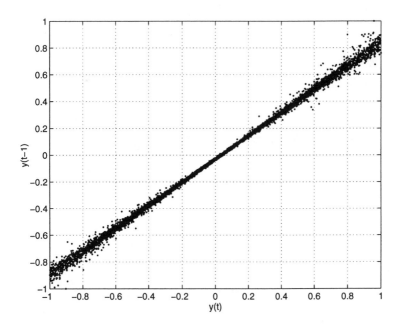

Figure 19: Filtered training sets (two input case)

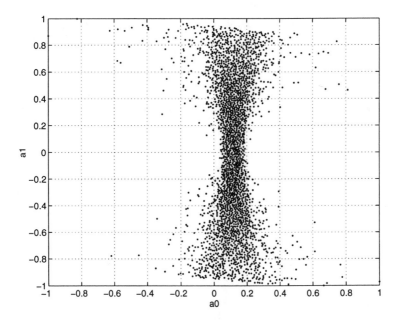

Figure 20: Rotated-filtered (right) training sets (two input case)

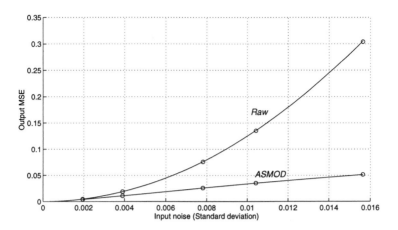

Figure 21: Output mean squared error (MSE) versus the standard deviation of the noise on the input.

$$b(\hat{u}_a(t), \hat{u}_r(t), u(t)) = \begin{cases} 1 & \text{if } (\hat{u}_a(t) - u(t))^2 < (\hat{u}_r(t) - u(t))^2 \\ 0 & \text{otherwise} \end{cases} \tag{24}$$

The MSE shows the *average* accuracy of the estimators (ASMOD and raw) over the entire test set. The relative performance measure (R_a) shows (as a percentage of the total number of data pairs tested) how many times ASMOD was more accurate than using the raw estimate (calculated using equation 20). Figure 21 through Figure 24 show how the performance varied with changes in the magnitude of the input noise. It should be noted that to obtain results for each point on these plots, ASMOD was re-trained and re-tested using training and test data generated with the corresponding values of σ.

It is possible to calculate the theoretical value of the MSE for the raw estimator using the following equation:

$$MSE_r = \left(\frac{\sqrt{2}\sigma}{\Delta t} \right)^2 \tag{25}$$

This equation was derived from the noise standard deviation (σ) in equation 20. The curve showing the performance of the raw estimator (Figure 21) was plotted using equation 25, but the data points shown were found using the test set (using equation 20). The results shown in Figures 21 and 22 show that ASMOD performed very well compared to raw estimation. It can be seen from equation 25 and from the curve in Figure 21 that raw estimation is very poor when input noise is large, and that the MSE is proportional to σ^2. By comparison, ASMOD always outperformed the raw estimator (with respect to MSE) and its MSE was approximately proportional to σ. Figure 22 confirms that ASMOD performed

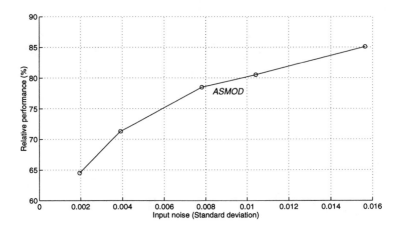

Figure 22: Relative performance of ASMOD versus the standard deviation of the noise on the input.

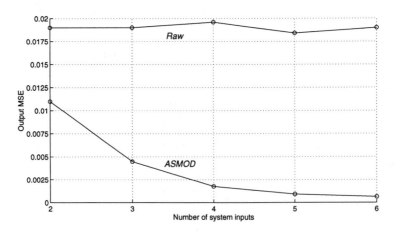

Figure 23: Output mean squared error (MSE) of both ASMOD and raw estimator versus number of system inputs.

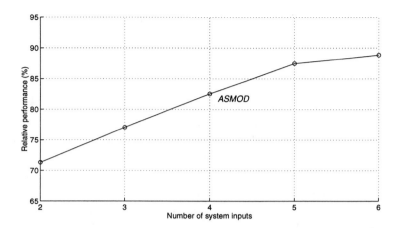

Figure 24: Relative performance of ASMOD versus number of system inputs.

better than raw estimation 85% of the time when input noise was very high. These results imply that ASMOD did not only successfully learn the basic input-output function, but also learned something about the noise characteristics of the system being modelled. ASMOD can therefore be thought of as a filter in this case.

A common characteristic of filters such as the Kalman and extended Kalman filters is that their performance improves with time. It is also possible to improve the performance of ASMOD by presenting it with a time history, in the form of extra inputs. Figures 23 and 24 show how ASMOD performed when trained and tested on an increasing number of inputs (*i.e.*, longer time histories). For example, when the number of system inputs equaled four, the inputs were $y(t)$, $y(t-1)$, $y(t-2)$ and $y(t-3)$. Figures 23 and 24 clearly show that there was a large increase in performance associated with an increase in the number of system inputs. It can also be seen from Figures 23 and 24 that the performance of ASMOD begins to level out when using six inputs (both with respect to MSE and relative performance). As compared with the raw estimation, the MSE was reduced by a factor of 30 using six inputs compared to a reduction of 1.7 using just two inputs.

The implication of using a longer time history (with regard to Kalman filter initialisation) is that initialisation will be delayed by $(N-2)\Delta t$ seconds, where N is the maximum number of inputs and Δt is the time between input samples. If the maximum number of inputs used is six in this example (as suggested by the results shown above), then the initialisation delay is relatively small. Would a Kalman filter initialised using raw estimates or lower order ASMOD estimates be more accurate than a six input ASMOD estimator when it comes on-line (*i.e.*, after $4\Delta t$ seconds)? Results from extended Kalman filters run on the estimation problem considered here reveal that convergence takes considerably longer than $4\Delta t$ seconds. This question does not arise when re-initialising a Kalman filter after divergence because six inputs will be available (assuming it diverges after $5\Delta t$ seconds).

5.3.2   Performance of a Neuro-fuzzy Initialised EKF

To demonstrate that a neurofuzzy initialised extended Kalman filter (NF-EKF) is often superior to an EKF initialised using raw observations, the recession-rate of a tracked feature was estimated. Note that the recession-rate was used instead of the time-to-collision because it cannot be used to describe situations where there is no depth motion.

This section will show that an NF-EKF is superior to an EKF initialised using raw observations when applied to the estimation of recession-rate $\alpha(t) = -\frac{\dot{y}(t)}{y(t)}$ of a tracked feature. The EKF estimated both y and $\dot{y}$ when a feature moved with constant velocity in the real world. The EKF's state $(\underline{x}_{F1})$ was initialised using:

$$\underline{x}_{F1}(1) = \left[\begin{array}{c} y(1) \\ \frac{y(1)-y(0)}{\Delta t} \end{array} \right] \qquad (26)$$

It is proposed that neurofuzzy estimation (ASMOD) can provide more accurate initial estimates than those given by equation 26, $i.e.$,

$$\underline{x}_{F1}(1) = \left[\begin{array}{c} y_a(1) \\ \dot{y}_a(1) \end{array} \right] \qquad (27)$$

where y_a is the ASMOD estimate of y, and $\dot{y}_a$ is the ASMOD estimate of $\dot{y}$. This estimation problem therefore required an ASMOD with N inputs $(y(t), y(t-1), \ldots, y(t-N+1))$ and two outputs $(y_a(t)$ and $\dot{y}_a(t))$, which can be thought of as two separate ASMODs (one for each output). The overall system diagram of the NF-EKF is shown in Figure 25 where both ASMODs consist of $N-1$ individual ASMODs, one for the two input case, two for the three input case, and so on.

Figure 26 shows the performance comparison of the constant velocity EKF compared with that of a similar EKF initialised using neurofuzzy estimates (NF-EKF) in the results obtained from a single trajectory run. It can be clearly seen that NF-EKF provides the more accurate initial estimate and the subsequent shorter converge time. The result also implies that improved state initialisation can prevent filter divergence in some cases. This is graphically shown by the trajectory example in Figure 27.

6   Case Study 2:   Neuro-fuzzy Application to Driver Modelling

Automatic warning generation for potential collision threats is a vital component of an intelligent driver warning system, given that the computer human inter-

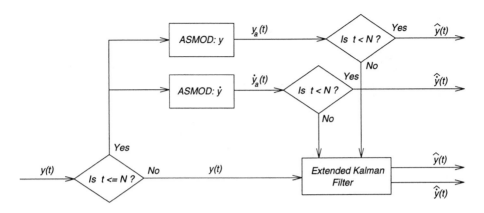

Figure 25: System diagram of a NF-EKF

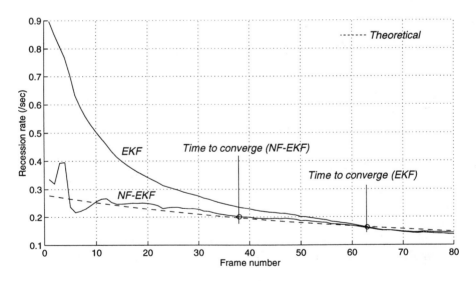

Figure 26: Shorter convergence time produced by the NF-EKF

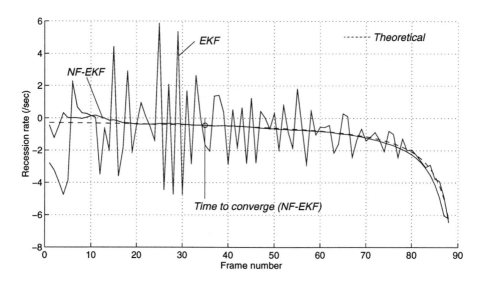

Figure 27: NF-EKF prevents repeated filter divergence

face is efficient enough that the driver can react promptly to the warnings. To improve the level of system intelligence, a time history of the driver's behaviour can be in parallel registered and analysed such that any anomalous driving style can be discovered and fed back to the driver. The evaluation process must be carried out over a properly chosen time scale, and the warning effectiveness is highly dependent on how the behaviour is characterised and correlated.

Figure 28 shows a block diagram for a driver modelling support system. To carry out the longitudinal car-following driving objective, the inputs to the driver model are currently restricted to controlled vehicle's speed, range/range rate to the front vehicle, and past history of throttle angle. These data are generated in the local perception module and measurement unit within the controlled vehicle. The model output is currently chosen to be the current throttle angle. Apart from the driver model, a reference model is also incorporated mainly as a 'safety net' in order to ensure that any short-term maneuvering in reaction to any unexpected movement of nearby obstacles is well within the vehicle's kinematic constraints. The reference model output provides a minimum range margin measured between the controlled vehicle and the front vehicle at every sampling interval.

Let $v_f(t)$ and $v_c(t)$ be the speed of the front and the controlled vehicle at sampled time t respectively. Also, let $\bar{a}$ be the maximum longitudinal acceleration and $\underline{x}(t)$ be the reference model output. Based on standard Newtonian equations, $\underline{x}(t)$ can be computed as

$$\underline{x}(t) = \frac{v_f(t)^2 - v_c(t)^2}{2\bar{a}} \qquad (28)$$

To account for the worst case scenario, the front vehicle is commonly assumed to be stationary $(v_f(t) = 0)$ and this generally results in an excessive minimum range margin, especially when $v_c(t)$ is large. When $v_f(t)$ can be detected accurately using Doppler radar, (28) generally produces a more realistic $\underline{x}(t)$ for safety net purposes. The risk assessment module then generates an appropriate warning to the driver when the detected range distance at sample t exceeds $\underline{x}(t)$, or when the deviation of the driver's behaviour from the norm is significant.

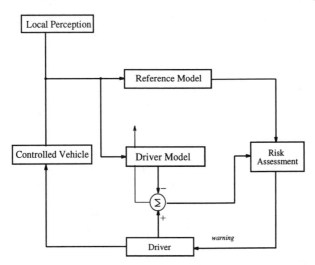

Figure 28: A block diagram for a driver modelling support system. The inputs to the driver model are controlled vehicle's speed, r ange and range rate to the front vehicle, and the past histo ry of throttle angle. Whereas the output is the current thro ttle angle. The inputs to the reference model are the vehicl e's speed and range rate whereas its output is the minimum r ange required for avoiding collision.

In general, the consistency evaluation on the driver's behaviour can be difficult because his/her responses to identical situations are never exact. The nonstationary characteristic can be caused by coarse estimation of the input/output variables, missing relevant variables, and more importantly the inherent randomness in human driving. Thus, the risk assessment module must be able to distinguish between the estimation error due to insufficient training and modelling error due to driver's noncausality. Adopting a single performance measure is likely to provide biased information about the driver's behaviour. In this study, three evaluation methods are used to validate the modelling performance. They are: one-step ahead prediction errors based on training/testing sets, learning curve and one-step ahead correlation based model validation techniques [7]. These methods can generally provide useful insights into the degree of error correlation.

One-step Ahead Prediction Output Errors (Training/Testing) - In each training cycle, every sample in the training set is cyclically presented once to the network for parameter adaptation. After sufficient training, the network response is computed for every sample in the training set (recalling performance), and every unseen sample in the testing set (generalisation performance).

Learning Curve - At the end of every training cycle, a root-mean-square (RMS) value of the one-step ahead prediction errors is computed for every sample in the testing set. This learning curve generally provides a reasonable measure of the convergence rate characteristic and the degree of uncertainty overfitting provided that the distribution of the training and testing data is *similar*. Note that the steady state error generally converges to a non-zero minimum when modelling error or measurement noise exist in the sampled data.

Normalised Correlation Function - The one-step ahead prediction errors are generally autocorrelated or correlated with the model inputs due to inadequate process and/or noise model. A normalised correlation function can be used as a baseline indicator to examine the one-step ahead modelling performance on the training set (with L training samples), and is especially well suited to models based on Volterra series [7]. This function computes the degree of correlation between variable f and g, and can be formulated as

$$\Phi_{f,g}(k) = \frac{\sum_{t=1+k}^{L}(f(t)g(t-k))}{\sqrt{(\sum_{t=1}^{L}f(t)^2)(\sum_{t=1}^{L}g(t)^2)}} \tag{29}$$

where k is the correlation time lag, and f and g can be based on one-step prediction errors or model inputs at sample t over the data set. These correlation functions are self normalised so that they are invariant with respect to the size of the prediction errors and input samples, and the degree of correlation is generally considered acceptable when the function lies within its confidence limits of $\pm 1.96/\sqrt{L}$ [7]. It should be emphasised that the one-step correlation functions only provide necessary conditions for an adequate model given the specific data set.

In the driver modelling study, the size of the input dimension is moderate and training samples are abundant. To satisfy the real-time learning and replanning constraints, the CMAC network was thus chosen as a compromise. In addition to the CMAC, a conventional linear model (CLM) was also used to model the driver's behaviour as a form of control benchmark. Besides the definition of a proper network structure, a selection of relevant input variables is equally important, and is highly critical for any model which generalises properly to a wide range of traffic scenarios. The modelling study adopts a "bottom-up" approach in which the driving objective is restricted to longitudinal car-following on test track and motorway environments. This provides a compromise between dealing with problems encountered in real world situations as well as ideal ones, and also allows important input variables to be identified. Much insight can thus be gained on the model input-output relationship before more complicated objectives/scenarios, such as lane changing in highstreets, are studied.

7   Driver Modelling Experiment

To evaluate the car-following modelling performance, two sets of data (TEST A,B) were generated by a single driver on the straight segment of a test track (average speed around 25 mph) and another two sets of data (MOTOR A,B) by the same driver on motorways (average speed around 55 mph). [3] These sampled data were generated at a rate of 10Hz, and are used to examine the effect of road environment on the driver's behaviour. A multivariate CMAC and CLM were independently used to adapt to the driver's behaviour. The inputs in these models were the previous normalised throttle angle, speed of the controlled vehicle (Jaguar model), range and range rate to the front vehicle whereas the output was the current normalised throttle angle, lying between 0 (zero acceleration) to 10 (maximum acceleration). The range and range rate inputs were obtained by sampling a 94GHz single-beam microwave radar sensor whereas the speed input was computed based on the wheel speed measurement. It should be noted that inferring the driver's behaviour by means of the throttle angle could be undesirable especially if the road gradient or the number of passengers vary significantly in the course of driving. In this study, the data were generated on road surfaces which had insignificant gradient, constant car load and minimal amount of gear shifting, and thus the effect of such nonstationary disturbances can be safely ignored.

7.1   Modelling Results

The driver modelling problem can be mathematically formulated as

$$T(t) = f(\mathbf{x}(t - n_{srr})) + \alpha T(t - n_{thr}) \qquad (30)$$

where $T(t)$ is the current normalised throttle angle, n_{srr} and n_{thr} are the time lags associated with $\mathbf{x} = $ [speed, range, range rate] and previous normalised throttle angle respectively. This chosen representation of driver model is based on the assumption that the throttle dynamics are relatively slow and thus the relationship between $T(t)$ and $T(t-n_{thr})$ is approximately linear. This structure produces a parsimonious representation where linear relationships are *explicitly* modelled, and can be easily modified to account for higher order linear throttle dynamics without increasing the complexity of the CMAC model.

A three-input-one-output CMAC model was chosen to fit $f(\cdot)$ with the receptive field partitioning scheme suggested in [45]. In the model, the speed, range and range rate limits were [0 80 mph], [0 50 meters], and [-12 12 mph] respectively, and a linear univariate field shape and product operator were used to form the multivariate basis function. The network output was normalised by the sum of ρ active basis function outputs (partition of unity), and the learning

---

[3]It should be noted that these data were generated when the driver was in closed loop control and thus the similarity in experience provided in the training and testing data can only be examined crudely, without knowing the set of relevant variables at hand.

rule for the weight vector $\mathbf{w}$ and α was based on the stochastic NLMS algorithm with monotonically diminishing learning rate (31)

$$\sum_{i=0}^{\infty} \delta_i = \infty, \quad \sum_{i=0}^{\infty} \delta_i^2 < \infty \tag{31}$$

The adaptive learning rate allows the network to trade off the influence of the measurement noise and modelling error. In each training cycle, each of the samples in the training set was cyclically presented once to both models for parameter adaptation.

7.1.1   Case 1: Test Track Scenario

In this case study, the training and testing sets were based on TEST A and TEST B respectively. The CMAC generalisation parameter ρ was chosen to be 7 whereas the number of quantisation intervals was chosen to be 30 along the speed and range rate axes and 20 along the range axis. The data samples in both the training and testing sets were sub-sampled so that two consecutive samples were 0.4 second apart (or equivalently 2.5 Hz). n_{srr} and n_{thr} were chosen to be 1 and 2 respectively.

The CMAC learning curve settled to its minimum after ten cycles of training were iterated. Throughout the training, 110 out of 645 weights were used, and the throttle input coefficient (α) converged to 0.7204. Figures 29a and 29c depict the CMAC recalling performance over TEST A and generalisation performance over TEST B respectively. Figure 29e depicts the training correlation curves ($\Phi_{\epsilon,\epsilon}, \Phi_{\epsilon,speed}, \Phi_{\epsilon,range}, \Phi_{\epsilon,rangerate}$) based on TEST A where the solid threshold lines represent the confidence limits of the correlation within which its standard deviation is considered acceptable. The CLM recalling and generalisation performances are shown in Figures 29b and 29d respectively, and the corresponding error correlation curves are shown in Figure 29f. The least squares weights were found to be -0.0016 (speed), -0.002 (range), 0.0089 (range rate), 0.2993 (bias), and 0.894 (previous throttle) using standard matrix inversion techniques.

By examining the one-step recalling and generalisation performances for both models (Figure 29a to 29d), one would be tempted to conclude that the CLM can perform just as well as the nonlinear CMAC model. However, these performance measures are generally insufficient, and can be highly dependent on the dynamics of the driver. For rapid sampling rate, the recalling and generalisation performances are likely to be satisfactory because the throttle angle rarely changes from one sample to another. Consequently, both models will be biased toward the previous throttle input ($\alpha \approx$ unity), and will thus no longer encapsulate the reactive driver's dynamics to the road environment. The correlation based validation techniques provide one basis for choosing an appropriate sampling rate which minimises the standard deviation of the correlation function. For both models, the errors and input/error were found to be excessively correlated when the sampling rate exceeded 2.5 Hz (0.4 second apart), and this

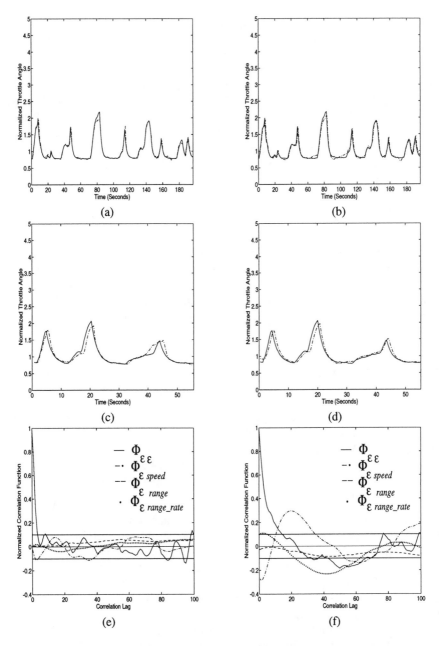

Figure 29: (a) CMAC training performance on test track data. (b) Linear model training performance on test track data. (c) CMAC testing performance on test track data. (d) Linear model testing performance on test track data. (e) CMAC correlation functions on test track training data. (f) Linear model correlation performance on test track training data. For training and testing performances, solid lines represent actual data, and dashed lines represent model output.

justified the preparation of the sub-sampled data set. Given the chosen sampling rate, the errors and input/error in the CLM were found to remain highly correlated, suggesting a considerable degree of nonlinearity of the throttle angle in relation to the speed, range and range rate variables. In this case study, a range of CMAC parameters and lag numbers were tested, and the chosen CMAC parameters and the lag numbers were found to produce the *best* modelling performance. It is interesting to note that the final previous throttle coefficients for both models were less than unity, implying that the autonomous driver's response is temporally stable. In particular, the CMAC throttle coefficient was less than that of the CLM, suggesting that the CMAC model was better able to extract the range and range rate information.

7.1.2   Case 2: Motorway Scenario

The training and testing sets in this case were based on MOTOR A and MOTOR B respectively. Similar to the previous case, the initial CMAC network parameters remained unchanged, except that the generalisation parameter ρ was reset to 9. The data samples in both the training and testing sets were sub-sampled so that two consecutive samples were 1.2 seconds apart (or equivalently 0.8 Hz). n_{srr} and n_{thr} were each chosen to be 1.

As in Case 1, the CMAC learning curve reached its minimum after ten cycles of training were iterated. 106 out of 441 weights were used throughout the training, and the resulting throttle coefficient converged to 0.591. Figure 30a and 30c depict the CMAC recalling performance over MOTOR A and generalisation performance over MOTOR B respectively, and the training input/error correlation curves are shown in Figure 30e. The CLM recalling and generalisation performances are shown in Figure 30b and 30d respectively, and the corresponding error correlation curves are shown in Figure 30f. The least squares weights were found to be -0.0004 (speed), 0 (range), 0.0109 (range rate), 0.1801 (bias), and 0.883 (previous throttle).

Similar to the test track scenario, the recalling and generalisation performances for both models are comparable although the generalisation performance of the CMAC model had slightly larger one-step prediction errors. Interestingly, the correlation curves for both models are very similar, suggesting that the CLM *might* be sufficient for the set of training data. Additional validation methods are needed to search for missing variables which might have contributed to the slightly larger error correlation. Again, the chosen CMAC parameters and the lag numbers were found to produce the *best* modelling performance. It is interesting to observe that the final previous throttle coefficients were less than those of the test track case, suggesting that the driver might have been more alert in the motorway environment.

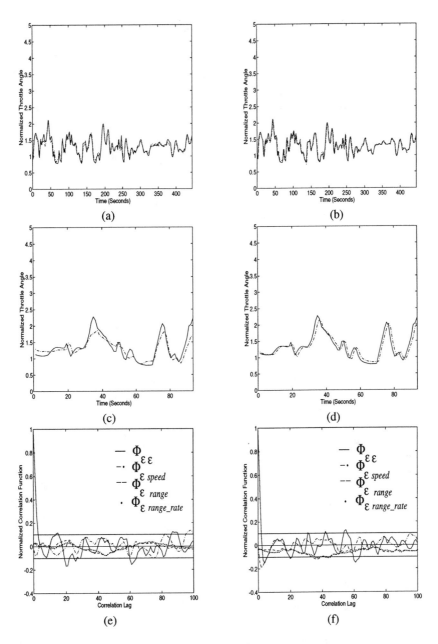

Figure 30: (a) CMAC training performance on motorway data. (b) Linear model training performance on motorway data. (c) CMAC testing performance on motorway data. (d) Linear model testing performance on motorway data. (e) CMAC correlation performance on motorway training data. (f) Linear model correlation performance on motorway training data. For training and testing performances, solid lines represent the actual data and dashed lines represent model output.

7.1.3   Case 3: Modelling Without Throttle History

To examine the relevance of the past history of throttle angle as the model input, it was deliberately removed from the driver model ($\alpha = 0$), and the resulting input variables became speed, range and range rate. The training set was based on TEST A, and only the CMAC model was used to model the throttle data. The initial network parameters and the lag number were identical to those described in Case 1. Figure 31a and 31b show the CMAC recalling performance over TEST A and the training error correlation curves after ten cycles were iterated. Without the throttle past history, the one-step prediction errors were considerably larger, and the errors and input/error were found to be excessively correlated, indicating that the dynamics of the throttle angle was highly autocorrelated in the course of driving.

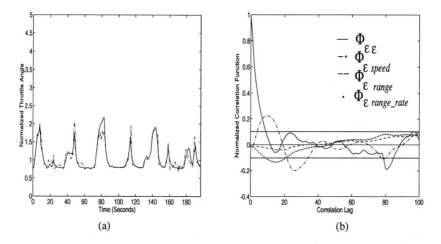

Figure 31: (a) CMAC training performance on test track data without throttle input. (b) CMAC correlation performance on test track training data without throttle input. Solid line represents actual data and dashed line represents model output.

8   Summary

In this chapter, the role of an intelligent driver warning system within the overall goal of the Intelligent Vehicle Highway Systems was discussed. To provide useful insights into how the IDWS can be implemented, two independent case studies were presented, and their roles within the IDWS were discussed. Both studies require accurate real-time nonlinear modelling capabilities with which to characterize the driver's behaviour and estimate multiple independent vehicle trajectories. It is proposed that a class of neurofuzzy systems, such as B-Splines and CMAC, can provide a real-time solution to these problems. These modelling techniques have fast adaptation and local replanning capabilities, and their structures are *linear in weights* so that learning rules can be based on standard linear feedback theory which is well understood. To deal with the curse of dimensionality, it is proposed that a network construction algorithm (ASMOD) can be used to initialise the neurofuzzy model structure. The initialisation process is generally not real-time compliant because a large volume of observations are required for determining how the overlays are to be partitioned.

The first case study addressed the problem of detecting multiple independently moving objects from a moving observer using a visual sensor. In particular, corners were used as feature tokens, and the concept of *attentive vision* was used to reduce the quantity of feature detection performed. Performance results from the implementation of the attentive strategy (not included in this chapter) show that more than 80% of features can be tracked using less than 30% of image data. The warning signal was based on *time-to-collision* or *recession rate* motion estimate which has been identified as an important visual cue for an average driver [32]. The time-to-collision estimation performance of the MMAE was shown to be improved by initialising the state vector in the EKF with more accurate estimates using ASMOD-based neurofuzzy systems.

The three motion models used for the MMAE were chosen for their simplicity and ease of implementation rather than for their realistic description of typical motions experienced by features in a driving scenario. Further research is therefore needed to investigate how features might actually move in typical driving scenarios when undergoing maneuvering, such as overtaking, braking and accelerating. It is possible that the three motion models used as part of the research may locally model the actual motion adequately. As features undergo changes in motion, as would be expected when maneuvering, it is important that these changes are observed by the MMAE algorithm and adaptation is performed as the motion switches between models.

In the second case study, the basic idea of adaptive driver modelling was described, and the role of such an adaptive driver model within the IDWS was discussed. A proper driver model can be employed to evaluate the consistency of the driver's behaviour over time, and thus can provide a useful feedback to regulate the driver's state of alertness. This driver modelling study was based on longitudinal car-following, and the real data were taken from the test track and motorway environments. The inputs of the driver model were the previous normalised throttle angle, controlled vehicle's speed, range and range rate to the front vehicle whereas the model output was the current normalised throttle angle. The resulting driver model objective can be roughly interpreted as one which estimates *only* the rate of change of the throttle angle, rather than the throttle angle itself.

The CMAC network and the CLM were independently used to model the driver's behaviour, and the evaluation techniques were based on one-step ahead prediction error performances over the training and testing sets, learning curve and one-step ahead normalised correlation functions. Modelling results suggest that the past history of the throttle angle can significantly reduce the deviation of the error correlation, implying that the throttle dynamics are generally slow for road driving. Also, the time scale dependency of the driver model was found to vary considerably from the test track to motorway environment. Correlation based model validation techniques allow one to choose an appropriate time scale such that the correlated errors are minimised. The modelling performance of both models on the test track data suggests that the chosen inputs are indeed relevant variables, and their nonlinear interactions with the throttle output are noticeable. It should be remembered that the correlation based validation techniques only provide a necessary (but not sufficient) condition under which the modelling performance is acceptable. For the motorway data, both models resulted in similar characteristics of error correlation although they were consistently larger than those for the test track case. This might be caused by factors such as missing input variable(s), human estimation errors for range and range rate variables, nonlinear coupling between the time shifted throttle angle and nonstationary characteristics, such as tiredness and agitation. Further work is needed to investigate the robustness of the modelling performance using a range of drivers with more relaxed driving objectives.

Acknowledgement - The authors wish to thank Dr. Z.Q. Wu from the Department of Electronics & Computer Science at Southampton University, UK, for his valuable comments and suggestions in improving the quality of this chapter.

References

[1] Abdelnour G., Chand S., Chiu S., Kido T. (1993), On-Line Detection and Correction of Kalman Filter Divergence by Fuzzy Logic, *Proceedings of the American Control Conference*, pp.1835-1839, San Francisco, CA.

[2] Albus J. (1975), A New Approach to Manipulator Control: The Cerebellar Model Articulation Controller (CMAC), *Transactions of ASME*, pp.220-227, September.

[3] An P.E., Miller W.T., Parks P.C. (1991), Design Improvements in Associative Memories for Cerebellar Model Articulation Controllers (CMAC), *Proc. Intl. Conf. on Artificial Neural Networks*, Helsinki, North Holland, Vol.2, pp.1207-1210.

[4] An P.E., Harris C.J., Tribe R., Clarke N. (1993), Aspects of Neural Networks in Intelligent Collision Avoidance Systems for Prometheus, *Joint Framework for Information Technology*, University of Keele, UK, pp.129-135, March.

[5] An P.E., Aslam-Mir S., Brown M., Harris C.J. (1994), Theoretical Aspects of the CMAC and its Application to High Dimensional Aerospace Modelling Problems, *Proceedings of IEE, International Conference on Control*, Vol.2, pp.1466-1471, Coventry, UK.

[6] Arain M., Tribe R. (1990), Application of Neural Networks for Traffic Scenario Identification, *4th Prometheus Workshop*, University of Compiegne, Paris, France.

[7] Billings S.A., Voon W.S. (1986), Correlation Based Model Validity Tests for Non-Linear Models, *Int. Journal of Control*, Vol.44, No.1, pp.235-244.

[8] Bossley K.M., Mills D.J., Brown M., and Harris C.J. (1995), Neurofuzzy high-dimensional modelling. In Alfred Walle, editor, *Adaptive Computing: Neural Networks*, pp.297-332, Henley-on-Thames.

[9] Bossley K.M. (1997), Neurofuzzy modelling approaches in systems identification, *Ph.D. thesis*, University of Southampton, UK.

[10] Broqua F. (1992), Impact of Automatic and Semi-Automatic Vehicle Longitudinal Control on Motorway Traffic, *Intelligent Vehicles 92*, pp.144-147, June, Detroit, Michigan.

[11] Brown M. and Harris C.J. (1994), Neurofuzzy Adaptive Modelling and Control, Prentice Hall, Hemel Hempstead.

[12] Catling I., McQueen B. (1991), Road Transport Informatics in Europe - Major Programs and Demonstrations, *IEEE Trans. on Vehicular Technology*, Vol.40, No.1, pp.132-140.

[13] Charnley D., Harris C.G, Pike M., Sparks E., Stephens M. (1988), The DROID 3D Vision System - Algorithms for Geometric Integration, *Technical Report 72/88/N488U at Plessey Research Roke Manor*, December.

[14] Charnley D., Blisset R.J. (1989), Surface Reconstruction From Outdoor Imagery, *Journal of Image and Vision Computing*, Vol.7, No.1, pp.10-16.

[15] Chui C.K. and Chen G. (1987), *Kalman Filtering, With Real Time Applications*, Springer-Verlag, Berlin.

[16] Collier C., Weiland R.J. (1994), Smart Cars, Smart Highways, *IEEE Spectrum*, pp.27-33, April.

[17] Cybenko G. (1989), Approximations by superpositions of a sigmoidal function, *Mathematics of Control, Signals and Systems*, Vol.2, No.4, pp.303-314.

[18] Dickmanns E.D. (1989), Subject-Object Discrimination in 4D Dynamic Scene Interpretation for Machine Vision, *Workshop on Visual Motion*, pp.298-304, Irvine, CA.

[19] Dickmanns E.D. (1991), 4-D Dynamic Vision for Intelligent Motion Control, *Journal of Engineering Application Artificial Intelligence*, Vol.4., No.4, pp.301-307.

[20] Fitzgerald R. J. (1971), Divergence of the Kalman Filter, *IEEE Transactions on Automatic Control*, Vol.16, No.6, pp.736-747.

[21] Graefe V., Blochl B. (1991), Visual Recognition of Traffic Situations for an Intelligent Automatic Copilot, *5th Prometheus Workshop*, Munich, October.

[22] Harris C. G., Stephens M. J. (1988), A Combined Corner and Edge Detector, *Proceedings of the Fourth Alvey Vision Conference*, pp.147-151, Manchester, UK.

[23] Harris C. G., Pike J.M. (1988), 3D Positional Integration from Image Sequences, *Journal of Image and Vision Computing*, Vol.6, No.2, pp.87-90.

[24] Harris C.J., Moore C.G., and Brown M. (1993), Intelligent Control: Aspects of Fuzzy Logic and Neural Nets, *World Scientific Press*, Singapore.

[25] Harris C.J., Brown M., Bossley K.M., Mills D.J., and Feng M. (1996), Advances in Neurofuzzy Algorithms For Real-Time Modelling And Control, *J. Engineering Application of AI*, Vol.9, No.1, pp.1-16.

[26] Haykin S. (1994), Neural Networks - A Comprehensive Foundation, *IEEE Press*.

[27] Hopfield J.J. (1984), Neurons with Graded Response Have Connective Computational Properties of Two State Neurons, *Proc. Nat. Acad. Sci*, Vol.81, pp.3088-3092, May.

[28] Iu S. and Wohn K. (1991), Recovery of 3D Motion of a Single Particle, *Journal of Pattern Recognition*, Vol.24, No.3, pp.241-252.

[29] Roger Jang J.-S. (1991), Fuzzy Modeling Using Generalized Neural Networks and Kalman Filter Algorithm, *Proceeding of the Ninth National Conference on Artificial Intelligence (AAAI-91)*, pp.762-767, July.

[30] Kavli T. (1994), Asmod - An Algorithm for Adaptive Spline Modelling of Observational Data, C.J. Harris, editor, *Advances in Intelligent Control*, pp.141-161, Taylor and Francis, London.

[31] Kay J.L. (1990), Advanced Traffic Management Systems - An Element of Intelligent Vehicle Highway Systems, *Convergence 90*, pp.73-84, October, Michigan.

[32] Lee D.N. (1976), A Theory of Visual Control of Braking Based on Information About Time-to-Collision, *Perception*, Vol.5, pp.437-459.

[33] F.L. Lewis, Yesildirek A., and Liu K. (1995), Neural Net Robot Controller with Guaranteed Tracking Performance, *IEEE Trans. Neural Networks*, Vol.6, No.3, pp.703-715.

[34] Lund E.J., Balchen J.G., Foss B.A. (1991), Multiple Model Estimation with Inter-Residual Distance Feedback, *9th Symposium on Identification and System Parameter Estimation*, Vol.2, pp.889-894, Budapest, Hungary.

[35] Marino R. (1990), Adaptive Observers for Single Output Nonlinear Systems, *IEEE Trans. AC.*, Vol.35, No.9, pp.1054-1058.

[36] Maybeck P.S. (1982), *Stochastic Models, Estimation and Control*, Academic Press, New York.

[37] Maybeck P. S., Hentz K. P. (1985), Investigation of Moving-Bank Multiple Model Adaptive Algorithms, *24th IEEE Conference on Decision and Control*, Vol.3, pp.1874-1881, Fort Lauderdale, Florida.

[38] Mealey G. L., Tang W. (1983), Application of Multiple Model Estimation to a Recursive Terrain Height Correlation System, *IEEE Transactions on Automatic Control*, Vol.28, No.3, pp.323-331.

[39] Miller W.T., Sutton R.S., Werbos P.J., ed. (1991), *Neural Networks for Control*, MIT Press, Cambridge, MA.

[40] Mirmehdi M., Ellis T.J. (1993), Parallel Approach to Tracking Edge Segments in Dynamic Scenes, *Journal of Image and Vision Computing*, Vol.11, No.1, pp.35-48.

[41] Moore C.G. and Harris C.J. (1994), Aspects of Fuzzy Control and Estimation, C. J. Harris, editor, *Advances in Intelligent Control*, Taylor and Francis, London.

[42] Murray-Smith R. and Johansen T.A. (1997), *Multiple Approaches To Modelling and Control*, Taylor and Francis, London.

[43] Products Developed at Neural Computer Sciences, UK.

[44] Onken R., Kopf M. (1991), Monitoring and Warning Aid for Driver Support on the German Autobahn, *Prometheus ProArt, der Bundesrepublik Deutschland fur das*, aweite Halbjahr.

[45] Parks P.C., Militzer J. (1991), Improved Allocation of Weights for Associative Memory Storage in Learning Control Systems, *Proceedings of 1st IFAC Symposium on Design Methods for Control Systems*, Zurich, pp.777-782, Sept. 4-6.

[46] Pomerleau D.A., Gowdy J., Thorpe C. (1991), Combining Artificial Neural Networks and Symbolic Processing for Autonomous Robot Guidance, *Journal of Engineering Application Artificial Intelligence*, Vol.4, No.4, pp.279-285.

[47] Roberts J. M. (1994), Attentive Visual Tracking and Trajectory Estimation for Dynamic Scene Segmentation, *Ph.D. Dissertation*, December, University of Southampton, UK.

[48] Rumelhart D.E., Hinton G.E., Williams R.J. (1986), Learning Internal Representations by Error Propagation, in *Parallel Distributed Processing: Explorations in the Microstructure of Cognition*, D.E. Rumelhart and J.L. McClelland, Eds., MIT Press, Cambridge, MA, pp.318-362.

[49] Schumaker L.L. (1981), *Spline functions: Basic theory*, New York, Wiley.

[50] Shapiro L.S., Wang H., Brady J.M. (1992), A Matching and Tracking Strategy for Independently-Moving, Non-Rigid Objects, *3rd British Machine Vision Conference*, Leeds, UK.

[51] Shepanski J.F., Macy S.A. (1988), Teaching Artificial Neural Systems to Drive: Manual Training Techniques for Autonomous Systems, *Neural Information Processing Systems*, American Institute of Physics, Editor, D. Anderson, pp.693-700.

[52] Shladover S.E. (1992), The California PATH Program of IVHS Research and Its Approach to Vehicle Highway Automation, *Intelligent Vehicles 92*, pp.347-352, June, Detroit, Michigan.

[53] Smith S.M. (1992), A New Class of Corner Finder, *Proceedings of the British Machine Vision Conference*, pp.139-148, Leeds, UK.

[54] Smith S.M., Brady J.M. (1993), A Scene Segmenter; Visual Tracking of Moving Vehicles, *1st IFAC International Workshop on Intelligent Autonomous Vehicles*, pp.119-126, Southampton, UK.

[55] Smith S.M., Brady J.M. (1994), A Scene Segmenter; Visual Tracking of Moving Vehicles, *Journal of Engineering Applications of Artificial Intelligence*, Vol.7, No.2, pp.191-204.

[56] Thomas B.T., Dagless E.L., Milford D.J., Morgan A.D. (1991), Real-Time Vision Guided Navigation, *Journal of Engineering Application Artificial Intelligence*, Vol.4, No.4, pp.287-300.

[57] Thorpe C.E. (1989), *Vision and Navigation - The Carnegie Mellon NavLab*, Kluwer Academic Publishing.

[58] Tobin D.M., Maybeck P.S. (1987), Substantial Enhancements to a Multiple Model Adaptive Estimator for Target Image Tracking, *26th IEEE Conference on Decision and Control*, Vol.3, pp.2002-2011, Los Angeles, CA.

[59] Traffic Safety Facts (1995): An Annual Compilation of Motor Vehicle Crash Data from the Fatal Accident Reporting System and the General Estimates System.

[60] Ullman S. (1979), *The Interpretation of Visual Motion*, MIT Academic Press.

[61] Wang L. X. (1994), *Adaptive Fuzzy Systems and Control: Design and Stability Analysis*, Prentice Hall, Englewood Cliffs, NJ.

[62] Wang H., Liu G.P., Harris C.J., Brown M. (1995), *Advanced Adaptive Control*, Pergamon Press.

[63] Watson G.A., Blair W.D. (1993), Track Maneuvering Targets with Multiple Sensors using the Interacting Multiple Model Algorithm, *5th Conference on Signal and Data Processing of Small Targets*, pp.438-449, Orlando, Florida.

[64] West M.M. (1994), Safety and Social Aspects of Intelligent Vehicle Highway Systems, *Technical Report*, School of Computer Studies, University of Leeds.

[65] Young E., Tribe R., Conlong R. (1992), Obstacle Detection for Collision Avoidance, *Third Prometheus Collision Avoidance Workshop*, Stuttgart, pp.190-195, June.

[66] Wu Z.Q., Harris C.J. (1997), A Neurofuzzy Network Structure for Modelling and State Estimation of Unknown Nonlinear Systems, *International Journal of Systems Science*, Vol.28, No.4, pp.335-345.

Chapter 2:

Knowledge-Based Scheduling Techniques in Industry

KNOWLEDGE-BASED SCHEDULING TECHNIQUES IN INDUSTRY

Jürgen Sauer
Universität Oldenburg, Fachbereich Informatik
Escherweg 2, D-26121 Oldenburg, Germany
sauer@informatik.uni-oldenburg.de

Scheduling is one of the crucial tasks to be done in order to guarantee the efficient execution of activities. The task is to find a temporal assignment of orders for performing specific activities to selected resources regarding several hard and soft constraints. In nearly all industrial areas scheduling problems have to be solved. Scheduling systems are embedded in the activities of industrial companies, e.g., in the production area scheduling is part of the production planning and control. Within scheduling systems simple, OR-based and - increasing in the last years - artificial intelligence techniques are used to solve scheduling problems.

This chapter gives an overview of the tasks of scheduling, the techniques used to solve scheduling problems and some issues in the design of scheduling systems together with two examples of scheduling systems.

1 Scheduling

In this section different dimensions of the scheduling problem are described. First we look at predictive, reactive and interactive scheduling which are tasks to be done in every scheduling environment. In the second subsection global and local scheduling are considered as organizational dimensions of scheduling leading to problems like coordination and communication. Finally, a simple example of a scheduling problem from an industrial scheduling environment is presented.

1.1 Predictive, Reactive and Interactive Scheduling

The task of **scheduling** is the temporal assignment of activities to resources where a number of goals and constraints have to be regarded. Scheduling covers the creation of a schedule of the activities over a longer period (**predictive** scheduling) and the adaptation of an existing schedule due to actual events in the scheduling environment (**reactive** scheduling) [1]. Scheduling problems can be found in several different application areas, e.g., the scheduling of production operations in manufacturing industry, computer processes in operating systems, truck movements in transportation, aircraft crews, refurbishment of Space Shuttles, etc. In all these areas "good" orderings to perform a series of given tasks have to be found [2], whereby in some cases specific objective functions shall be optimized.

Throughout the rest of the paper we will take manufacturing as the example and therefore use the notions of this area, but the results are valid for other application domains as well. The scheduling of production processes of a manufacturing organization is one of the significant tasks required to achieve competitive production, which means, for example, to deliver products in time or to use resources efficiently. A scheduling problem can be described by the 5-tuple (O, P, R, HC, SC) [3] with the following components:

- O is a set of **orders** to manufacture products which are to be scheduled subject to several constraints, e.g., due dates, amounts, user priorities.
- P is a set of **products** with information about (alternative) process plans, operations or steps within the process plans, duration of steps, raw materials used, machines that may be used alternatively within the steps, etc.
- R is a set of **resources** with different functional capabilities, e.g., machines with given capacity, personnel, raw materials.
- HC is a set of **hard constraints** that must be fulfilled, e.g., production requirements, time and capacity limitations.
- SC is a set of **soft constraints** that should be fulfilled but may be relaxed, e.g., meeting due dates, use preferred machines. Most of the objectives of scheduling can be formulated by means of soft constraints.

The result of scheduling is a (production) **schedule** showing the temporal assignment of operations (steps) of the process plan to the resources to be used, i.e., which resources should be used when for the manufacturing of a particular product for which an order exists.

Often objective functions are used to evaluate the schedule in order to find the "best" or an optimal schedule. These objective functions are mainly time oriented, e.g., sum of lateness, sum of tardiness which is defined as

$$STA := \sum_{i \in orders} TA_i \text{ with } TA_i = \max(0, (due\_date_i - scheduled\_end_i)).$$

Nearly the same information is needed for predictive and reactive scheduling and the same conditions must hold for the result (e.g., concerning the goals to be fulfilled).

In reactive scheduling all the events occurring in the scheduling environment have to be regarded, e.g., events from the shop floor like machine breakdowns or maintenance intervals, or events from the logistics level such as new or cancelled orders. Reactive

scheduling then means adapting the schedule to the new situation with the appropriate action to handle each of the events. All the objectives of scheduling have to be regarded as well as specific objectives of reactive scheduling which are:
- conserve as much as possible of the former schedule,
- react almost immediately.

When looking at the scheduling process in an organization we always find humans who have to decide, interact or control within the process. Thus scheduling has also a very important interactive dimension. **Interactive** scheduling then means that several decisions have to be taken by the human scheduler (the user of the scheduling system), e.g., introducing new orders, cancel orders, change priorities, set operations on specific schedule positions, and these decisions have to be regarded within the scheduling process. A support of the system is necessary to keep consistency and to present all information needed in an adequate manner (see also Section 3).

Thus the complexity of real-world scheduling scenarios is mainly determined by
- the requirements imposed by numerous details of the particular application domain, e.g., alternative machines, cleaning times, set-up costs, etc.,
- the dynamic and uncertain nature of the manufacturing environment, e.g., unpredictable set-up times, machine breakdowns, etc.,
- conflicting organizational goals, e.g., minimize work-in-process time, maximize resource utilization, and
- the need of interaction with a human scheduler.

The problem space of a scheduling problem can be visualized by an AND/OR-tree. It is constructed by combining the production requirements of the products (regarding alternative process plans and machines) with the orders given and the scheduling horizon (see Figure 1). Finding a solution to the scheduling problem is equivalent to finding a solution of the AND/OR-tree where the constraints are met. A solution consists of the root node, all successors of an AND-node (if the node belongs to the solution) and one successor of an OR-node (if the node belongs to the solution). In Figure 1 a solution is indicated by bold nodes and solid lines.

The number of possible solutions for such a tree can be estimated by [4]

$$\left((\#RI \bullet \#R)^{\#S} \bullet \#V \right)^{\#O}$$

with
#RI	mean number of possible intervals for resources,
#R	mean number of possible resources per step,
#S	mean number of steps per variant,
#V	mean number of possible variants for products,
#O	number of orders for products.

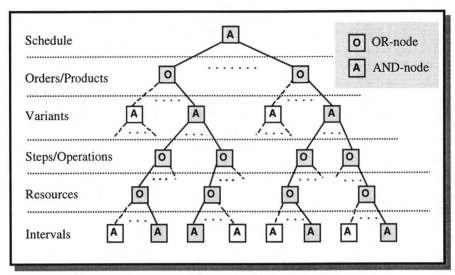

Figure 1: Problem space of scheduling

In the next section we look at another dimension, which is important for scheduling problems, especially when different sites have to cooperate to perform the activities.

1.2 Global and Local Scheduling

Industrial scheduling is embedded in the logistics chain responsible for the creation of a feasible schedule for performing the production processes in order to achieve the economical goals of the company. Scheduling integrates different tasks of production planning and control (PPC) systems to plan and carry out the manufacturing of products on the available resources respecting time, capacity, and cost restrictions. It can be assigned to the phases resource/material management, time management, job release, and production control of PPC. MRP or MRPII based systems provide the input data for scheduling. Systems controlling machines and collecting data from the shop floor provide data which are necessary for adjusting the schedules to the actual situation.

Scheduling problems are usually treated in a single plant environment where a set of orders for products has to be scheduled on a set of machines. However, within many industrial enterprises the production processes are distributed over several manufacturing sites, which are responsible for the production of various parts of a set of final products. This problem scenario is true especially for the industrial partners in the EUREKA-project PROTOS [5]. Some specific features of multi-site scheduling caused by the distribution of the production are:
- Complex interdependencies between the production processes performed in different plants.

- Cumulative and not precise information on the global level, e.g., capacity information.
- Coordination and rescheduling on the global level is necessary in order to provide the local schedulers with time intervals that will avoid and solve problems on the local level.

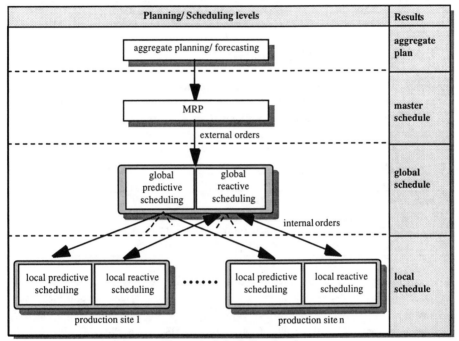

Figure 2: Scheduling levels

Multi-site scheduling [6] is characterized by scheduling tasks on two levels. On the global level products must be distributed to plants where the intermediates have to be produced. On the local level the intermediates have to be scheduled within the local production sites. If difficulties are encountered rescheduling has to be performed either on the local or the global level. Figure 2 illustrates the scheduling tasks on the different levels.

The goals within a multi-site scheduling system are twofold. The system has to regard
- the goals of the global scheduling activities such as meeting due dates of final products, minimizing transportation costs and work-in-process times, and
- the goals of the local scheduling level such as optimizing machine utilization, set-up times and meeting due dates of intermediates, which are often in contrast to each other.

Additional goals, especially for the effectiveness of a multi-site scheduling system, are the early detection of capacity problems and the coordination of the scheduling activities of the production sites. If a global schedule has to be rescheduled, one of the main goals is to preserve as much as possible of the existing global schedule in order to minimize the subsequent effort on the local level. Therefore, the multi-site scheduling problem can be divided into global and local scheduling tasks. On both levels predictive and reactive scheduling are necessary to create and maintain, respectively, the global or local schedules. Additionally, the coordination between these tasks has to be supported in order to provide all components with actual and consistent information.

1.3 A Scheduling Example

The following example uses data from the application domain "chemical industry". Table 1 shows the given orders (from the master schedule or the global scheduling system) A1 to A4 for three different products P1 to P3 with the given amount together with the earliest start, the due date and a priority denoting user preferences.

Table 1: Orders

order	product	amount	start	due	priority
A1	P1	300	02 04 97	12 04 97	1
A2	P2	400	04 04 97	12 04 97	1
A3	P3	200	02 04 97	12 04 97	1
A4	P1	200	03 04 97	09 04 97	1

Table 2 shows some of the production requirements for the three products. Each product has 2 or 3 alternative production variants; within each variant, several steps have to be performed. These three attributes build the key of the data entry. For every step the relative start time, the duration for the typical lot size and a final cleaning duration together with the set of alternative machines are given. Variant 0 denotes a so-called stem-variant which preferably should be used. The first machine in the list of possible machines should be preferred.

Some other typical information is missing in the example, for example, additional information on products, resources, personnel, stocks, raw materials.

The most important hard constraints are:
- One of the variants with all the steps has to be used. Only one of the alternative machines has to be used. After each step we have to clean the machine; exception: if the same step is performed several times then cleaning is necessary only once.
- Overlaps are not allowed, i.e., each machine can only perform one step at a time.
- Process oriented production has to be regarded, i.e., the steps of one variant have to be performed strictly one after another without preemption using the given relative start times with respect to the start of the first step, i.e.,
  $Start_i := Start_1 + Start_i - 1$

Table 2: Production requirements

product	variant	step	start	duration	setup/clean	machines
P1	0	1	1	1	2	[M1 M2]
P1	0	2	2	2	2	[M3]
P1	0	3	4	1	2	[M4 M5]
P1	1	1	1	1	2	[M1]
P1	1	2	2	2	2	[M4 M5 M6]
P1	1	3	4	1	2	[M1 M2]
P2	0	1	1	1	2	[M2 M4]
P2	0	2	2	1	2	[M3 M5]
P2	1	1	1	1	2	[M1 M6]
P2	1	2	2	1	2	[M2 M7]
P3	0	1	1	1	2	[M2 M4 M3]
P3	0	2	2	2	2	[M4 M5]
P3	0	3	4	2	2	[M2]
P3	1	1	1	1	2	[M3]
P3	1	2	2	2	2	[M4]
P3	1	3	4	2	2	[M5]
P3	2	1	1	1	2	[M4 M5 M6]
P3	2	2	2	2	2	[M2 M3]
P3	2	3	4	2	2	[M1 M7]

Important soft constraints are:
- Meet the due dates.
- Use the preferred variants and the preferred machines.

Figure 3 shows two of the about $3,5 \cdot 10^{10}$ { $((3 \cdot 2)^3 \cdot 2)^4$ in the above formula} possible schedules for the given problem. Each bar shows when one or a combination of single steps use a specific machine (the first digit denotes the order and the second the step number) and the cleaning time at the end of the production. Different patterns show the different orders, and dd_x their due dates. Evaluation functions can be used to compare the outcomes, for example, when using sum of tardiness then solution 2 is better $(4 < 7)$:

- $STA_{Solution1} = 7$
- $STA_{Solution2} = 4$.

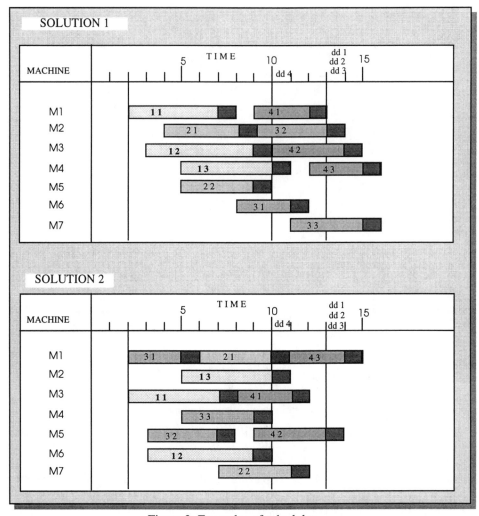

Figure 3: Examples of schedules

2 Scheduling Techniques

From the theoretical point of view scheduling is regarded as the problem of optimizing an evaluation function with respect to a given scheduling problem, i.e., scheduling is a combinatorial optimization problem. Most of the problems requiring an optimal solution to a resource scheduling problem belong to the class of NP-complete problems

[7], which means that no deterministic algorithm is known yet for solving the problem in polynomial time. Traditionally, production scheduling research has focused on methods for obtaining optimal solutions to simplified problems in the predictive scheduling domain. Well known problems are job-shop scheduling (all jobs use all machines with different routings) or flow-shop scheduling (all jobs use all machines in the same order/ routing). For a job-shop scheduling problem with 10 jobs and 5 machines the number of possible solutions is $10!^5 = 6.3 \cdot 10^{32}$. Thus it is not possible to enumerate all solutions to find an optimal one.

In order to determine an optimal solution, different restrictions may be imposed on the problem domain (e.g., on the number of orders or machines), which makes the application of the results to real-world scheduling problems very difficult or even impossible because most of the constraints of the scheduling environment are not regarded.

In scheduling theory the reduced scenarios are therefore normally used to find complexity notations and algorithms for optimal solutions. For an overview on scheduling theory see [8], [9].

Due to the difficulty of the problem domain, the objective in a real-world scheduling environment should be the determination of a "good" and feasible solution, not an optimal one. Very important for this task is the (heuristic) knowledge of the human domain expert who is able to solve distinct scheduling problems and to judge the feasibility of schedules by virtue of his/her gained experience. Several knowledge-based approaches have been developed using the experience of the human experts and problem-specific knowledge of the application domain. Scheduling problems have been investigated intensively in artificial intelligence (AI) and operations research. In AI approaches a variety of paradigms are used, in particular constraint-based search, heuristic search and rule-based techniques. The vast majority of approaches have been developed for predictive scheduling problems. Only recently, an increasing number of algorithms for reactive scheduling have been reported. Some of the approaches are presented in this section; for further information see, e.g., [1], [10], [11], [12].

AI provides not only new paradigms for problem solving but also new representation formalisms which allow the explicit representation and use of the knowledge of the domain, mainly by rule-based and constraint-based representation of scheduling knowledge. Thus scheduling research focuses on representational and problem solving issues (Figure 4).

The Knowledge Involved in Scheduling
Different kinds of knowledge are used in solving a scheduling problem. This knowledge can be divided into the areas of domain, situation, scheduling and meta-scheduling knowledge:

- The **domain knowledge** contains static information about the application environment, i.e., the structure of the **scheduling problem**, for example, the set of orders, the possible products, their recipes, the available resources etc.

- The **situation knowledge** represents the current state of scheduling, for example, the existing schedule, the remaining capacities of resources etc.
- The **scheduling knowledge** is divided into static and dynamic approaches for scheduling and rescheduling. Hard and Soft Constraints often are modeled within the scheduling knowledge.
  - The **static scheduling knowledge** contains complete algorithms, for example, operations research algorithms but also knowledge-based ones. These algorithms are firmly implemented and not changeable any more.
  - The **dynamic scheduling knowledge** denotes chunks of heuristic scheduling knowledge, which can be used together or alternatively in finding solutions to scheduling problems. It provides the possibility for adequate description and integration of multiple algorithmic approaches in one system.
- The **meta-scheduling knowledge** contains information about scheduling, i.e., knowledge necessary to determine the "best" algorithm due to the current scheduling problem.

Dynamic and meta-scheduling knowledge are used in the meta-scheduling approach presented in Section 3.2.

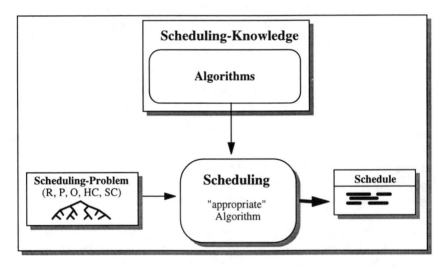

Figure 4: Scheduling

2.1 Heuristic Scheduling

Heuristic scheduling is based on heuristic search techniques and general heuristics such as problem decomposition together with problem specific knowledge adopted from scheduling experts in order to guide the search process. Knowledge representation is rule- or frame-based (object-oriented). Most of the predictive approaches can be characterized by the underlying perspective of the problem decomposition as shown in Table 3:

- *order-based*, i.e., one order is selected from all unscheduled orders and all operations of this order are completely scheduled before continuing with the next order, e.g., PROTOS [13], ISIS [14].
- *resource-based*, i.e., a resource is selected and then the appropriate operation is chosen out of the set of possible operations on this resource, e.g., [15].
- *operation-based*, i.e., one operation after another is selected and scheduled, e.g., [16].

Table 3: Strategies for scheduling

order-based	resource-based
WHILE orders to schedule	
select order	**select** variant for every order
select variant for order	find operations of orders
WHILE operations to schedule	WHILE operations to schedule
select operation	**select** resource
select resource	**select** operation
select interval	**select** interval
schedule operation	schedule operation
END WHILE	END WHILE
END WHILE	
time-order-based	**operation-based**
find earliest start of all orders	
WHILE orders to schedule	**select** variant for every order
select actual day	find operations of orders
WHILE orders to schedule	WHILE operations to schedule
for actual day	**select** operation
select order	**select** resource
select variant for order	**select** interval
WHILE operations to schedule	schedule operation
select operation	END WHILE
select resource	
schedule operation	
END WHILE	
END WHILE	
END WHILE	

Selection rules can be adopted from existing systems (e.g., priority rules), from literature e.g., [17], or from experts. Weighted combinations of simple rules are also possible. Some examples are:

1. for the selection of orders
   - schedule order with earliest start time first
   - schedule order with shortest processing time first

- schedule order by increasing number of alternatives (critical products first)
- schedule order by increasing slack intervals
- schedule order by increasing user priority

2. for the selection of routings
   - use stem variant first
   - select in inverse order (LCFS)
   - use critical routing first
   - use simple routing first

3. for the selection of operations
   - select by increasing operation number (FCFS)
   - select by decreasing operation number (LCFS)
   - select by increasing number of alternative resources (critical operation first)
   - select by decreasing number of alternative resources (simple operation first)

4. for the selection of resources
   - use stem first
   - use simple resource first
   - use critical resource first

5. for the selection of intervals
   - forward from given release date
   - backward from due date.

The algorithms differ essentially in the problem-specific heuristic knowledge applied to determine the appropriate decisions during problem solving, often specifically tailored to just one special problem scenario. Heuristic algorithms using priority rules are investigated in the OR as well; thus there is no clear distinction between AI and OR in this area.

2.2 Constraint-Based Scheduling

Constraints are the most important part of every scheduling problem. Thus constraint-based approaches have rapidly evolved and are now the dominant technique in representing and solving scheduling problems [18]. Two aspects of constraint use are important. The first is the representational aspect. Constraint formalisms (e.g., [14]) are used to explicitly represent the hard and soft constraints of the problem area. The constraints then are used to guide the search process. In the first applications this was heuristic search.

The second and newer aspect is the use of constraint programming techniques to solve scheduling problems. Here a scheduling problem is represented as a constraint satisfaction problem (CSP), i.e., the scheduling problem is described by a set of variables of certain domains and a set of constraints restricting these domains. The constraints often connect variables thus leading to constraint nets of nodes (representing variables) connected by arcs (representing constraints). For the solution of problems presented as constraint nets efficient systems have been developed implementing fast constraint handling algorithms, e.g., CHIP or ILOG. The systems provide features for definition and propagation of constraints, especially those of the scheduling area. With these systems even the optimization of certain objective functions is possible. Specific problem solving strategies have to be implemented additionally, e.g., to guide the search for the next variable to be tackled. Here textures [19] or heuristics may be used.

2.3 Scheduling with Fuzzy and Neural Network Approaches

Fuzzy scheduling deals with the inherent dynamic and incompleteness of the scheduling area. It allows the representation (by fuzzy sets and linguistic variables) and the inference (by fuzzy rules) from vaguely formulated knowledge. The main types of imprecise information addressed by fuzzy sets are
- vaguely defined dates or durations, e.g., due dates,
- vague definitions of preferences, e.g., preferences between alternatives,
- uncertainty about the value of scheduling parameters, e.g., process times,
- aggregated knowledge, e.g., machine groups instead of individual machines.

To handle the imprecise information with fuzzy controllers the following steps have to be performed:
- Transformation of scheduling data into a knowledge representation that can be handled by a fuzzy controller (fuzzification). Imprecise knowledge is represented by linguistic variables denoting the possible values, e.g., capacity of machine groups by {very low, low, normal, high, very high}. For each of the possible values a membership function (e.g., triangular) is given, which is used in combining and processing the fuzzy sets.
- Processing of the fuzzy scheduling knowledge towards a decision by means of given rules and integration of fuzzy arithmetics to deal with imprecise or vague data. Fuzzy rules then look like
    /* rule to determine the importance of orders */
    IF   Time-demand(very low)
            FUZZY_AND Priority(normal)
            FUZZY_AND Date(soon)
    THEN Importance(normal);
- Transformation of the fuzzy scheduling decision into crisp scheduling data (defuzzification), e.g., determine concrete dates for operations.

First approaches had promising results and research is ongoing [20], [21], [22].

Neural networks are mainly used for pattern recognition but are also useful in other application domains. In scheduling up to now only few problems have been investigated for the use of specific neural networks allowing optimization [12]. One main disadvantage is the inflexibility of the networks, i.e., for slightly changed situations new networks have to be established. Thus most of the approaches present neural networks for the predictive scheduling domain.

2.4 Iterative Improvement Techniques

Once a solution is found and there is enough time, several techniques can be used to improve the solution. The improvement techniques look at scheduling as a combinatorial optimization problem; start with any solution and try to find an optimal or near optimal solution by iterative improvements [23]. Genetic algorithms, simulated annealing, tabu search and iterative deepening belong to this approach.

Iterative improvement methods start with an initial solution or a set of initial solutions and try to improve them by modifications that shall result in a solution with a "better" objective value. Table 4 shows a general algorithm for iterative improvement [23]. The techniques differ in how the procedures "modify(s)" and "acceptable(new_s, s)" are designed and used.

Table 4: Scheme of an iterative improvement algorithm

```
BEGIN
s:= initialSchedule()
REPEAT
        sbest:= s;
        REPEAT
            new_s := modify(s)
            if acceptable(new_s, s)
                then s:= new_s;
        UNTIL better(s, sbest)
UNTIL stopping_criteria
END
```

Genetic algorithms (GA) are used widely, so they shall be described in more detail. GA imitate natural selection and genetics. They start with a set of solutions (individuals) forming a population. The modify procedure here consists of three parts: first, a subset of the individuals is selected for recombination, second, with the genetic operator crossover new individuals are created, and third, with the genetic operator mutation the new individuals are slightly changed. The new population is evaluated by an objective function and can be compared to the previous population.

The scheduling approaches using genetic algorithms differ in the representation of the individuals (schedules), e.g., as binary digits, and the operators used for selection, crossover and mutation [24].

Iterative improvement techniques lead to good results with simple objective functions but because of their runtime they are often not useful in reactive scheduling scenarios.

2.5 Distributed AI and Scheduling

Distributed AI (DAI) [25] is a newer field of research. DAI emphasizes the cooperative character of problem solving. Thus the results should also be useful for scheduling problems because some of the problems mentioned are inherently distributed (e.g., global and local scheduling). The systems developed are based on the idea of cooperating intelligent agents, each of them responsible for solving a specific task of the whole scheduling problem. Thus the main questions are how to divide the system into agents and how the agents communicate.

To distribute tasks among agents, several approaches are possible, e.g.,
• Agents can be subsystems of a scheduling system, e.g., predictive agent, reactive agent etc.
• Agents can represent single objects of the scheduling area, e.g., machine agents performing all the tasks fitting to a machine, or order agents performing all the tasks important for a single order.

Every agent has to perform a set of tasks with goals specific for the agent or a class of agents. Often a control agent is necessary to control the performance of the whole system and the fulfillment of the global goals of the whole system. Within the agents, all the problem solving techniques mentioned here may be used to perform the scheduling or other tasks of the agent.

For communication two architectures are widely used:
• the blackboard approach: all agents use a central data structure for communication. Each agent reads from the blackboard and checks if he can solve the problem and writes his results to the blackboard.
• contract nets: agents use a structured protocol to communicate to each other.

2.6 Reactive Scheduling

Reactive scheduling deals with the repair of a schedule which has become inconsistent due to specific events. The events can be of external type, such as a short-term acceptance of a high-priority order or delay of material delivery, or internal, such as a machine breakdown.

The importance of reactive scheduling is due to its real-time character. Consequences of events shall be monitored immediately and the schedule has to be adjusted as fast as possible. Because the actual situation in the shop floor is affected, i.e., raw material is already transported to machines for manufacturing a specific operation, the changes in the schedule shall be as minor as possible. As a third factor the overall goals of scheduling shall be regarded as well.

Only few approaches for reactive scheduling have been presented [26] but the area is growing. Some approaches use heuristic repair strategies regarding the events of the shop floor [27]. Others try to find more general approaches, because some specific rescheduling problems suggest an emphasis on either order- or resource-based algorithms [28], [29]. The early Leitstand systems [30] are used to monitor the situation on the shop floor and help the human scheduler in rescheduling by hand. The combination of the Leitstand approach for visualizing the effects of events or scheduling actions (automatic as well as interactive) and sophisticated reactive scheduling algorithms seems to be the most promising approach for reactive scheduling. Many algorithmic approaches may be used within the schedulers, but heuristic and constraint-based approaches seem to be most useful.

2.7 Appropriateness of Scheduling Techniques

Due to the variety of scheduling problems it has been shown that it is impossible to find a single general purpose scheduling algorithm that works well in all cases [1]. Thus Table 5 tries to conclude this section with an overview of the scheduling areas mentioned and the most suitable techniques within these areas.

Table 5: Appropriateness of scheduling techniques

Scheduling Area	Techniques
Global Predictive Scheduling	Heuristics, Constraints, Genetic Algorithms, Fuzzy-Logic
Global Reactive Scheduling	Interaction, Heuristics, Constraints
Local Predictive Scheduling	Constraints, Heuristics, Genetic Algorithms, Neural Networks, OR-Systems
Local Reactive Scheduling	Interaction, Heuristics, Constraints, Multi-Agents
Meta Scheduling	Heuristics, Neural Networks

3 Scheduling Systems

A Scheduling system shall support the human scheduler in his daily work in creating and revising schedules of the production. Several criteria influence the requirements for such a system, e.g., the area of production and the preferences of the producing company as well as the need for presentation of specific information and sophisticated scheduling algorithms. In spite of a large number of developed scheduling methods, only a few practical applications have entered into everyday use in industrial reality. Our experience obtained in projects addressing real-world scheduling problems showed that not only the applied scheduling methods but also several other features play a significant role in the acceptance of scheduling systems, including user interface, possibilities for manual interaction and information presentation [31]. Hence, a knowledge-based scheduling system should meet the following requirements [32]:

- information presentation
  The information necessary for the scheduling task must be presented in an appropriate manner, showing specific information at a glance on capacities or alternative process plans. Moreover, it should be possible to monitor all scheduling actions in order to see the immediate consequences of specific decisions and to maintain consistency.

- interaction
  Interaction shall allow for full manual control of the scheduling process. All decisions may be made by the user (e.g., selecting orders, operations, or machines). However, the support of interactive scheduling merely by information presentation and consistency control seems not to be sufficient due to the combinatorial complexity of the problem domain. Pure automatic scheduling, on the other hand, is not realistic either since it neglects the important role of the human expert who has the ultimate responsibility for all decisions. Thus, industrial scheduling systems should support the interactive as well as the automatic part of predictive and reactive scheduling (also called mixed-initiative scheduling [33]).

- incorporation of scheduling expertise
  One of the main features of a knowledge-based scheduling system is the identification and application of problem-specific knowledge for the solution of the addressed problem. By using this knowledge the system can employ heuristics for the problem solving process that are similar to the ones used by the human expert, who, in turn, can verify the plausibility of the solution. However, it is not sufficient to merely mimic the decision-making of a human expert since his/her decisions are often myopic, aimed at solving small sub-problems immediately instead of global optimization.

- integration in the organizational environment
  An existing complex information technological infrastructure can be found in every modern industrial enterprise. Scheduling systems cannot be designed as stand-alone components since they have to communicate, interact, access the same data, and share information with their organizational environment. Therefore,

knowledge-based systems have to be an integrated part of an existing information system, thus providing well defined interfaces to standard application systems such as database systems and computer networks.

- participation of the user
  The incorporation of the user in all phases of the system design process is extremely important for the final acceptance of the scheduling system.

- communication between scheduling levels
  This is a crucial task in order to maintain consistency, coordinate the activities between the different scheduling systems on the two scheduling levels, and to inform the participating systems of events which might affect them.

Within our research group several scheduling systems have been designed for specific problem domains in industry and medicine [27], [32], [34] (Figure 5 gives an overview of three of the systems). The objective of the projects was the enhancement of the problem solving capabilities of the human domain experts by means of computer-based scheduling systems. Primary characteristic of all three systems is the combination of a graphical user interface with knowledge-based algorithms, thus enabling interactive as well as predictive and reactive scheduling.

Project application area	PROTOS chemical industry	PSY/REAKTION metal industry	MEDICUS hospital (heart surgery)
production area:	produce dyes	produce fittings	treat patients
special features:	alternative routings, alternative machines	alternative routings, alternative machines	operation, intensive-, intermediate-, normal-care
resources:	machines, apparatuses	machines	operating theater, hospital beds
production process:	continuous flow production	discrete part manufacturing	fixed number of operations, beds
soft constraints:	use stem variants, meet due dates	minimal flow-time and work in process	waiting time max. 6 weeks, weekends for emergency
special features of user interface:	selection of alternative routings and apparatuses	capacity diagram, master scheduling, reactive scheduling	capacity diagram, zooming, reactive scheduling

Figure 5: Overview of scheduling systems

The systems are based on a common architecture (see Figure 6) consisting of:

- a user interface responsible for the tasks of information presentation and interactive scheduling, based on a Gantt-chart representation of the current schedule, as well as tools for manual interaction such as selection, insertion, deletion, relocation and substitution of resource allocations.
- a scheduling component containing scheduling knowledge both for predictive and reactive scheduling tasks, the knowledge base and a consistency checker.
- a database component which implements an interface, typically to an existing database system, and
- interfaces to other scheduling levels responsible for communication with the systems on those levels.

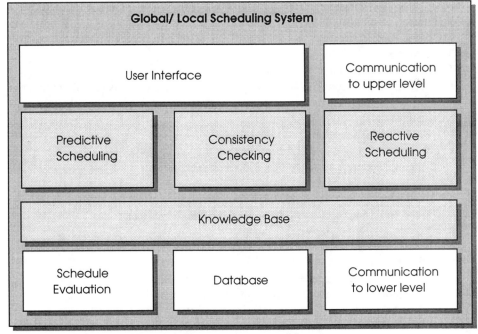

Figure 6: Common system architecture

As an example, the PSY system is presented in more detail (Section 3.1). Based on the experiences with the previously implemented scheduling systems a meta-scheduling system has been developed which guides the user in finding the appropriate strategy for a given scheduling problem (Section 3.2).

3.1 PSY/REAKTION - Production Scheduling in Metal Industry

The scheduling system PSY (Production Planning and Scheduling System) [32] was developed in cooperation with a company of the metal industry producing fittings for pipelines. More than 10,000 different products may be produced ranging from standard fittings (e.g., 90 degrees arches for water mains) to special fittings for power plants. The lot sizes reach from one for the special fittings to several thousands for standard fittings. The system was developed to support the scheduler in long- and short-term predictive scheduling. In long-term scheduling (one year) the orders (customer orders and orders for stock) have to be placed in weeks regarding the capacity of the machines. In short-term scheduling a detailed schedule of one week showing hours of production and consisting of about 100 orders each with about 6 to 10 operations has to be created.

The Problem

The problem description is as follows:
- a set of orders from the long-term schedule is given consisting of information about the products to be produced, the amount, the week when they should be finished, and a user given priority.
- products are fittings for pipelines or mains.
- resources are machines for cutting, heating, or forming pipes.
- the hard constraints describe the production requirements including:
  - all orders have to be scheduled,
  - all operations of an order have to be scheduled,
  - the preference constraints between operations have to be met,
  - overlaps are not allowed,
  - orders must not be split.
- soft constraints are:
  - orders should be scheduled within the given weeks,
  - work-in-process and flow times should be minimal,
  - critical machines should be utilized efficiently.

The System

The user interface (Figure 7) presents the information of the scheduling area and supports interactive scheduling. The orders that must be scheduled (and those which have already been scheduled) are presented in the upper left window (Betriebsauftraege), where an order can be selected and changed or new orders may be inserted (long-term scheduling). The user can attach priorities to certain orders. The upper right window (Woechentliche Auslastung) contains the capacity information of all machines. Here the capacity diagram of one machine over 5 weeks is presented and weeks and machines can be selected. Additionally, the week and a single order or all orders to be scheduled in detail are selected. The effect of the scheduling algorithm (one of three possible strategies may be chosen in an additional window) is shown in the central window (Wochenfeinplanung) presenting the whole schedule. System information is listed in the bottom window (Systemmeldungen). Additional windows (shown as icons) present information about the routings, the calendar, the shifts, the long-term scheduling and the possible scheduling strategies. The system supports long-term scheduling by checking the capacities of the critical machines involved in the production of a desired product in the week it shall be manufactured. If a given capacity limit is violated the order is proposed to be shifted to another week.

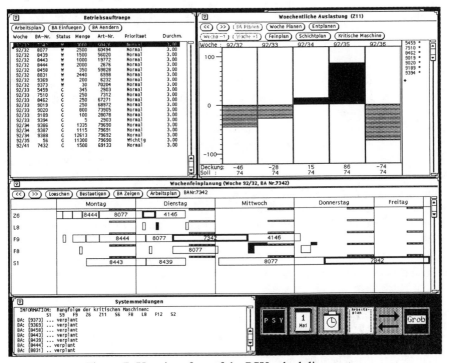

Figure 7: User interface of the PSY scheduling system

```
sort orders by priorities
WHILE orders to plan
    select order
    WHILE operations to plan
        select operation and resource
        select interval
        schedule operation or solve conflict
    END WHILE
END WHILE.
```

Figure 8: Scheme of the PSY algorithm

Three predictive scheduling strategies based on a common scheme (Figure 8) are implemented for short-term scheduling from which the user can select one. Orders are selected by using priorities. The differences are in the selection of operations, resources and intervals. The so-called "basic" strategy implements a strategy where the week is filled from left to right (Monday to Friday) by the "first in first out" principle and the shortest processing time rule. The operations are scheduled on the earliest possible position trying to optimize the flow times and to meet the due dates. The two other strategies first look at critical machines. Orders are selected by priorities and the operations using the critical machines are scheduled first. In the "first fit" variant the operations are scheduled on the earliest possible position trying to minimize flow time; in the "best fit" variant the operations are scheduled on the smallest possible position trying to optimize utilization.

Using one of the strategies a single order or all orders of one week may be scheduled. The schedule is presented as a Gantt-chart and the user has the ability to alter the schedule by deletion, substitution or relocation of orders or operations. To improve the reactive scheduling capabilities of the system, an extension was implemented in the system REAKTION [27] realizing a concept for reactive scheduling in detailed schedules which have become inconsistent due to unexpected events. The events can be of external type, e.g., short-term acceptance of a high-priority order or delay of material delivery, or of internal type such as a machine breakdown. The system is realized as a leitstand [30] with a Gantt-chart representation of the schedule, where the schedule is repaired interactively or by an algorithm using heuristics to solve the constraints violated. The heuristic repair strategy implemented regards the priorities of the orders when deciding which inconsistency (caused by an event) has to be treated first. Several event specific heuristics have been combined to treat any event individually.

3.2 A Meta-Scheduling System

When solving the scheduling problem in the projects mentioned above we identified some general problems independent of the underlying production structure. Although a huge variety of algorithmic solutions has been proposed, it is hard to find the appropriate algorithm or algorithmic component in a given situation. There is no system providing support in selecting the appropriate algorithm. Another problem is that most of the algorithms are developed for specific problem situations; if the situation changes they are no longer useful and there is no support in customizing the algorithms. These problems are the motivation for meta-scheduling and dynamic scheduling knowledge. A meta-scheduling system should offer multiple alternative algorithms applicable to varying circumstances in connection with a support in selecting the most appropriate approach for a given problem. In our approach we use the types of scheduling knowledge mentioned in Section 2, including meta-knowledge to represent the appropriateness of strategies in given situations, and dynamic scheduling knowledge to separate the scheduling knowledge into modules that can be connected to "new" scheduling algorithms.

Meta-scheduling then looks like (Figure 9): if a scheduling problem is given then meta-scheduling knowledge is used to select the appropriate scheduling knowledge on the basis of goals or events either by choosing a static, predefined algorithm or by dynamically creating a "new" algorithm using a skeleton of a scheduling algorithm and rules within the skeleton.

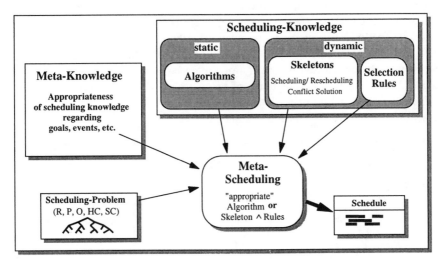

Figure 9: Meta-Scheduling

To find the chunks of knowledge we look especially at the heuristic search approaches. Each of them can be viewed as a scheduling strategy using different heuristic rules for the selection of orders, machines etc. It is possible to extract the rules from the strategies and represent both explicitly. The strategies can be described as **skeletons** (adopted from [35]), where special parts can be refined with appropriate rules regarding the actual scheduling problem (see Table 3). **Rules** are used for the selection of orders, variants, operations, resources, and time intervals. They can be adopted from OR (e.g., priority rules [17]) as well as from human experts.

The dynamic combination of scheduling skeletons and appropriate rules for selections provides us with a huge library of different scheduling and rescheduling approaches. A crucial problem is then the selection of the "best" approach in a given problem situation.

Meta-knowledge can be used to support this task. One approach was presented by the OPIS system [29] where one algorithm out of four possible ones is selected based on the values of several parameters describing the actual scheduling situation. In our approach meta-knowledge is more general and can be used to select:
- appropriate strategies for scheduling and rescheduling both as fixed algorithms or as skeletons,
- the rules within the skeletons, and

• conflict solution strategies useful within the skeletons for scheduling and rescheduling.

Different sources of meta-knowledge may be exploited covering the goals which shall be achieved, the events, and other information specific to the situation.

Representation of Scheduling Knowledge

A language called HERA (heuristics for representation of scheduling knowledge) has been developed [4], [3] for the representation of the scheduling and meta-scheduling knowledge. HERA is based on Prolog providing all the features of declarative knowledge representation and the integration of Prolog code as well as calls to other languages. The "classical" representation of heuristics as IF-THEN rules is extended by an explicit representation of goals and events and by control constructions usable in the action part to describe scheduling strategies.

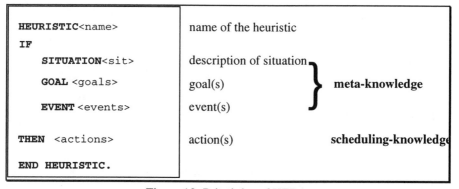

Figure 10: Principles of HERA

Figure 10 shows how heuristics then look. <name> denotes the name of the heuristic, <sit> contains the description of the situation to use the heuristic, <goals> the description of the goals that can be achieved, <events> the description of the events that can be tackled, and <actions> the description of the strategy (the heuristic scheduling knowledge). The IF-part of the heuristic contains the meta-knowledge which is used to select the appropriate strategy. The THEN-part represents the scheduling knowledge ranging from the call of predefined strategies to the description of the scheduling and rescheduling strategies to be used.

The prototypical system META_PLAN [3], [4] implemented in Prolog is designed to support a human scheduler in the selection and simulation of knowledge-based scheduling algorithms for given problem situations.

The *User-Interface* (Figure 11) provides a user-friendly and problem-adequate graphical presentation of the information currently in the knowledge base, e.g., a Gantt chart representation of the existing schedule (in the window "Scheduling Result"), the evaluation of the current schedule, and multiple tools for interaction, e.g., the selection and comparison of predefined scheduling strategies or skeletons together with rules (in the window "Predefined Skeletons and Rules").

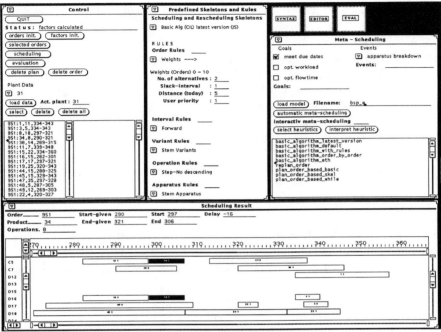

Figure 11: User-interface of META_PLAN

The *Meta-Scheduling* component is the most important component of the system, since it implements the selection and interpretation of the appropriate scheduling strategies as follows:

1. It starts with the input of a new scheduling problem (tasks, goals, and events). To identify appropriate heuristics the actual goals and events are compared to the corresponding descriptions in the heuristics represented in HERA. Appropriate are those where at least one of the actual goals is met and where all actual events are tackled.

2. The alternative algorithms (static as well as dynamically created ones) are judged and the applicable approaches are ranked with respect to their appropriateness for the current problem. The "best one" of these is the algorithm where most of the actual goals are met.

3. The best strategy is applied first. If the interpretation of a heuristic succeeds, a new schedule has been generated. If the interpretation of a heuristic fails, the next heuristic is chosen (2.) until a solution is found or no appropriate heuristic is available. In this case no solution is found.

This component implements a meta-scheduler since it may build schedulers as well as schedules [11].

An *Evaluation* component provides several functions for evaluating schedules, e.g.,
- information about scheduled intervals and lateness of the orders,
- information about used capacities,
- evaluation functions such as sum of delays, number of tardy orders, mean tardiness etc.

A *Heuristic-Editor* enables the acquisition of new knowledge and the alteration of current knowledge represented with HERA. The knowledge base of META_PLAN contains the dynamic scheduling knowledge consisting of strategies, skeletons and rules represented with HERA and several fixed scheduling algorithms which can be selected by the meta-scheduler or by the user. Fixed algorithms cover:
- the order-based approach of PROTOS,
- a time/ order-based approach [36],
- reactive approaches due to order cancellation and high priority orders [4],
- the first two approaches as "fixed" skeletons with a given set of rules useable as parameters that can be selected manually.

To integrate fixed scheduling algorithms (e.g., from operational research) written in other languages together with the meta-knowledge necessary for their application, an interface is implemented giving META_PLAN features of a hybrid scheduling system.

The system provides flexibility for scheduling and rescheduling. Various different scheduling algorithms are available, each showing selective advantages for specific problems The user is supported in selecting the "best" strategy and can create his/her "own" scheduling algorithm and extensions are possible (other skeletons and rules can be integrated easily). META PLAN is a hybrid scheduling system providing for flexible use of dynamic scheduling knowledge as well as meta-scheduling knowledge. The system is implemented in Prolog (Quintus-Prolog) using features including definite clause grammars for the description of HERA, meta-programming for the interpreter, and tools for building user-interfaces (ProWindows).

4 Conclusion

Scheduling is a fast growing research area. This is supported not only because scheduling is economically interesting (good schedules can save millions of dollars [2]) but also by a huge variety of application domains and the applicability of nearly all problem solving techniques to problems in this domain. The scheduling problem has been presented in different dimensions and some of the most used problem solving techniques in scheduling have been presented.

Two examples of scheduling systems developed have been described. The first is based on the experience that the acceptance of scheduling systems is influenced not only by sophisticated (knowledge-based) scheduling algorithms but also by system features such as the design and functionality of the user interface, the possible interaction, and the information presentation. A common architecture for scheduling systems is deduced, incorporating knowledge-based scheduling algorithms and user friendly interfaces presenting all relevant information and allowing user interaction to control the entire scheduling process.

The second system is a meta-scheduling system appropriate for designers of scheduling systems. A basic concept of the system is the decomposition of scheduling algorithms in the underlying strategies and heuristic rules for selections. These strategies and heuristic rules are represented separately by means of skeletons and rules. Scheduling algorithms are created dynamically by combining skeletons and rules providing a huge variety of possible scheduling algorithms.

In our research project we have attempted to expand the meta-scheduling idea to the design support of complete scheduling systems [37]. A knowledge-based system is under development that guides the user in designing a knowledge-based scheduling system. It supports all phases of system development:

- the modeling of the problem area, e.g., the database, and the requirements definition of the system ranging from the functional requirements to the look of the user interface. Reference models, e.g., for the database and the requirements are used to guide the process.
- the configuration of the scheduling system from predefined components that may be slightly changed. This is supported by an object-oriented system architecture. Here the meta-scheduling approach mentioned earlier is incorporated.
- the test of the system using test data created according to the requirements defined.

References

[1]   Smith, S.F. (1992), Knowledge-based production management: approaches, results and prospects, *Production Planning & Control*, Vol. 3, No. 4.

[2]   McDermott, D., Hendler, J. (1995), Planning: What it is, What it could be, An Introduction to the Special Issue on Planning and Scheduling, *Artificial Intelligence*, Vol. 76, No. 1-2, July.

[3]   Sauer, J. (1995), Scheduling and Meta-Scheduling, Beierle, C., Plümer, L. (eds), *Logic Programming : Formal Methods and Practical Applications*, North-Holland, Amsterdam.

[4]   Sauer, J. (1993), *Wissensbasiertes Lösen von Ablaufplanungsproblemen mit expliziten Heuristiken*, Dissertation, Universität Oldenburg, DISKI 37, Infix Verlag, Sankt Augustin.

[5]   Beierle, C. (1992), Knowledge Based PPS Applications in PROTOS-L, Comyn, C., Fuchs, N.E., Ratcliffe, M.J. (eds), *Logic Programming in Action*, Springer, Berlin.

[6]   Bruns, R., Sauer, J. (1995), Knowledge-Based Multi-Site Coordination and Scheduling, Schraf, R.D. et al. (eds.), *Flexible Automation and Intelligent Manufacturing 1995*, Begell House, New York.

[7]   Garey, M., Johnson, D. (1979),*Computers and Intractability: A Guide to the Theory of NP-Completeness*, W. H. Freeman, New York.

[8]   Blazewicz, J., Ecker, K.-H., Schmidt, G., Weglarz, J. (1994), *Scheduling in Computer and Manufacturing Systems*, Springer, Berlin.

[9]   Pinedo, M. (1995), *Scheduling*, Prentice-Hall, Englewood Cliffs.

[10]   Dorn, J., Froeschl, K.A. (1993), *Scheduling of Production Processes*, Series in Artificial Intelligence, Ellis Horwood, Chichester.

[11]   Kempf, K.G. (1989), Manufacturing planning and scheduling: Where we are and where we need to be, *Proceedings of the Fifth IEEE Conference on Artificial Intelligence Applications*.

[12]   Zweben, M., Fox, M.S. (1994), *Intelligent Scheduling*, Morgan Kaufman, San Mateo.

[13]   Sauer, J. (1991), Knowledge Based Scheduling in PROTOS, *Proc. IMACS World Congress on Computation and Applied Mathematics*, Trinity College, Dublin.

[14]   Fox, M. (1987), *Constraint Directed Search: A Case Study of Job-Shop Scheduling*, Pitman Publishers, London.

[15]   Liu, B. (1989), *Knowledge-Based Production Scheduling: Resource Allocation and Constraint Satisfaction*, DAI Research Paper 436, University of Edinburgh.

[16]   Keng, N.P., Yun, D.Y., Rossi, M. (1988), Interaction Sensitive Planning System for Job-Shop Scheduling, Oliff, M.D. (ed.), *Expert Systems and Intelligent Manufacturing*, Elsevier, Amsterdam.

[17]   Haupt, R. (1989), A survey of Priority Rule-Based Scheduling, *OR Spektrum*, No. 11.

[18]   LePape, C. (1994), *Constraint-Based Programming for Scheduling: An Historical Perspective*, Working Paper, Operations Research Society Seminar on Constraint Handling Techniques, London, UK.

[19]   Beck, J.C. et al. (1997), Texture-Based Heuristics for Scheduling Revisited, *Proc. of AAAI-97*, National Conference on Artificial Intelligence.

[20]   Sauer, J., Appelrath, H.-J., Suelmann, G. (1997), Multi-site Scheduling with Fuzzy-Concepts, submitted *for Approximate Reasoning in Scheduling*.

[21]   Slany, W. (1994), *Fuzzy Scheduling*, Dissertation, Technische Universität Wien, Christian Doppler-Laboratory for Expert Systems.

[22]   Kerr, R.M., Slany, W. (1994), *Research Issues and Challenges in Fuzzy Scheduling*, Technical Report 94/68, Technische Universität Wien, Christian Doppler-Laboratory for Expert Systems.

[23] Dorn, J. (1995), Iterative Improvement Methods for Knowledge-Based Scheduling, *AICOM*, Vol. 8, No. 1, March.

[24] Bruns, R. (1997), Scheduling, *Handbook of Evolutionary Computation*, Bäck, T., Fogel, D., Michalewicz, Z. (eds.), Oxford University Press, Oxford.

[25] Chaib-Draa, B. et al. (1992), Trends in Distributed Artificial Intelligence, *Artificial Intelligence Review*, No. 6, pp. 35-66.

[26] Kerr, R.M., Szelke, E. (1995), *Artificial Intelligence in Reactive Scheduling*, Chapman & Hall, London.

[27] Henseler, H. (1995), REAKTION: a system for event independent reactive scheduling, Kerr, R., Szelke, E. (eds.), *Artificial Intelligence in Reactive Scheduling*, Chapman & Hall, London.

[28] Ow, P.S., Smith, S.I., Thiriez, A. (1988), Reactive Plan Revision, in: *Proceedings of AAAI-88*, Morgan Kaufman, San Mateo.

[29] Smith, S.F., Ow, P.S., Matthys, D.C., Potvin, J.-Y. (1990), OPIS: An Opportunistic Factory Scheduling System, *Proceedings of the Third International Conference on Industrial & Engineering Applications of Artificial Intelligence & Expert Systems*, Charleston.

[30] Adelsberger, H. et al. (1992), The Concept of a Knowledge-based Leitstand - Summary of First Results and Achievements in ESPRIT Project 5161 (KBL), *CIM-Europe, 8th Annual Conference*, Birmingham, UK.

[31] Kempf, K.G. et al. (1991), Issues in the Design of AI-Based Schedulers: A Workshop Report, *AI Magazine*, Special Issue, January, 1991.

[32] Sauer, J., Bruns, R. (1997), Knowledge-Based Scheduling Systems in Industry and Medicine, *IEEE-Expert*, February.

[33] Hsu, W.L., Prietula, M., Thompson, G., Ow, P.S. (1993), A mixed-initiative scheduling workbench: Integrating AI, OR, and HCI, *Journal of Decision Support Systems*, 9(3), pp. 245-247.

[34] Sauer, J., Bruns, R. (1994), Knowledge-Based Scheduling Systems in Prolog, Proc. of 2. Int. Conf. *The Practical Application of Prolog*, London.

[35] Friedland, P.E., Iwasaki, Y. (1985), The Concept and Implementation of Skeletal Plans, *Journal of Automated Reasoning*, Vol. 1, No. 1.

[36] Nussbaum, M., Slahor, L. (1989), Production Planning and Scheduling: A Bottom-up Approach, Rzevski, G., *Artificial Intelligence in Manufacturing*, Computational Mechanics Publ., Southampton.

[37] Sauer, J., Appelrath, H.-J., (1997), Knowledge-Based Design of Scheduling Systems, *Proc. of World Manufacturing Congress*, Auckland.

Chapter 3:

Fuzzy Image Analysis for Medical Applications

FUZZY IMAGE ANALYSIS FOR MEDICAL APPLICATIONS

J. Hiltner
University of Dortmund
Department of Computer Science, Chair I
44221 Dortmund, Germany

M. Jäger, M. Moser
VITRONIC Bildverarbeitungssysteme GmbH
65189 Wiesbaden, Germany

C. Tresp
Aachen University of Technology
LuFG Theoretical Computer Science
52056 Aachen, Germany

In this chapter a way of using vague knowledge for image understanding is presented. Often there is only vague information about the content of an image and to handle this vague information one cannot use a classical image processing system which only works with crisp descriptions. In the last few years fuzzy logic has shown very promising methods to handle the different kinds of uncertainties and vague information. Here some possible operators for image segmentation and attribute description are given. This interpretation of the concept results from the practical analysis of images given from the field of medical MR-tomography.

1 Introduction

The field of image processing is becoming more and more important in many applications. As examples one can find systems for image processing in industry, e.g., in quality checking or part recognition. Also in medicine, particularly radiology, many methods of image processing are applied.

1.1 Image Processing

To understand the meaning of "image processing" one must make the distinction between low-level image processing and high-level image processing. Between these two there is a soft transition, but a possible distinction is given by the resulting data structure or the goal of the processing. Low-level image processing, also known as image preprocessing, normally transforms image data to image data, for example, quality improvement or contrast enhancement. On the other hand, high-level image processing (image recognition, image understanding, image analysis) transforms image data to an interpretation of the content of the image. Image analysis systems are mostly knowledge-based systems.

Menhardt [19] defines that image analysis deals with "... the automatic recognition of objects in a digital image of a real scene". This means that a set of points is assigned to an object name (or vice versa). Generally systems for image analysis are application dependent, because for each scope special knowledge is necessary. In Figure 1 a typical model for image analysis is shown.

1.2 Image Analysis Model

The model (see Figure 1) consists of a processing line and a knowledge base. All parts of this processing line work on the knowledge base. The fundamental part of image preprocessing improves the image data for further steps. There are two kinds of preprocessing known as image enhancement and image restoration.

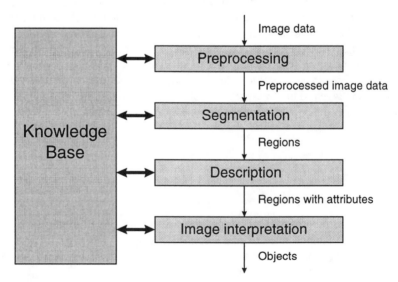

Figure 1: Typical model for image analysis

The segmentation part divides the image into different regions where, in the classical case, an overlapping is not permitted. The regions should correspond to the searched objects. This is very difficult, because image data can contain uncertainties (see Section 3). As a criterion for segmentation each region should be homogeneous in its interior and be separable from the surrounding regions. A large number of segmentation operators are known, which could be divided into the two groups, region-oriented and edge-oriented.

Region-oriented methods for image segmentation search for connected regions which consist of points with similar attribute values (for example the gray value). The region-oriented methods again can be divided into the region-growing methods and the thresholding-methods. Region-growing methods (see Figure 2) use a starting point which the growing process starts from. All points around this starting point are viewed and those which are similarly colored are added to the list of points which belong to the searched region. The new added points are selected as new starting points and the process restarts. For each wanted region a starting point is needed. Big problems are: when to stop the growing process and how to select number and position of the starting points. As shown in Figure 2 the number of starting points can significantly affect the outcome.

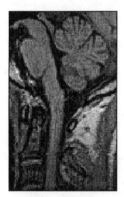  

Figure 2: Example for region-growing: original image (a), segmentation results with 10 starting points (b) and 11 starting points (c)

Thresholding methods (see Figure 3) use one or more threshold values to segment a given image. The assignment of points to regions is defined by the membership of their feature values to the intervals between neighboring threshold values. A problem is the selection of the threshold values. A special case of thresholding is the binarization operation.

The edge-oriented methods (see Figure 4) for image segmentation search for changes in feature values on object borders. Generally the gradient of each point is determined, where a high gradient value is interpreted as an edge.

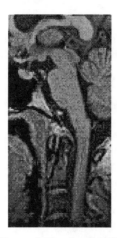

Figure 3: Example for thresholding with threshold-value 96 (gray value)

Many edge operators exist and all of them have advantages and disadvantages. Problems can be unclosed and thick edges (see e.g., Figure 4(b)). These operators can also be very noise sensitive and smooth transitions between two objects cannot always be found. Edges can be determined in different ways, for example the application of a high pass filter on the Fourier-transformed image or the consideration of surrounding points using a local convolution operator.

For the interested reader here are some examples of edge operators listed without further explanation [6][8]:
- Sobel-operator
- Kirsch-operator
- Laplace-operator

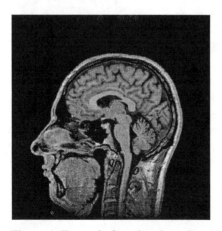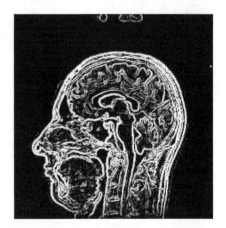

Figure 4: Example for edge detection (a) original image (b) application of the Sobel operator

The next part in the processing line of the model is the description of regions resulting from the previous segmentation. Here the attribute values are determined. These attribute values describe the regions to compare them with the attribute values for the searched objects given in the knowledge base. Examples for attributes include mean gray value (brightness) of a region, its size, boundary shape and texture.

Finally the processing line in the interpretation step makes an analysis of the descriptions and compares them with the object descriptions in the knowledge base. Then object names are assigned to the regions. Because the regions may not correspond to the objects, this part contains the process of merging or splitting of some regions. In Figure 2(c) one can see that the brain stem is divided into different regions depending on the number of starting points. Hence some of the regions must be merged. In contrast to this the cerebellum was merged with another region and must be split.

The knowledge base of the model contains the knowledge about the problem solution. The knowledge can be divided into low-level and high-level knowledge. The low-level is procedural knowledge about skillful parameter selection for the image operators and must be provided by image processing experts. The high-level knowledge is used for the identification of regions. It contains descriptions of objects and relations between them and it must be provided by domain experts.

The interested reader can find a good introduction and overview of techniques for image processing and image segmentation in [5][6].

2 Medical Image Processing

In the last few decades many technologies for medical image acquisition have been developed. As a consequence the importance of image based diagnostics is growing continually. And proceeding with this evolution, a rising number of more and more complex image processing systems have been developed for physicians' assistance.

2.1 Medical Image Data

Medical image sources all have advantages and disadvantages relating to quality, costs and burden for the patient (e.g., with x-rays, radioactive medicines for contrasting etc). Some of these technologies will be discussed in the following sections..

2.1.1 X-ray Diagnostic

X-ray (discovered in 1895 by Wilhelm Conrad Röntgen) was the first way to look inside the human body without using a scalpel. Early on in radiodiagnosis use was made of three of the properties of X-ray: their ability to penetrate the tissues, their photographic effect, and their ability to cause certain substances to fluoresce. In penetrating tissues, the radiation is observed differentially, depending on the densities of the tissues being penetrated. The radiation emerging from tissues thus produces on a photographic film or a fluorescent screen an image of the structures (see Figure 5) of differing densities within the body. The limiting factor in this method of diagnosis is the similarity between the densities of adjacent soft tissues within the body, with a resultant failure to produce a significant contrast between the image regions of adjacent structures or organs [29].

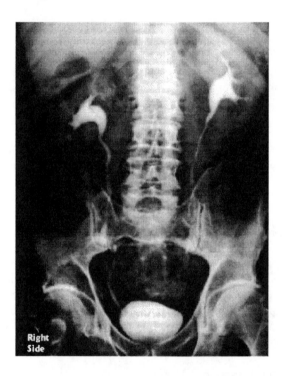

Figure 5: Example of an X-ray image

2.1.2 Computer Tomography (CT)

The CT scan is a procedure in which the body is X-rayed from many different angles. An X-ray source delivers a series of short pulses of radiation while it and an electronic detector are rotated around the body of the individual being tested. The responses of the detector are fed to a computer that analyzes and integrates the X-ray data from the numerous scans to construct a detailed cross-sectional image of the body. A series of such images enables physicians to locate tumors, cerebral abscesses, blood clots, and other disorders that would be difficult to detect using conventional X-ray techniques [29].

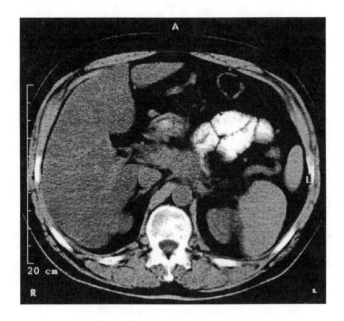

Figure 6: Example of a CT image

2.1.3 Nuclear Magnetic Resonance Tomography (NMR)

While computer tomography scanning is a pure X-ray technique, other computerized investigations yield data without the use of X-rays. In NMR imaging the patient is placed within a magnetic coil (see Figure 7) and radiofrequency energy is applied to e.g., the head (see Figure 4). These harmless radio waves excite protons that form the nuclei of hydrogen atoms in the examined part of the body (here the brain). The protons then give off measurable electrical energy, which, with the aid of the computer, can be used to construct a map of the tissue. Since NMR-imaging is relatively insensitive to bone, it gives excellent images of the intracranial and intraspinal contents [29].

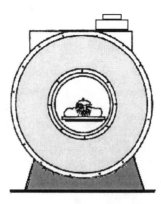

Figure 7: Patient in an NMR-tomograph

2.1.4 Ultrasonography

Ultrasonography (ultrasound diagnostic) is the use of high frequency sound (ultrasonic) waves to produce images of structures within the human body. The ultrasonic waves are produced by electrical stimulation of a piezoelectric crystal and can be aimed at a specific area of the body. As the waves travel through bodily tissues, they are reflected back at any point where there is a change in tissue density, as for instance in the border between two different organs of the body. The reflected echoes are received by an electronic apparatus that determines the intensity level of the echoes and the position of the tissue giving rise to the echoes. The images thus formed can be displayed in static form, or through the use of rapid multiple sound scans. They can in effect provide a moving picture of the inside of the body (see Figure 8).

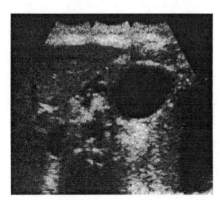 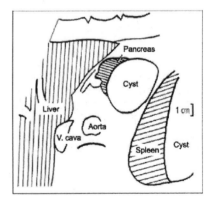

Figure 8: Example of an ultrasound image and schematic view

Part of ultrasound's usefulness is the fact that the sound waves cause no known damage to human tissues, unlike X-rays or other ionizing radiations used in diagnostic radiology. Because of its safety, ultrasound is most commonly used to examine fetuses in utero in order to ascertain birth defects or other abnormalities. Ultrasound is also used to provide images of heart, liver, kidneys, gallbladder, breast, eye, and major blood vessels [29].

2.1.5 Endoscopy

Endoscopy is a diagnostic method for the examination of the interior of a canal or hollow viscus by means of a special instrument (endoscope). The endoscope is a fixed or flexible tube with optical lenses, CCD-cameras and lights. Endoscopy is used in the field of minimal invasive surgery as well as for diagnostic imagery. Application fields include laparascopy, gastroscopy, thorascopy and cystoscopy. Example images of a normal colon can be seen in Figure 9.

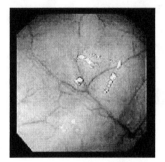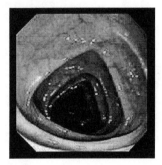

Figure 9: Examples of endoscopic images of the colon

2.1.6 Thermography

Thermography can be applied in medical imaging where the images map different surface temperatures on the body. There are different types of thermography: telethermography (recording with an infrared camera) or plate thermography (direct contact to the skin). The image temperature differences result from blood flow disturbances or tumors (see Figure 10).

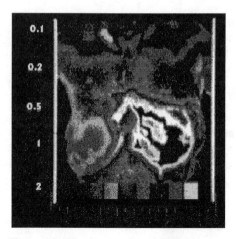

Figure 10: Thermography of female breast

2.2 Special Problems of Medical Image Processing

Of course problems which occur in general image processing also arise in medical image processing, but these problems, for example noisy data, location translations, different object sizes and so on, are often more extreme. For this reason some of the special problems of medical images will be presented in more detail.

2.2.1 Interindividual Variability

A special problem in medical image processing is the interindividual variability (see Figure 11). In this example one can see three median slices of an MR-tomography of a human head. All these slices contain the same structures, for example the brain stem, the cerebellum, and so on, but it is very easy to see the differences between these images. "Classical" (non-fuzzy) object recognition methods do often fail here.

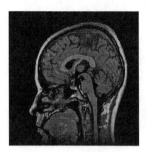 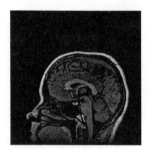 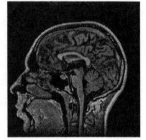

Figure 11: Example for interindividual variability

2.2.2 Fissured Borders

Most of the organs in medical images do not have simple shapes and it is hard to separate them exactly. This effect is exacerbated in the examination of 3-dimensional structures using NMR data (e.g., see all three examples of the cerebellum in Figure 11).

2.2.3 Smooth Transitions

The recorded object itself can contain uncertainties, for example at the transition between two or more single structures. It may be very difficult even for an expert to find a crisp edge between the cerebellum and the cerebrum. One can see this in the example zoom-in (see Figure 12).

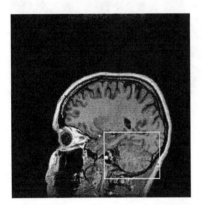 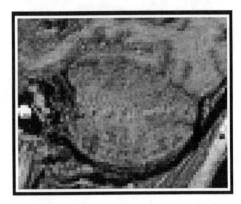

Figure 12: Example for smooth transition

3 Uncertainties in Image Analysis

Uncertainties in image analysis are a major problem and they occur in different ways in each step of the processing model. Handling these data as uncertain data implies that the subsequent steps should also handle their data as uncertain.

3.1 Occurrences of Uncertainties in Image Data

We now consider the different kinds of uncertainties beginning with the uncertainties in image data.

3.1.1 Noisy Image Data

As everyone knows amplitude recording cannot be exact. Generally image data are, depending on the recording technique, more or less noisy (see Figure 13). As one can see it is very difficult to find any structures in the noisy image.

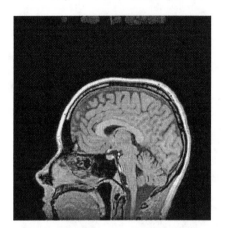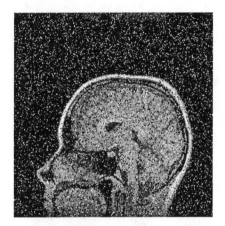

Figure 13: Example for noisy data (generated synthetically)

3.1.2 Digitalization Failure

Real valued signals are infinitely variable, but measure values can be represented only with finite precision in digital form. The more detailed the measure values are the more errors (e.g., noise) can occur and more computing time and memory is needed.

3.1.3 Vagueness of Localization

This phenomenon follows from an inexact digitizing step during the recording. On the one hand the recorded volumes, which are represented by a gray value voxel, are inexactly positioned. On the other hand the size and form of the volumes can vary. Often both these effects occur at the same time as represented in Figure 14.

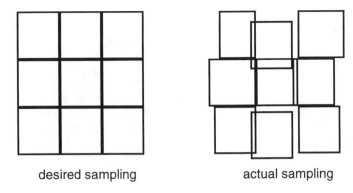

desired sampling   actual sampling

Figure 14: Vagueness of localization

A special kind of this type of uncertainty are motion artifacts (see Figure 15). These result from movements of the object during recording time. In the image presented here the recorded object (a human head) moves to the upper right during the recording process. The resulting image is smudged so that it is much harder to find any structures in the image.

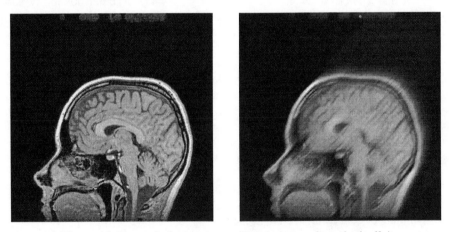

Figure 15: Example for motion artifact (generated synthetically)

3.1.4 Partial Volume Effect

Another kind of uncertainty in image data is the partial volume effect caused by the limited spatial or volumetric resolution of the image sampling system. Each voxel (volume element, 3-dimensional pendant of a pixel) is represented by one single gray value in the image data, which results from the finite resolution of every recording technique. Sampling effects mask fine detail in the image, as shown in Figure 16, possibly leading to a loss of fine edges.

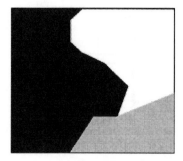 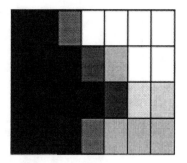

Figure 16: Partial volume effect – crisp edges get lost

3.2 Modeling of Uncertainties

There are methods for modeling the different types of uncertainty. One can assign each voxel its own fuzzy set from the universe of gray values, representing the degree of belief that a noise voxel has the respective gray value. Another possibility is an additional fuzzy value for each voxel (beside its gray value), as in [17] where this additional value is unclear. So we define this additional value as a measure of confidence in the gray value of the voxel.

But how to get this measure value? It should be clear that it not only depends on the gray value of the voxel itself but also on the size and form of the voxel (see the section on the partial volume effect and vagueness of localization). Another influence is the surrounding voxels. For example a voxel with a very high gray value should have a very low measure of confidence in its gray value if all surrounding voxels have a given low gray value. This voxel is likely to be noisy.

The determination of these confidence measures can be assigned to the conceptual part of the image preprocessing. Then the "Classical" operators of preprocessing such as smoothing or contrasting are not needed.

The main problem in the segmentation step is the smooth transition gray value between objects (see Figure 12). In this case it may be meaningful to allow the voxel to belong to different regions and so a fuzzy modeling of regions makes sense. In this context regions can be defined as not-empty and connected fuzzy subsets of voxels [23][25]. Each of the voxels has a degree of membership to a given region and overlapping regions can be modeled. Since the regions are defined fuzzy, the attributes of the regions should also be fuzzy.

But there is also another reason to allow fuzzy attributes. It allows the modeling of more complex attributes or hard to define attributes (see Figure 17). Here one can see the problem of the crisp definition of the attribute "oblong" based on a fixed width to height ratio. Why should the second rectangle have the attribute value "oblong" as true, but the third one not?

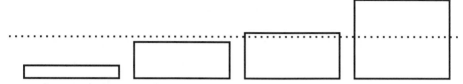

Figure 17: Problem of the crisp classification "oblong"

Here the fuzzy logic allows the modeling of attributes such as oblong, round, etc. using linguistic terms. Rosenfeld shows some fuzzy determination methods for easy to determine attributes [23][24].

Another type of uncertainty can be found in the modeling of the knowledge. Here one can see the uncertainty in the linguistic description of objects with concepts like "round", "big", "dark" and so on and the knowledge itself is uncertain, too. This is a major issue in NMR (nuclear magnetic resonance) tomography where the problem of interindividual variability (see above) can be found. Further uncertainty can also result from different expert opinions.

Many techniques exist for processing uncertain knowledge, including fuzzy expert systems. In the field of image processing the work of Menhardt is significant [19][20].

Since there are likely to be problems of uncertainties in image data it does not make any sense to define objects as crisp structures (see the partial volume effect). More meaningful is the representation of an object by its name and a fuzzy region with an additional confidence measure.

4 Fuzzy Logic for Image Segmentation

The process of segmentation is divided into two sub-tasks, filtering and flooding, a process based on region growing extended with fuzzy methods.

4.1 Application of Vague Filters

The given problem is to connect each pixel on the image with a membership value belonging to the object that we look for, e.g., the *brain stem* as in Figure 18. When we look for the *brain stem*, we have vague knowledge about the location of the object and even vague knowledge of a plausible interval of gray values that can be assigned to every pixel belonging to the *stem*. To model this vague knowledge, we describe the filters through fuzzy functions applied to the image of interest. We introduce a mapping M on the image that translates the input image into a modified one, where now each pixel x from the image X receives an (estimated) fuzzy membership to the object:

$$M: X \rightarrow [0,1] \text{ where } M(x):= \mathbf{TQ}(F_1(x), F_2(x), ..., F_n(x)) \tag{1}$$

$M(x)$ calculates for each pixel x of the image in which way it fulfills the conditions demanded by F_1 to F_n. The general quantor $\mathbf{TQ}$ is a so called t-quantor that simulates the necessary number of t-norm connections on all demanded conditions. In our example, the function F_1 stands for the presumed location of the *brain stem* and F_2 defines the supposed vague interval of gray values the *brain stem* may have.

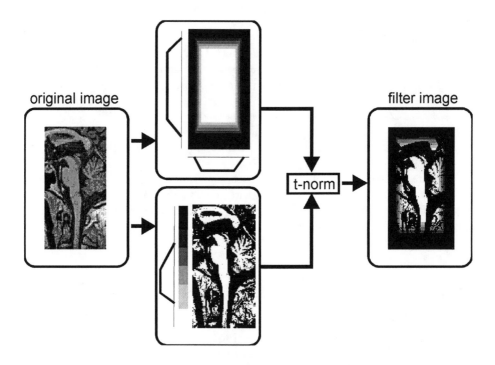

Figure 18: Application of vague filters for location and gray values

Both functions are describing fuzzy sets. The approximated values should be obtained by experts or by manually evaluating a number of tomograms. During the next step, the values have to be encoded into fuzzy sets. Figure 18 gives an example how to apply the filter method if one wants to locate the *brain stem* in the 2-dimensional case.

4.2 Application of Vague Flooding

The resulting image from fuzzy filtering serves as input into the procedure for fuzzy region growing. Even within the crisp case of this method, there is the problem of choosing the appropriate starting pixels. The basic idea is to select only starting pixels that have a membership degree larger than 0. The next step to select starting pixels is to begin with pixels that are lying within a homogenous region. Such a region does not have large variations of gray values of its pixels and consists of pixels that have a high plausibility value obtained by the fuzzy filtering procedure. Since no further information is available, we then start with each pixel that meets the conditions. A pixel x is connected to a starting pixel x_0, if and only if there is a path of high quality between them. The fuzzification of this yields a degree $R_{x_0}(x)$ of fuzzy-connectivity:

$$R_{x_0}(x) = \mathbf{SQ}_{p \in \Pi(x_0, x)} \{pathrate(p)\} \tag{2}$$

$\mathbf{SQ}$ is a fuzzy existential quantifier that implements a t-conorm connection on all possible paths p that lead from x_0 to a single pixel x. $\Pi(x_0, x)$ is the set of all paths from x_0 to x. A path p is a sequence $(p_0=x_0, p_1, p_2, .., p_{n_p}=x)$ of pixels, whereas pixels neighbored in this sequence are also neighbored in the image. The function $pathrate$ then rates a given path according to its quality:

$$pathrate = \mathbf{TQ} \{A_1, ..., A_m\} \tag{3}$$

A_k stands for one of m different attributes that determine the degree of the quality of a given path (i.e., the pixels that are crossed by moving from x_0 to x). Since we demand that if one attribute is not adequate the overall quality of the path is equally low, we chose the fuzzy generalization $\mathbf{TQ}$. Among other possible and sensible attributes, we suggest the following ones:

- **Membership to the filter region**

The whole path must be part of the region filtered as described above. To fuzzify this attribute, we use the fuzzy generalization $\mathbf{TQ}$ over all pixels belonging to the path. This yields the following degree of membership of the path p to the fuzzy region M:

$$m_M(p) := \mathbf{TQ} \{ M(p_i) \mid i = 0, ..., n_p \} \tag{4}$$

- **Global homogeneity**

Each point of the path must have a gray value similar to the starting point. The similarity can be described by a fuzzy set f_g of possible gray value differences. This gives the following measure of global homogeneity of a path p:

$$gh\ (p) := \mathbf{TQ}\ \{f_g(|g(p_i)\text{-}g(p_0)|)\ |\ i = 1, ..., n_p\ \} \tag{5}$$

- **Local homogeneity**

The difference between the gray value of two neighbored points of the path must be small. The term small can be described by a fuzzy set f_l. This results in the measure of local homogeneity of a path p:

$$lh(p) := \mathbf{TQ}\ \{f_l\,(|g(p_i)\text{-}g(p_{i\text{-}1})|)\ |\ i = 1, ..., n_p\ \} \tag{6}$$

This leads to an assignment of fuzzy regions (also known as iconic fuzzy sets) for each starting pixel. Obviously, those starting points with degrees that come close to another starting point with a high path-connectivity will lead to very similar segmentation results. Therefore, it is easy to further optimize the strategy. Figure 19 shows some results, applying the strategy to the search of the *brain stem*.

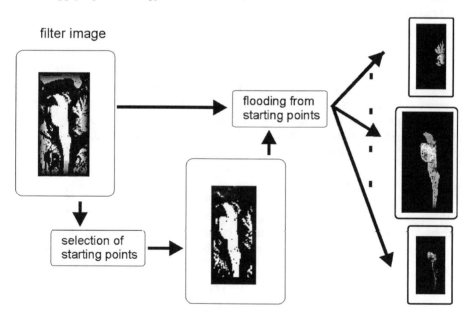

Figure 19: Vague region growing with different starting pixels

5 Fuzzy Logic for Object Description

5.1 The Valuation Procedure

After the core step of segmentation, the obtained objects must be rated. In the example, one wants only to find the *brain stem* and not the large number of potential candidates. It is important to have a description of the object *brain stem* that hopefully applies a number of fuzzy concepts like "The *brain stem* is very bright and has a medium size". Now we need operators on the description levels for brightness and size that directly use the fuzzy rated segmentation results and choose the one result that has the highest degree of plausibility. Therefore, a fuzzy knowledge base using the defined operators is sensible. If the result after defuzzification is smaller than demanded, we have to apply a strategy to obtain better starting pixels, e.g., by readjusting the parameters of our filter.

Instead of a sequential model of image analysis, in knowledge-based image analysis the single components interact in a more mutual manner. To select the most appropriate segmentation result, we need the knowledge from the level of object recognition. Therefore, the sequential model that starts with image enhancement, segmentation, object description and recognition - similar to that proposed by [6] - has to be modified in the following way. The step of image enhancement is no longer as important as before since enhancement tries to correct fuzziness on images where our approach explicitly deals with it. Nevertheless, one can combine the process of filtering as well as image enhancement under the component of image preprocessing. On the other hand, the unidirectional connection from segmentation to object recognition must be complemented by one from recognition to segmentation. The reason for this comes from the observation that the recognition process has a strong influence on the selection of appropriate starting points for the fuzzy region growing. Object description and even stronger object recognition as a component is additionally supplied with a knowledge base where one can find not only information about the different operators and relations that are relevant for the objects of interest but also about a directive on how to proceed after obtaining results from the segmentation component.

5.2 Vague Attributes

For the description of objects in natural languages one often uses linguistic terms like "more or less small", "very round", etc. Generally these are vague descriptions of specific attribute values. Therefore, fuzzy subsets offer themselves as a way to handle this information. For example "very round" can be modeled by a fuzzy set on the degrees of roundness as shown in Figure 20.

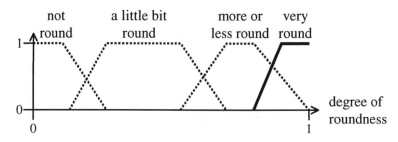

Figure 20: Linguistic terms for roundness and corresponding fuzzy sets

Many kinds of attributes like "size" and relations like "is smaller than" are possible. Their suitability depends to a high degree on the field of application, but in all cases an important requirement for these operators is their intuitive comprehensibility. For example, everyone can imagine the meaning of the attribute "round", but what the second centroid moment means is very hard to comprehend.

Another problem in the case of tomogram segmentation is the 3-dimensionality. While there are many terms in natural language describing 2-dimensional forms, for 3-dimensional descriptions the corresponding words are missing in many cases. Here, natural descriptions often make use of 2-dimensional cuts or projections of the current object. Therefore, in the following the focus is centered on 2-dimensional attributes, and only when there is a simple extension is a 3-dimensional variation presented. The implementation of relations is omitted within this article but is similar to those of the attributes since we consequently use fuzzy sets to rate the results.

Subsequently, the following definitions are used:

- n: number of pixels the region consists of
- x_i, y_i, z_i: coordinates of these pixels ($i = 1, ..., n$)
- d_x, d_y, d_z: distances between pixels in x-, y- and z-direction

5.2.1 Size

The simplest attribute is the size of a region which is the number of pixels belonging to the region. Size (resp. *area* in the 2-, *volume* in the 3-dimensional case) obviously can be defined as follows:

$$area(R) := n \cdot d_x \cdot d_y \tag{7}$$

$$volume(R) := n \cdot d_x \cdot d_y \cdot d_z \tag{8}$$

5.2.2 Compactness

Compactness is a measure that indicates whether the region has a smooth or a fissured border. The longer the border of a region with fixed size, the lower its compactness. A circle has highest possible compactness.

There are different definitions for compactness, but all of them use the ratio between area and square of perimeter. Normalization to the interval [0, 1] usually used in fuzzy logic yields:

$$compactness_{2D}(R) := \frac{4\pi \cdot area(R)}{perimeter(R)^2} \tag{9}$$

This definition can easily be extended to the 3-dimensional case. Instead of *area* and *perimeter, volume* and *surface* must be used. Analogous considerations result in the definition of 3-dimensional compactness:

$$compactness_{3D}(R) := \frac{6 \cdot \sqrt{\pi} \cdot volume(R)}{surface(R)^{3/2}} \tag{10}$$

For the determination of *perimeter* (resp. *surface*) the pixels of the region which are lying on its border must be counted.

5.2.3 Roundness

Another attribute is the roundness of a region. Therefore, one must define the meaning of the concept roundness. If defined as "not cornered", an ellipse has a high measure of roundness. Alternatively, it can be defined as circular. Then one must decide whether a ring structure is round, or only a filled circle has a high measure of roundness. This definition depends on the application field for the description operator and, for the following example, the definition is the similarity to a filled circle. The similarity between two regions can be defined by their difference in area. To calculate the roundness of a region R a reference circle C_{2D} is needed and we use a circle with the same size and the same center of gravity as the object. To obtain a size independent measure of roundness the value of the difference area must be normalized by the region's size, where it is reasonable to define the similarity as zero when difference areas are larger than the half size of the region. This interpretation of roundness is presented in equation 11.

$$roundness_{2D}(R) := \min\left(1 - \frac{area(K_2 \cap \overline{R}) + area(\overline{K_2} \cap R)}{area(R)}, 0\right) \tag{11}$$

An adaptation to the 3-dimensional case can easily be obtained. One must only use a reference sphere C_{3D} instead of a reference circle C_{2D} (see eq. 12).

$$roundness_{3D}(R):= \min\left(1 - \frac{volume(K_3 \cap \overline{R}) + volume(\overline{K_3} \cap R)}{volume(R)}, 0\right)$$ (12)

Some examples of the roundness measure are shown in Figure 21. For each one the first picture shows the found object and the reference circle. In the second picture the black pixels show the difference area.

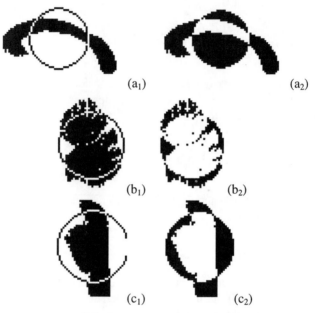

(a₁)   (a₂)

(b₁)   (b₂)

(c₁)   (c₂)

Figure 21: Example for calculation of roundness
(a) roundness = 0,169; (b) roundness = 0,757; (c) roundness = 0,702

5.2.4 Orientation

Another attribute is the orientation of an object. The determination of the orientation is only sensible in case of extended objects. The principal axis of orientation can be calculated by minimizing the mean square distance of each point of the structure to a straight line. The function to calculate this distance is derived from the standard straight line equation $y = mx + b$ and is shown in equation 13 for a single point (x,y).

$$distance(x, y, m, b) = \sqrt{\frac{(mx + b - y)^2}{m^2 + 1}}$$ (13)

By using the distance function (eq. 13), the goal function that must be minimized can be calculated with equation 14. The variable n represents the number of points belonging to the structure for which the principal axis of orientation is to be determined.

$$f(m,b) := \frac{1}{n}\sum_{i=1}^{n} distance(x_i, y_i, m, b) = \frac{1}{n}\sum_{i=1}^{n}\sqrt{\frac{(mx_i + b - y_i)^2}{m^2 + 1}} \qquad (14)$$

This straight line can be interpreted as the principal axis of orientation. Examples for the orientation of different structures are shown in Figure 22.

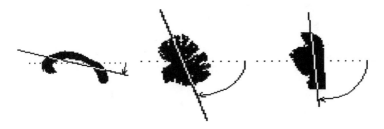

Figure 22: Examples for principal axis of orientation

6 Fuzzy Reasoning in Image Analysis

There are different possibilities to represent knowledge. Our first approach was to explicitly represent the relevant knowledge with some kind of a semantic network. Relevant knowledge means the knowledge about the different features of the object of interest. If one is looking for the *brain stem*, one has to know, for example, that it is very homogenous and long. Furthermore, the *brain stem* has relations to other objects, for example the *corpus callosum* or the *cerebellum*.

Within the knowledge base, one can define linguistic variables and linguistic terms for the description of typical object features. Furthermore, since the relations between the objects can also be fuzzy, the definition of fuzzy relations with arity 2 is allowed. An object of interest is then recognized by its features and relations to other already recognized objects. There are two kinds of relevant features, the low level features, also called vague filters, are those used during segmentation and the features calculated during the step of object description are called vague attributes.

The disadvantage of a semantic network is that each single facet of knowledge has to be explicitly stated which means that the system has no ability to reason with knowledge, i.e., to infer implicit knowledge from explicit knowledge. Knowing the vague observation that the *cerebellum* is at least 3 pixels below the *corpus callosum*, and further knowing that the location of *cerebellum* is left of the *brain stem*, it would be possible to automatically infer the relation of location between *brain stem* and *corpus callosum*.

As seen above, the high-level knowledge type of relations provides a basis for inferring new relationships from a basic knowledge base. For this reason, we have started to develop and integrate some fuzzy knowledge representation logic, based on a fragment of fuzzy predicate calculus. The language extends those from the family of KL-ONE based terminological knowledge representation systems also called description logics [9].

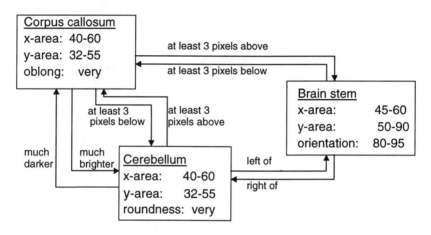

Figure 23: Example for a fuzzy knowledge base

6.1 Knowledge Base Extension and Consistency Check

The underlying fuzzy knowledge representation language is described in [10]. The basic reasoning mechanism is founded in [11]. Today, we only use a heuristic inference strategy, i.e., the inferences seem to be sound, but are definitely not complete from a logical point of view. Nevertheless, since we only need enough knowledge to recognize structures, a complete computation of all possible inferences is not really essential. This is opposite to some other crisp approaches (e.g., Baader and Hollunder in [13]) with sound and complete inference algorithms. But even in the crisp case, completeness is often not really required, as seen in [13]. A simple example for an extension of a given knowledge base is shown in Figure 23 where the location relations between *brain stem* and *corpus callosum* are computed.

The reasoning mechanism also enables further functionality since the system can verify new integrated relations with some consistency. When the *cerebellum* is defined much darker than the *brain stem*, feature definitions for the brightness degree of both objects that differ from the relation will lead to some inconsistency, directly traced by the system. Whereas in classical logic only consistent or inconsistent statements are allowed, the system now supports different consistency/inconsistency degrees. A fuzzy brightness interval with a support defined on [50..120] for the cerebellum is more consistent than one of [70..140] with respect to [80..150] for the brightness support of the *cerebellum*.

6.2 Applying the Knowledge

Object recognition is not as straightforward as one may think. Let us consider the following example. Since the basic strategy first is to look for the more simple to recognize objects, the system starts to search for the *brain stem*. Normally, it is imperative for the detection of more complex objects to take note of their relationships to already recognized ones. For example, the *corpus callosum* can be detected by using the defined relations to the *brain stem*. But in some rare cases caused by the different factors of fuzziness, it is more difficult to detect some simple objects than some with a more complex structure. This may result in all possible candidates for the *brain stem* to receive very low membership degree values. Therefore, the confidence in the ultimately selected object to represent the *brain stem* is very low. The applied strategy is then to detect other objects, e.g., the *corpus callosum*, without using the relation that the *corpus callosum* is at least three pixels below the *brain stem*. If the system nevertheless is able to obtain a good result for this object, it can now use the computed relation "at least 3 pixels above" to search for the *brain stem* again. Since this relation among others changes the search parameters, completely different and hopefully better results for the *brain stem* will be obtained.

6.3 Fuzzy Control for Image Processing

As supplement to the fuzzy operators presented above there is the possibility of using fuzzy controllers with fuzzy rules. These rules can contain instructions to optimize the parameters for the operators. The premise and conclusion of the rules are linguistic variables and linguistic terms. An easy example is the following rule:

IF found_object = very_small THEN search_area_increasing = very_high

IF image_data = very_dark THEN brighten_factor = very_high

A lot of rules like this can be found to further improve the results of the fuzzy operators.

7　Practical Experiences with Fuzzy Image Processing

Our research on automatic evaluation of MR-tomograms and the resulting application has its origin in a concrete request (see Figure 24) made by the brain research institute of the University of Düsseldorf when there is a requirement to analyze several hundreds of heads a year. Aim of the medical research is to prepare a map of the human brain with respect to interindividual variability across the wide span of possible variations of human brains.

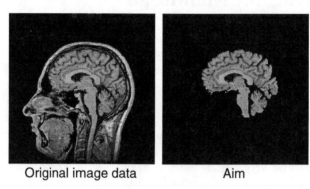

Original image data　　　　　　　Aim

Figure 24: The desired result

At present the processing of tomograms, in the course of which the brain is divided from remaining tissue, is performed manually. The working time required per head is of the order of three hours and the work is executed by scientific auxiliaries whose services are very expensive. At the brain research institute Düsseldorf several hundreds of hours per annum go to pay for this work and the high cost factor motivates the development of methods to automate the manual process requiring no creativity.

Another very important topic is that the manual work requires a division into brain and remaining tissue by a line drawn with a light pen. This division is not always reliable since there are many different factors such as the daily condition of the physician influencing the quality of segmentation. Hence a correct automatic segmentation is preferred, because a computer does not have a daily condition. The processing system described above has proven to give good results. For example, the whole brain in Figure 25 has been segmented successfully.

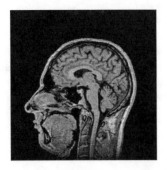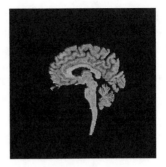

Figure 25: Results of the system BRAINY

The next example (Figure 26) shows results obtained with the system CATS [28], which has found the single structure cerebellum in both samples. This system uses fuzzy relations besides the fuzzy descriptions of the searched structures. As a further extension the search can be performed for 3-dimensional objects instead of the search on single slices.

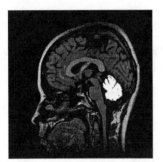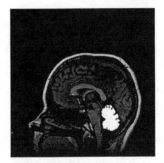

Figure 26: Results of the system CATS

8 Outlook

The field of image processing has many applications in industry and medical diagnostics. As we have shown above conventional methods have problems with the processing of medical images, which results from different uncertainties existing in the data. Here fuzzy logic shows a promising way to improve the results, but the use of fuzzy logic for image processing is still at its beginning.

However with progressing technologies in hard- and software the applications for image processing are a growing market. And with increasing application fields new kinds of technology like fuzzy logic have a good chance to become important.

The acceptance of the users must also be a goal of research at image processing. Physicians and radiologists must accept that computers and software applications can improve their diagnosis. They must put away their fear that fuzzy systems make "fuzzy" decisions and equate fuzzy with wrong. And they must put away their general fear of computers. Computers are used in many different areas of medicine, and fuzzy systems are expected to become more widely accepted as a significant aid to the physician in his daily work.

References

[1]   Fathi, M., Tresp, C., Hiltner, J. and Becker, K. (1994), Fuzzy Set Optimization in Use of Medical MR-Image Analysis based on Evolution Strategies, *IEEE-WWW*, Japan

[2]   Zadeh, L.A. (1965), Fuzzy Sets, *Information and Control 8*, pp. 338-353

[3]   Haralick, R.M. and Shapiro, L.G. (1985), Survey - Image segmentation techniques, *Computer vision, graphics, and image processing*, Vol. 29, pp. 100-132

[4]   Borisenko, V.I., Zlatopol'skii, A.A. and Muchnik, I.B. (1987), Image segmentation (state-of-the-art survey), *Automation and remote control*, Vol. 48, pp. 837-879, Plenum Publishing

[5]   Pal, S.K. and Pal, N.R. (1993), A review on image segmentation techniques, *Pattern recognition*, Vol. 26, No. 9, pp. 1277-1294

[6]   Gonzalez, R.C. and Woods, R.E. (1994), Digital Image Processing, Addison-Wesley

[7]   Abele, L. (1982), Statistische und strukturelle Texturanalyse mit Anwendungen in der Bildsegmentierung, *Nachrichtentechnische Berichte*, Vol. 6, Lehrstuhl Nachrichtentechnik, TU München

[8]   Wahl, F. (1989), Digitale Bildverarbeitung, Springer Verlag

[9]   Brachman, R.J. and Schmolze, J.G. (1985), An overview of the KL-ONE knowledge representation system, *Cognitive Science*, 9(2), pp. 171-216

[10] Tresp, C. (1996), A Knowledge Representation Formalism to Process Vague Medical Queries, *Annual report of the Graduiertenkolleg Informatik & Technik*, Aachen, Germany

[11] Tresp, C., Becks, A., Klinkenberg, R. and Hiltner, J. (1996), Knowledge Representation in a World with Vague Concepts, *Intelligent Systems 96*, Gaithersburg, MD

[12] MacGregor, R.M. (1994), A description classifier for the predicate calculus, *Proceedings of the Twelfth National Conference on Artificial Intelligence*, Seattle, pp. 213-220

[13] Baader, F. and Hollunder, B.A (1991), Terminological Knowledge Representation System with Complete Inference Algorithm, *Proceedings of the Workshop on Processing Declarative Knowledge*, PDK 91, pp. 67-86, Springer-Verlag

[14] Pal, S.K. (1982), A Note on the Quantitative Measure of Image Enhancement Through Fuzzy Sets, *IEEE Transactions on Pattern Analysis and Machine Intelligence*, Vol. PAMI-4, No. 2, March

[15] Li, H. and Yang, H.S. (1989), Fast and Reliable Image Enhancement Using Fuzzy Relaxation Technique, *IEEE Transactions on Systems, Man and Cybernetics*, Vol. SMC-19, No. 5 (September/October)

[16] AlShaykh, O.K., Ramaswamy, S. and Hung, H.-S. (1993), Fuzzy Techniques for Image Enhancement and Reconstruction, *2nd IEEE Conference on Fuzzy Systems and Neural Networks*

[17] Pal, S.K. and King, R.A. (1980), Image enhancement using fuzzy sets, *Electronic letters*, Vol. 16, No. 10, pp. 376-378

[18] Mogahddamzadeh, A. and Bourbakis, N.G. (1995): A Fuzzy Approach for Smoothing and Edge Detection in Colour Images, IS&T/SPIE's Symposium on Electronic Imaging: Science and Technology, San Jose, California, Feb. 5-10

[19] Menhardt, W. (1989), Bildanalyse und ikonische Fuzzy Sets, KI 1/89, pp. 4-10

[20] Menhardt, W. (1990), Unscharfe Mengen (Fuzzy Sets) zur Behandlung von Unsicherheit in der Bildanalyse, *Thesis*, University of Hamburg, Germany

[21] Bezdek, J.C. and Pal, S.K. (1992), Fuzzy Models for Pattern Recognition, *IEEE Press*

[22] Price, K., Russ, T. and MacGregor, M. (1994): Knowledge Representation for Computer Vision: The Veil Project, *ARPA Image Understanding Workshop*

[23] Rosenfeld, A. (1984), The fuzzy geometry of image subsets, *Pattern recognition letters*, Vol. 2, S. 311-317

[24] Rosenfeld, A. (1979), Fuzzy digital topology, *Information and control*, Vol. 40, pp. 76-87

[25] Prewitt, J.M.S. (1970), Object Enhancement and Extraction, In: Lipkin, B.S.; Rosenfeld, A. (Hrsg.): *Picture Processing and Psychopictories*. Academic Press

[26] Pschyrembel (1994), Klinisches Wörterbuch 257. Auflage 1894 - 1994,   Verlag Walter de Gruyter, Berlin und Porta Coeli GmbH, Hamburg, Germany

[27] Wleklik, T. (1996), Medizinische Bilddaten, *Seminar PG Bambus*, University of Dortmund, Germany

[28] Jäger, M. and Moser, M. (1996), Ein Modellentwurf zur wissensbasierten Analyse von 3D-Bildern unter Berücksichtigung von Unsicherheiten, *Diploma Thesis*, University of Dortmund, Germany

[29] The New Encyclopædia Britannica (1991), 15th edition, Encyclopædia Britannica Inc., USA

Chapter 4:

Fuzzy Logic in Communication Networks

FUZZY LOGIC IN COMMUNICATION NETWORKS

Hans Hellendoorn

Production and Installation
Siemens Nederland N.V.
P.O. Box 16068, The Hague
The Netherlands

Rudolf Seising

History of Sciences
Faculty of Social Sciences
University of Federal Armed Forces Munich
Germany

We present a number of applications of fuzzy logic in the area of modern communication networks, notably fuzzy routing in general communication networks, fuzzy CAC, and fuzzy UPC in ATM networks. Most of the older routing strategies are analytical and therefore only one or two input parameters can be considered due to complexity reasons. In the last few years there has been a general tendency towards more parameters using non-analytic methods to master the complexity. Fuzzy logic is an excellent heuristic method to come to grips with the complexity problem in communication and computer networks. Two examples show the use of fuzzy logic to routing; first we will show the use of explicitly available information in the form of routing tables, then we will show the use of implicitly available information in the form of experience and heuristic knowledge in distributed networks. We also use fuzzy methods for traffic management in ATM (Asynchronous Transfer Mode) networks. The ATM concept requires two main functions regarding traffic control: Call Admission Control and Usage Parameter Control. We present a fuzzy logic solution for both control tasks and show the success by presenting simulation results and heuristic valuations.

1 Introduction

In this chapter we introduce fuzzy set theory [20] in the field of computer networks. Fuzzy theory is particularly appropriate to deal with linguistic notions and uncertainty and enables inferencing of linguistic variables in rule-based systems. Fuzzy methods have been very successful in many fields including intelligent control, data analysis, multicriteria analysis, and decision support. Here we focus on two problems in communication networks: the first problem is an optimization problem, viz., the routing problem in communication networks. This problem is encountered in every network that does not allow the sender to reach the receiver in a single transmission hop but, instead, must pass a path of intermediate links. The second problem has to do with traffic management of modern broadband networks, viz. call admission control (CAC) and policing (UPC).

In general, computer networks offer different routes to a given destination. Traditional routing techniques are based on graph-theoretical solutions which find the shortest path connecting a source node to a destination node. In ARPANET, the predecessor of INTERNET, the routing algorithm was a distributed adaptive and asynchronous distance vector algorithm which is based on the Bellman-Ford algorithm [7]; in 1979 it was replaced by a link state algorithm based on the Dijkstra original algorithm [6]. Today in INTERNET, routing algorithms called RIP (Routing Information Protocol) and OSPF (Open Shortest Path First) are used in a single routing domain. RIP is a distance vector algorithm and OSPF is a link state algorithm. Routing algorithms that operate between routing domains are BGP (Border Gateway Protocol) and IDRP (Inter Domain Routing Protocol). As far as broadband networks are considered the use of traditional routing techniques may be too simplistic since all conventional routing strategies are based on the analysis of only one routing metric. Integrated broadband communication networks based on the Asynchronous Transfer Mode (ATM) will have to handle a great variety of services, different load classes, and variable bit-rates. These new requirements need new routing strategies to consider a variety of parameters like topological and load-specific parameters. Fuzzy methods can be used to solve this complex task. We will suggest fuzzy routing for modern communication networks depending on local and global parameters.

To compare the fuzzy routing systems with traditional ones, we have developed network simulations. The results are analyzed to estimate the impact of the systems on the performance of the networks. To continue the use of fuzzy theory in the area of modern communication networks we focus on the traffic management of broadband networks which supports a wide range of multimedia traffic. In ATM networks, traffic from various sources such as video, voice, and data is split up into cells of a fixed size (53 bytes) and a fixed format. These cells share a common link by being statistically multiplexed. Thus, such a high speed multimedia network handles various classes of traffic with different bit rates and different quality of service requirements. Voice traffic is delay-sensitive and uses the speed of several kilobits per second, whereas file transfer is loss-sensitive and uses the speed of megabits per second. The ATM transport protocol is based on cell switching without flow control or retransmission. The required bandwidth of a connection is not allocated in advance but the network makes use of the statistical multiplexing scheme. In case of congestion the network performance or the quality of service may quickly degrade and might result in queueing delay and cell loss. Thus, it is a necessary traffic management task to avoid congestions. This is done by two basic functions: CAC (call admission control) and UPC (usage parameter control).

Section 2 gives a brief survey of the field of computer networks. Then we consider traffic problems associated with the transmission of information, especially the routing problem and traffic management in ATM-networks.

In Sections 3 and 4 we present two fuzzy routing systems for computer networks. The first system considers global parameters to propagate the data to the destination node; the second system is specialized in the use of local information.

Section 5 gives an introduction to network management and its parameters in broadband networks. It deals with two traffic control mechanisms of broadband ISDN networks with ATM, notably fuzzy call admission control (CAC) and fuzzy usage parameter control (UPC). It also presents some simulation results from these fuzzy CAC and UPC.

2 Elements of Modern Communication Networks

2.1 A Reference Model for Networks

Today, computer networks are highly complex systems. They usually contain many thousands of components providing interconnections between computers, printers, terminals, and others. Whereas traditional computer systems contain computers with only one manufacturer's equipment and technology, modern computer systems are built by components of different manufacturers. These heterogeneous networks have to be designed in a highly structured way especially if these heterogeneous networks are connected. If a message has to be propagated from the sender to the receiver in another network, many problems arise: different network addresses, different protocols, and many more. Standards for connecting heterogeneous computer systems for distributed applications processing are given in the reference model of the Open System Interconnection (OSI) defined by the International Organization for Standardization (ISO). This model organizes the communication functions for open systems. Therefore it is designed as a series of layers in a hierarchical way. The OSI model has seven layers. Each one has been created by need of a different level of abstraction and performs a well defined function. The interface between two layers is defined by the specification of the services the lower layer offers to the upper one. The communication between equal layers on different systems is defined by protocols, which can be seen as a set of rules and conventions.

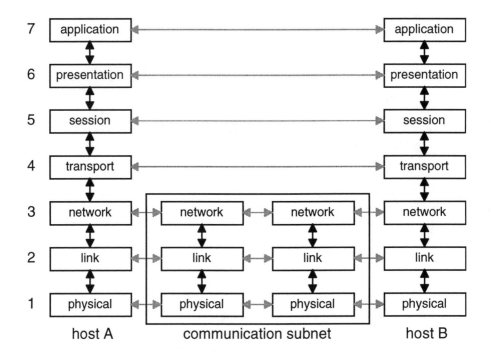

Figure 1: ISO-OSI reference model

Figure 1 illustrates this reference model. Layers 1, 2, 3, and 4 constitute the transport system to handle the message transmission from the sender to the receiver whereas the three remaining layers 5, 6, and 7 (resp. session layer, presentation layer, and application layer) present the application system. In this chapter we are interested in the routing function of the third layer. Routing is managed in this network layer. The routing function selects each link in the network across which a message is to be transmitted. Choosing the best route from the sending node to the destination node is one of the main functions of the third layer in the ISO-OSI reference model.

To transmit traffic, two general approaches, known as *circuit switching* and *store-and-forward switching*, can be used. Circuit switching establishes an exclusive physical connection between the communication partners. This is the technique used in telephone systems, and in ISDN, too. Circuit switching leads to inefficient utilization of channels, because the required bandwidth has to be statically set in advance. That is why it is rarely used for data networks. An alternative possibility is store-and-forward switching. With this technique, blocks of data sent by a source are stored in the first switching node and then forwarded later when the outgoing link is free, one hop at a time. Each block is received entirely, inspected for errors, and retransmitted in case of error. We can divide this store-and-forward technique into *message switching* and *packet switching*. In the first case messages are sent as unit entities; in the second case messages are broken into packets. These packets have to be buffered in the switching node memories. Circuit switching and packet switching differ in many ways, but the key advantage of the latter is that it acquires and releases the bandwidth as it is needed; each communication link is fully utilized whenever it has any traffic to send. In circuit switching, unused bandwidth on an allocated circuit is just wasted; in contrast to packet switching it may be utilized by other packets from unrelated senders to unrelated receivers. The Broadband Integrated Services Digital Networks (B-ISDN) and its standard Asynchronous Transfer Mode (ATM) will be based on multiplexing and switching of fixed-size labeled packets of information, called *ATM-cells*. With regard to future networks discussed in this chapter, we only deal with packet switching networks.

The OSI-layers can offer two different types of services to the layers above them: connectionless and connection-oriented. The prototype of a connectionless service is the postal system. Each packet or letter is routed through this system irrespective of all other packets or letters and each of them carry the full destination address. If two packets are sent to the same addressee they may arrive in reverse order, whereas the order in connection-oriented services cannot change. This kind of service operates in the same way as the telephone system. If a connection is established, it can be used as long as it is terminated. Instead of connection-oriented services, the term *virtual circuit service* is used and instead of connectionless service the term *datagram service* is used.

2.2 Internetworking

To connect different subnetworks coordination authorities are required. Therefore a new sublayer called internet sublayer was created as part of the network layer. Now, special nodes called gateways or routers can combine the subnets to an internet. The beginning of internetworking was the ARPANET project in the seventies. Four computers of the University of California, connected by telephone cable, made up this first internet in 1969. In 1971, ARPANET consisted of 15 nodes; in 1972 already 37 computers were connected. Later, local area networks and workstations were affiliated. In 1986, the National Science Foundation (NSF) established a distributed union for supercomputers in USA, the NSFNET. This INTERNET backbone encloses the old ARPANET and many other networks. Today, more than 30000 computer networks in more than 70 states of the world belong to this INTERNET.

Several aspects can be used to classify communication networks. We already mentioned the division associated with different switching techniques. Another division can be made with regard to the area they cover, their total data rate, or their ownership. These characteristic features lead to the distinction in LANs (Local Area Networks), and WANs (Wide Area Networks). LANs link computers and peripheral devices within a limited geographical area. Often they provide communication facilities within a building or a campus and only span several kilometers. An extension of a network over several thousand kilometers is named a WAN. Apart from the LANs and WANs, another category of communication networks are MANs (Metropolitan Area Networks). MANs cover an entire city; they share some of the characteristics of both LANs and WANs. MANs provide interconnection of LANs.

Another classification of computer networks is according to its topology, that means the way, how the nodes are interconnected. The cost of a fully meshed network is high. To provide common access to shared resources at low cost the topologies of local area networks usually have the form of a bus, ring, star, and tree. Further classifications are possible.

2.3 Routing Strategies

To handle the routing of packets as they move through the network, a path or a set of paths must have been set up to connect a given source with a given destination. Routing tables, indicating the appropriate outgoing link for an individual packet with a given destination address, are stored within each node.

To establish the appropriate routing table entries in each node along a path, specific routing strategies have been developed. Here, we give some classifications. One of the simplest strategies to find a path to a given destination is *fixed routing*, which uses fixed routing tables. The quality of this route does not depend on dynamic network conditions, but it is practicable to determine the best route this way for an estimated network traffic. A new decision on optimal paths has to be made if the network topology is modified. In case of stable load the advantages of this strategy are simplicity and reliability, but the lack of flexibility is a drawback in situations of congestion or error events.

Another simple routing strategy is *broadcasting* each data packet from the destination to all other network nodes. This is a necessary procedure in case of topological changes like errors or repairing to inform all network members, but it is a primitive routing strategy, for example if the sender could not localize the receiver. A variation of broadcasting is *flooding*. Here, the source node sends the packets to its neighbor stations and each neighbor station transmits it on all outgoing links with the exception of the link it has come from. This flooding technique is very robust: all packets will reach their destination if there is at least one connection between source node and destination node. The disadvantage of this technique is the generation of very high traffic load in the network. A consequence of this is a high delay for all messages in the network.

Less traffic is generated by *random* routing, where each network station chooses only one link to transmit an incoming packet by chance, except the input link. Random routing is robust like flooding, but it only makes sense in certain topologies.

The opposite of fixed routing is *adaptive* routing that means accommodated changes of routing decisions in case of dynamical changes in network topology or in traffic load. Adaptive routing strategies may be classified by the used network information. *Global* strategies utilize all available information about the network to decide for the optimal path. If there is a central station in the network to collect and evaluate all routing information, it is called *centralized* routing.

A *local* routing strategy uses local accessible information, for instance the queuing lengths of all outgoing links. Algorithms using these strategies are called *isolated* routing algorithms. For example, the Hot-Potato-Algorithm is isolated and adaptive. In this routing algorithm each station tries to forward an incoming packet as fast as possible. To that end it compares the queuing lengths for all outgoing links to append the packet to the shortest queue.

Distributed routing strategies are mixtures of global and local routing. An example is the delta routing. Here, each station sends information to a central network station via each path. This central station computes a set of best paths which differ in their initial link cost by at most a delta-value. When this delta is very small, there is only one best path; otherwise all best paths are equivalent. The first case leaves the routing decision to the central station; in the second case each node determines the outgoing link by local information.

Most routing strategies need information about the network topology, the traffic load, and the cost of paths. If centralized routing is used, there is a central node, called *routing control center*. This central node collects status information of each network node (e.g., a list of neighbors, current queue lengths, current topology, the amount of traffic processed per line since the last report, etc.). Then the routing control center can build new routing tables and distribute them to all stations. One drawback of centralized routing is the vulnerability of the central station. To have a second computer as a substitute routing center is a possible solution. Decentralized routing is more complex but also more robust.

Another kind of routing strategy is *multipath* routing or *bifurcated* routing. Delta routing is a good example for bifurcated routing when delta is big enough. If there is more than one optimal path, the load can be distributed. One can weight the possible paths by probabilities or reserve various paths for different load classes. Multipath routing minimizes the delay for propagating data packets through the network. The minimum delay may be another routing decision parameter besides cost and length of a path. In Section 3 we will see which criterion can be used to determine an optimal path through the network. Such a criterion is called a routing metric.

2.4 Elements of ATM Networks

Integrated broadband communication networks based on the Asynchronous Transfer

Mode (ATM) will have to handle a great variety of services, different load classes, variable bit-rates, connection-oriented and connectionless communication, and simplex, duplex, point-to-point, and multi-cast connections, These new requirements need new routing strategies to consider a variety of parameters like topological and load-specific parameters. Fuzzy methods can be used to solve this complex task.

There is a reference model for ATM based on the ISO-OSI reference model mentioned in Section 2.1, but not each layer of this ATM-reference model corresponds to a layer of the former. So, there are the ATM layer and the ATM adaptation layer that were defined to ensure the corresponding transport to adapt the data to the ATM cell format. The physical layer embodies the management of the bit transport depending on the hardware (fibre optic cable, coaxial cable). Here, we will not discuss details about the ATM-reference model shown in Figure 2. Our fuzzy systems work solely on the ATM layer. The transport principle in ATM networks is an easy connection-oriented packet switching. Useful data and signalling data have to be filled in ATM cells. The ATM switching technique is founded on so-called virtual channels (VC). When a connection between two ATM end systems is established, a logical channel will be produced. For each hop between two switching nodes there is a logical "virtual" channel which can be identified by its *virtual channel identifier* (VCI) in the header of each ATM cell. As a lot of virtual connections may use the same hop, there may be a lot of virtual channels in this hop. Therefore, the switching nodes of ATM networks read the VCI of a ATM cell occurring in a virtual channel, connect this virtual channel with the outgoing virtual channel it needs and write the corresponding new VCI into the cell header. Very often ATM cells coming in a switching node on the same virtual channel also need the same outgoing virtual channel. Therefore ATM networks have a further switching concept to connect fusions of virtual channels called *virtual paths* (VP) in so-called ATM cross connects with other virtual paths. There are path connections in ATM networks which are built by virtual paths with their *virtual path identifiers* (VPI).

In ATM networks, traffic from various sources such as video, voice and data is split up into cells of a fixed size (53 bytes) and a fixed format. These cells then share a common link by being statistically multiplexed. Thus, such a high speed multimedia network handles various classes of traffic with different bit rates and different quality of service requirements. Voice traffic is delay-sensitive and uses the speed of several kilobits per second, whereas file transfer is loss-sensitive and uses the speed of megabits per second. The ATM transport protocol is based on cell switching without flow control or retransmission. The required bandwidth of a connection is not allocated in advance but the network makes use of the statistical multiplexing scheme. In case of congestion the network performance or the quality of service may quickly degrade which might result in queuing delay and cell loss. Thus, it is a necessary traffic management task to avoid congestions. This is done by two basic functions: CAC (call admission control) and UPC (usage parameter control).

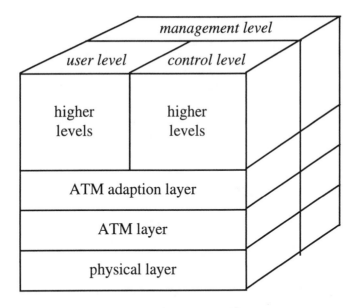

Figure 2: ATM reference model

The procedure to establish a connection in ATM networks includes the negotiation of a traffic contract which specifies the characteristics of the data traffic on this connection. A so-called *source traffic descriptor* includes a specification of traffic parameters which are qualitative or quantitative descriptions of traffic profiles, i.e., the *peak cell rate*, the *sustainable cell rate*, the *maximum burst size*, the type of the traffic source (video, audio, fax, ...). First of all in the traffic contract the *quality of service* parameters (QoS) and the parameter *cell delay variation* have to be negotiated depending on the hardware, the requirements of the users, the load and the state of the network. The *call admission control* institution is established to decide about the implementation of a new connection in ATM networks whereas *usage parameter control* institution decides whether traffic contract requirements are met. The CAC algorithm is an instrument to decide whether an incoming call can be accepted or has to be rejected. This decision is based on a set of traffic descriptors that characterize each connection. These parameters together with a QoS (Quality of Service) specification are part of the *traffic contract* between the network and the user (the connection). QoS requirements may concern tolerance values of *cell delay, cell delay variation, cell loss ratio*, etc. If the network receives a new connection request, the CAC has to decide whether the network has enough resources left to provide the QoS requirements to the new connection without affecting the QoS that have been guaranteed to the existing connections. Based on this estimation (there is no numerical analytical calculation method in the presence of statistical multiplexing) the call will be accepted or rejected.

The UPC algorithm supervises the established connections by checking and punishing violating connections. This is necessary because users of the network may not respect the agreed-upon traffic parameters and therefore the CAC is insufficient to prevent congestion. Once a new connection has been accepted, the UPC is required to ensure that traffic submitted into the network does not exceed the parameters negotiated within the traffic contract. The traffic policing procedure UPC has to detect a source that does not keep the negotiated parameters very quickly. Otherwise connections (that keep their negotiated parameters) might be affected by delay or even by cell loss. The UPC can react using various actions for punishment like dropping, delaying, or marking violating cells.

3   Global Fuzzy Routing

The subject of this section is the examination of the applicability of fuzzy methods to shortest path routing in computer communication networks. As already mentioned in Section 2 routing is an important performance factor in wide area networks (WANs). The goal of shortest path routing is to find the 'best' path through a network depending on a graph theoretical view of the network.

Shortest path routing strategies are based on information about the network topology. According to a metric (like transmission delay) a length or weight is assigned to each link in the network. Then a shortest path algorithm calculates the shortest paths from a given source node to any other node in the network [6, 7]. In a distributed, adaptive routing algorithm each node has to accomplish the following tasks: 1) share the information with other nodes, 2) calculate the 'shortest' paths to all other nodes (based on the topology information), and 3) collect information about the network.

The problem we are now facing is: Where are drawbacks of this strategy and where are sensible applications for fuzzy methods? Calculating the shortest paths is done by a shortest path algorithm - a problem which is well known and solved. Sharing the information is most commonly done by flooding: Every node in the network sends its routing information to all neighbors. Information which is already known is ignored. There are numerous criteria which can be used for the routing decision. This is exactly the area where fuzzy systems can show their strength.

In all common shortest path routing strategies only one parameter is used as routing information. Different routing algorithms use different parameters like transmission delay, number of hops, etc. But the routing decision is based exclusively on this one parameter, so the network traffic is optimized only considering, e.g., the delay time; other important criteria for a networking company like link costs are not taken into account.

The idea of our approach is to use more than only one parameter and to use a fuzzy system to obtain a crisp link weight from a set of parameters. This link weight can easily be used as input for a shortest path algorithm.

To show that this idea leads to a reasonable routing strategy we implemented a *fuzzy link evaluator* (FLE) with SIEFUZZY, a fuzzy development tool from Siemens [17]. We also implemented a network simulation model using the FLE with OPNET, a well-known simulation system for telecommunication and computer networks [14]. This fuzzy router is mainly based on the routing algorithm used in ARPANET. We chose the ARPANET routing algorithm as this is the best documented and because it provides a well-defined test environment. First, we will briefly describe the conventional part of the used routing algorithm and then we will discuss the fuzzy shortest path router in detail.

3.1 Conventional Solution

During the operating life of the ARPANET different routing algorithms were used: the first one (a distance vector algorithm, based on the Bellman-Ford algorithm) implemented in 1969 revealed severe disadvantages as the network grew from only a few stations in the beginning to several hundreds in the seventies. The major problems were long lived loops and oscillations due to too short measurement intervals and too long routing messages. In 1979 (ARPANET II) it was replaced by a link state routing algorithm which used a variant of the Dijkstra-algorithm to calculate the shortest paths (the shortest path first (SPF) algorithm). Routing in the ARPANET experienced its last revision in 1989 when a new link metric was installed.

Our fuzzy shortest path routing strategy is based upon the SPF-routing algorithm used in the eighties. It is an adaptive distributed algorithm in a datagram-oriented network: A message is split into several packets which are sent separately through the network. Every node decides autonomously where the arriving packets are to be sent to. This decision depends on the measured parameters and may change as the traffic situation in the network changes. The nodes need basically two data structures for the routing task:

1. The routing table - a list in which each other node in the network (the destination node) is assigned the neighbor (of the source node) to whom the packet has to be forwarded (see Table 1).

Table 1: Routing table

destination node	2	3	4	5
route traffic via node	2	3	2	2

For each arriving packet the node only has to check the packet's destination and the routing table indicates to which node the packet has to be sent.

2. The network database: in the simplest case a directed, weighted graph representing the network. Based on this database the routing table is calculated and kept up to date using a shortest path algorithm.

The ARPANET II routing strategy used the packet's transmission delay as parameter for the routing decision. The delay on each link to the neighbor nodes is measured using the acknowledgements for transmitted packets. We are using the following very similar method to measure the delay. Every packet is time-stamped with its arrival time and its sent time. The difference of these two values plus a constant for the transmission time yields the delay of the packet. In constant intervals of time the average delay of all packets which have passed a line is computed. If this average varies too much from the average of the previous period, the network database and the routing table are updated and the new link states are distributed to all other nodes so that they can also update their databases and routing tables.

The distribution of this information is performed by the simple flooding algorithm. Every node sends copies of the flooding packet containing the updated information to all its neighboring nodes except for the one the packet was received from. This algorithm guarantees that the update messages are spread fast enough over the network.

3.2 Fuzzy Shortest Path Routing in Detail

As already mentioned above we tried to improve the non-fuzzy routing strategy by using a FLE, which computes an evaluation for each outgoing link. This evaluation is then used as input for the SPF algorithm. After measuring the relevant parameters the FLE computes a quality number which is used to compute the routing table and which is flooded (as link state) over the network (see Figure 3).

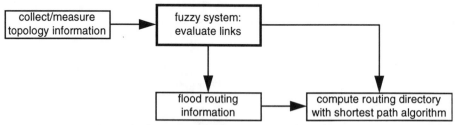

Figure 3: Structure of the fuzzy routing algorithm

As fuzzy systems can easily handle complex situations we selected the following eight parameters as sensitive input parameters for our fuzzy system:

*   *Link capacity:* A link with a high capacity can carry more traffic and is therefore less prone to overload in comparison to a link with low capacity.
*   *Transmission cost:* The transmission costs are an important factor in commercial networks: for some applications it might be useful/cheaper to use the less

expensive links even if they are slower than others.

- *Transmission time:* The transmission time is the time the signal needs to travel from one node to another. It is another important characteristic of a connection between two nodes. It depends on the physical properties of the link media (e.g., copper cable with a certain length or satellite connection).

- *Transmission delay:* The transmission delay is even of major importance for the routing decision as this parameter changes more frequently than all the others. It is the sum of transmission time, processing time and queueing time.

- *Change of transmission delay:* The change of transmission delay is considered, as one can assume that, e.g., an increasing delay will still increase in the next seconds.

- *Link security:* The link security is taken into account because a secure link can be regarded as a better choice in comparison to a link which is likely to fail.

- *Node security:* A node which often fails should be avoided if possible.

- *Packet security:* The packet security is the last security parameter, representing the security that a packet does not get lost in consequence of overload situations. Voice or picture transmission needs lower security than, e.g., the transmission of banking data.

In the FLE these parameters are represented with *linguistic variables* and grouped into three categories to get a systematical design. The first three parameters are used to represent the cost-performance relation of the evaluated link. The next two represent the delay situation on the link and the last three represent the security of the link, which may also be viewed as a trust in the link (see Figure 4).

For these three groups (performance, timing, security) three rule bases are designed to compute three intermediate variables describing the three link characteristics of interest and serving as input for the main rule base that computes the link evaluation.

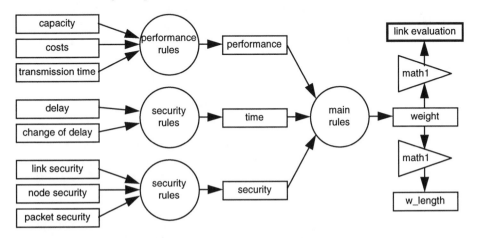

Figure 4: The fuzzy link evaluator

As the design of the linguistic variables and the rule bases are not yet optimized we do not describe them in detail. To get a usable crisp number as output from the fuzzy system we compute the reciprocal value of the defuzzified link weight, as the domain of the variable weight is the interval [0,1]; low values mean a 'good link' and high values represent 'poor links'. The general strategy of the FLE is: 1) Use links with low delay. 2) If there are two links with equal delay use the one with higher security and/or better performance. The FLE has been integrated into a simulation network to examine the behavior in a closed loop.

As our routing algorithm is distributed and adaptive each node performs the routing task. The node model is kept quite simple. Each node can be connected to up to three duplex links (receiver i is associated with the same link as transmitter i) and packets are generated in each node. The heart of each node is the processor module which performs the routing task as described above.

With this simulation network we tested how the fuzzy routing strategy reacted on a node failure, on 'bad' links with a high transmission time, rather high costs and low security, and how it acted in comparison with a router without a fuzzy component.

As we did not use quantities from real networks for our simulation, we can only judge the behavior of the fuzzy shortest path router as far as quality is concerned. However, the simulations show that using the FLE has an obvious influence on the routing decision. Especially the 'bad links' were better recognized by the fuzzy router than by the non-fuzzy router. We expected this result because the fuzzy router has better 'knowledge' about the situation in the network.

This is one of the main advantages of our fuzzy routing algorithm. A fuzzy system can easily handle more than just one input. The design and tuning of the FLE can easily be done by a network expert and changes to an existing system are quite simple because a well designed fuzzy system is easier to understand than huge sets of formulae. Furthermore a fuzzy router can easily be adapted to changing network conditions.

4   Local Fuzzy Routing

The algorithm in this section is designed to work in a distributed way based on node-local information and load parameters in packet switched networks. The advantage of this kind of algorithm is that they cause minimal additional load to the networks for forwarding routing information.

The algorithm shows that some advantages of the fuzzy theory are still maintained in the environment of communication networks, i.e., the use of many different parameters in a routing algorithm and the easy maintenance of fuzzy systems by the use of linguistic rules and variables. Common routing algorithms only use one parameter of the network to control the packet flow. Today's applications require more specific routing algorithms with the possibility to treat different kinds of load in a different and appropriate manner. Therefore the objectives for the design of the fuzzy routing algorithm are: optimizing the network-wide parameters packet loss rate and network latency, supporting different load classes by the use of appropriate packet headers, and supporting network management by easy maintenance of the algorithm.

4.1 Previous Work on this Topic

The starting point of the development is an earlier proposed two-level adaptive routing scheme for packet switched computer communication networks. It was developed by Boorstyne and Livne in 1981 [4]. They showed that under certain conditions this adaptive routing scheme optimizes the global average node delay in the network.

One could find an easy solution for this problem: A packet is to be put into the queue at the outgoing link, which has the lowest expected waiting time. Another strategy could be to put the packet into the shortest queue. Other reasonable strategies can be found. If the node operates in this way, packets will wander aimlessly through the network and the total performance will be abysmal. The Boorstyne approach combines the routing function with the benefit of higher performance at the node by choosing 'good' queues. Briefly, this approach is as follows. Consider a node as a single queue with several servers (output links). For a particular commodity, i.e., a packet with a certain destination, the use of some of these servers would cause the packets to be sent along 'bad' paths - either too long or too congested. Thus, for each commodity and each node a subset of allowable links is to be specified. So each commodity has its own subset of links. These restrictions force packets to use 'good' paths. This is the first level of the adaptive routing scheme.

The second level is to choose one out of these 'good' paths. This decision is based on the argument given above; the chosen queue is the one where the waiting time is to be expected lowest. This level is the dynamic part of the algorithm because it uses the current node situation for its decision.

This routing scheme causes a significant performance increase in average node waiting time and global average time delay. The algorithm does not use application specific parameters and load specific information. Also, the algorithm divides the parameters into two classes, static parameters in the first stage and dynamic parameters in the second stage. Dependencies between parameters of both classes do not influence the routing decision.

Based on this algorithm a fuzzy solution should eliminate these disadvantages. The algorithm deals with the output selection policy of a router. Therefore a model of a router has to be developed which is based on queuing theory.

4.2 A Model of a Router Node

The model of a router node in a communication network is held as simple as possible. All arriving packets are put into one waiting queue. This also holds for packets arriving from layer 4 of the OSI model. Thus, the input selection policy is a FIFO strategy. The server for this waiting queue is the routing algorithm itself. It determines the probability distribution of the service. For analytical reasons we have chosen an exponential distribution of the service time for each packet; other distributions would be more realistic. When a packet is served by the routing algorithm, it is put into the waiting queue attached to the outgoing link which is chosen by the routing algorithm. The servers of these waiting queues are located in layer 2 of the OSI model. So the routing algorithm does not influence these servers. We assume the servers of layer 2 to have an exponentially distributed service time for each packet. The queue lengths are bound to a finite value. Therefore it may happen that a packet will only find full packet queues, which may cause the loss of the packet. Figure 5 shows the model used in this work.

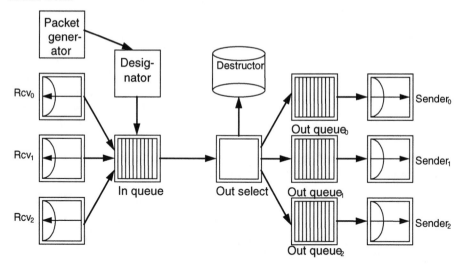

Figure 5: A detailed model for a router node

The following assumptions are made in the model: The packet header of OSI layer 3 contains the address of the target router node. This may be a three byte long address information; the length of this information is determined by the absolute number of router nodes and the inherent redundancy of this information. Furthermore we assume the packet to contain two two-bit fields for priority and loss tolerance information about this packet. This leads to four values for each of these parameters. Without this information a user influence on the routing strategy would be too difficult to realize. The algorithm stated here can be divided into pieces that represent the three functional components of a router. The first and second part are non-fuzzy; they represent the input selection policy and the switching policy of a router.

The output selection policy first uses a fuzzy decision module to determine a performance value for each outgoing link at the node. In a second step the outgoing link with the highest value is determined. The fuzzy decision module uses several parameters to determine a performance value for an outgoing link. Some of these parameters like the minimum number of hops to the target node are static, that means these parameters can be assumed constant for a long period. Here, however, long is relative: it depends on the speed of the communication network and the packet throughput. Other parameters may change with each packet, for example, packet priority or queue length. These parameters will now be discussed.

4.3 Network Parameters and Design of the Fuzzy Decision Module

The first of these parameters is the *relative queue length* at each outgoing link. It is defined as the absolute queue length (expressed in bits) divided by the maximum queue length. Therefore the relative queue length is independent of the maximum queue length and is defined on the interval [0,1]. This makes it easier to compare this parameter for different kinds of network installations in a router.

$$l_{Q,rel_{i,j}} := \frac{l_{Q_{i,j}}}{l_{Q,\max_{i,j}}}$$

where $l_{Q_{i,j}}$ is the absolute queue length at the queue which leads to the outgoing link from node i to node j, and $l_{Q,\max_{i,j}}$ is the maximum number of bits the queue can contain.

If all packets have the same length, it is possible to count the packets in the waiting queue:

$$l_{Q,rel_{i,j}} := \frac{N_{Q_{i,j}}}{N_{Q,\max_{i,j}}}$$

where $N_{Q_{i,j}}$ is the number of packets which are located in the queue at this moment and $N_{Q,\max_{i,j}}$ is the maximum number of packets which the queue can contain. This kind of measurement is considerably faster.

The next parameter is the *relative link load*: $\rho_{i,j} := \frac{\lambda_{i,j}}{C_{i,j}}$, where $\lambda_{i,j}$ is the current link load on the link from node i to node j in bit/s and $C_{i,j}$ is the link capacity of the link from node i to node j in bit/s. Therefore, $\rho_{i,j}$ is normalized on the interval [0,1].

The use of the link capacity leads to another problem which also shows the need of a fuzzy treatment of these parameters. The capacity of a link in OSI layer 3 can only be estimated; it depends on the overhead of the routing protocols of the lower OSI layers and their technical implementation. It may change with the degree of service or with other effects like transmission conditions for radio or satellite links. A model with a probabilistic view of these effects would cause too much complexity to the routing algorithm.

Another load-dependent parameter is the *load difference* between the load before and after a queue. The load before the queue is determined by the routing algorithm whereas the load after the queue is determined by the lower OSI layers. This may be viewed as a kind of internal congestion control but it is also an instrument to obtain an early warning system for faults on this link. If the link has a high fault rate, packets have to be retransmitted very often. So the serving rate of the lower OSI layers may decrease and the difference between the incoming packets per time at the queue and the transmitted packets will increase.

$$\Delta_{\rho_{i,j,in-out}} := \frac{\lambda_{1,j,in} - \lambda_{1,j,out}}{C_{i,j}},$$

where $\lambda_{1,j,in}$ is the load, which arrives at the queue, leading to the link from node i to node j, and $\lambda_{1,j,out} = \lambda_{1,j}$ is the load which is transmitted over this link.

Another parameter which can only be estimated is the expected *time delay* of a packet from the point where it is put into the outgoing waiting queue to the point when it joins the incoming waiting queue at the next node. This delay is influenced by the lower layers too.

$$t_{trans_{i,j}} := \frac{l_{Q_{i,j}}}{C_{i,j}} + t_{delay} + \frac{1}{2} \cdot \frac{l_{P,served}}{C_{i,j}} \cdot \frac{\lambda_{1,j,in}}{C_{i,j}} + \frac{l_{P,in}}{C_{i,j}},$$

where t_{delay} is the signal transmission time depending on the used media, $l_{P,served}$ is the length of the packet currently served by layer 2, the factor 1/2 considers the fact that half of the packet has already been served, and $l_{P,in}$ is the length of the currently handled packet within the fuzzy module.

Another time parameter is the difference of the *time zones* of nodes. This parameter is more static and the influence is not very big. The reason why this parameter can have influence on a decision is that the traffic through the node at normal job time, for example from 8 am to 4 pm, is much higher than at night hours. If the same value of the remaining parameters is assigned to two potential paths, it will be more reasonable to put the packet into the queue which leads to a node where it is night than into a queue which leads to a node where it is, e.g., 9 am. An observation is that this parameter is originally a topological and therefore a non-local parameter. The question is whether a topological parameter can be treated as a local parameter. Here, the instance of this parameter is a table in each node which contains the appropriate information. This table can be set up at node initialization time and must only be changed if a node changes its location, which does not happen very often in real networks. The cost of this information is the same as the cost of a local parameter because of the static behavior of this parameter. In that sense this parameter is a local one.

The next parameter is the *packet loss probability*, that means, a packet is totally lost and only higher layers of the OSI model may recognize this failure. This probability is usually very small and it is only measured for demonstration purposes and to inspect the function of an error rate dependent routing algorithm. Real applications have other criteria for avoiding links and the development of such application profiles is a field of current research. The header of each packet provides two more input parameters. These are the *packet loss tolerance* and the *packet priority*. Both represent the application needs. Packets with high loss tolerance may use links with a high packet loss probability. Packets with low tolerance have to use trustworthy links. Similarly, packets with a high priority should use links with a low expected transmission time but packets with a low priority have no restrictions on time conditions of a link.

The last input parameter of the fuzzy decision module is an array which contains the *minimum number of necessary hops* to each node in the network for each outgoing link. It differs from node to node and provides a minimum of topological information for the routing algorithm. It can be set up in the initialization procedure of each node. It is only to be altered if topological changes like link failures occur. The mathematical definition of the elements of the array is given by the graph theoretical formula

$$a_{j,n} := \begin{cases} \max(11 - hop_{\min}, 1) & \text{if} \quad \exists\, \wp_{i,n} \in \Gamma: \ \wp_{i,n} = \{i, j, ..., n\} \\ 0 & \text{else} \end{cases}$$

where $\wp_{i,n}$ is a path from node i where the packet is currently located to node n which is the destination node of the packet using the link from node i to node j, if this link exists. Another assumption concerns the path: every node appears only once which means that circles are not allowed. Γ is the connectivity graph of the network. Each connection in this graph represents a link in the real network. The parameter $hop_{\min}$ is the minimum path length based on counting the visited nodes which a packet has to pass. The number 11 results from the fact that we assume that if $hop_{\min}$ is greater than 10 the path length does not play a role anymore. Another convention is the zero element of this array. If an element $a_{j,n}$ is zero, there is no path from node i to node n using a link from node i to node j. From these parameters every input variable of the fuzzy routing algorithm can directly be derived. There are two more variables beside the input and output variables: These are used by the algorithm to represent abstract measures during the evaluation process. They may be eliminated after an optimization, but during the design of the algorithm they are helpful to check parts of the functionality of the algorithm. These variables represent the security rating and the speed rating of a link. For these reasons the fuzzy part of the algorithm is designed as given in Figure 6.

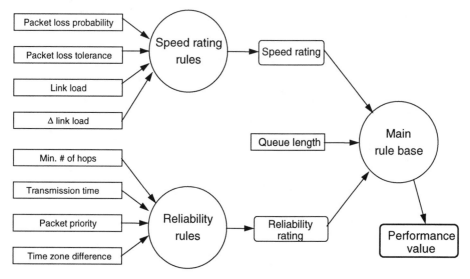

Figure 6: A fuzzy model to find a routing solution

As shown above, the fuzzy algorithm contains three rule bases. Rule base 1 determines the security rating of the link, rule base 2 the speed rating of the link. Both ratings are used with the relative queue length as an input for rule base 3. This rule base determines the performance value for the link. So, here is a point where a network provider can easily influence the weighting of the different criteria which finally determines the routing decision.

Let us examine rule base 3. It contains eleven rules where the first ten rules are all of the same kind. They have only one fuzzy set of the variables 'link security' and 'link speed' in their premise and a corresponding fuzzy set of the output variable in their conclusion, like

IF *link security* **IS** very small **THEN** *output value* **IS** very bad.

This allows to weight the security criteria relative to the speed criteria only by setting appropriate rule weights. The last rule of this rule base acts as an 'emergency break'. If an overflow of the waiting queue is likely it should not be used by packets which can use another link to reach their target node. Only those packets which have no choice may still use this link. The rule is

IF *relative queue length* **IS** full **THEN** *output value* **IS** very bad.

This rule has a hundred times higher weight than the other rules. So, if the situation at the waiting queue gets critical, the performance value will decrease. This does not hold when all waiting queues are congested; in this case this node is overloaded anyhow.

4.4 Results of Static and Dynamic Analysis

The analysis of the algorithm can be divided into a static and a dynamic part. The static analysis was done with SieFuzzy which was also used to build the fuzzy decision module. This analysis just sets all parameters to certain values and traces what happens to the output in the case one parameter is changed. The dynamic analysis uses a simulation of a network to examine the effects when many parameters change continuously in a time interval. We used OpNet where we linked fuzzy modules to perform the routing inside of the nodes. The fuzzy decision module shows the following behavior:

- the packet loss tolerance increases with the packet failure rate
- the influence of the packet priority increases with the transmission time
- the link performance value decreases with increasing transmission time
- the link performance value increases with the topological link value
- if the queue is filled more than ninety percent, the performance value decreases rapidly.

The results show that the routing algorithm behaves under static conditions in many parts in the wished manner. The problem is that some hidden dependencies may appear in a dynamic system. For these reasons a dynamic analysis of the algorithm has to be made. The analysis is based on simulations with an ideal node model. This model is given through the above-mentioned assumptions about the router node. In the recent work this model was used in two simulated networks. The first one has only four nodes and only one of these nodes, n_0, can put packets onto the network. The other three nodes just perform some measurement and protocol work. The structure is shown in Figure 7.

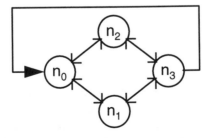

Figure 7: A simple network for dynamic analysis

Two aspects are verified using this network. The first is whether the decision module recognizes different load types, and, secondly, whether the packets are appropriately routed. Therefore, the following network parameters were varied: the load in packets per second, the packet priority and packet loss tolerance, the link capacities, the transmission times, and others.

During the dynamic analysis of this network the following results are obtained. The algorithm reacts very sensitively on changes of the loss tolerance and the packet loss rate. The sensitivity on these parameters decreases, if the load at this node increases and the node gets exhausted. Then packets are routed through all possible links. This is expected because if the load on one link gets too high, the attached queue will get filled. If still more packets travel through this link they may get lost because of queue overflow. This violates the objective of optimizing the packet loss. Therefore, the 'queue rule' is implemented which prevents the negative aspects load-specific routing.

The other load-dependent parameter is priority. In the beginning, the algorithm reacts sensitively on the packet priority. If a packet has a high priority, it is routed through links with a low-expected transmission time. But, as the system is now dynamic, this leads to longer queue lengths at these links which causes an increment in the expected transmission time. After a short time the expected transmission time on all links is nearly equal which makes priority-dependant routing impossible. The desired effect to have a low total transmission time for packets with a high priority cannot be guaranteed. Other means have to be added like reserving link capacities. Only in cases where the waiting time cannot compensate the difference between transmission times is priority dependent routing useful.

4.5 Comparison with Common Routing Schemes

The second network is an eight-node network (see Figure 8). The nodes are connected with full duplex links. All links have the same characteristics. They have a link capacity of 64 kbit/s. The error rate and the transmission time are set to zero. The routing algorithm has a service rate of 256 kbit/s; the lower layers have a service rate of 64 kbit/s which is equal to the link capacity. The packet lengths are exponentially distributed with an average of 1 kbit. As packet lengths are exponentially distributed, the service time of a packet is exponentially distributed too. Each waiting queue at the outgoing links has a maximum capacity of 64 kbit; each waiting queue at the arriving links has a maximum capacity of 256 kbit. It follows that the maximum waiting time of a packet in each waiting queue is 1 second.

Two types of nodes can be recognized, nodes with two attached links, and nodes with three links. Each node generates packets for all other nodes; the target addresses are equally distributed. All nodes create the same average number of packets in a time interval. Therefore, this network has a high degree of symmetry and the mathematical analysis is relatively simple.

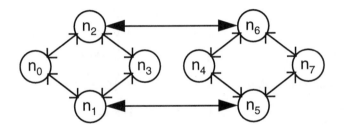

Figure 8: The simulation network

This network is used to compare the fuzzy decision module with the RIP routing algorithm and a simple implementation of the Boorstyne solution. Finally, the performance of the fuzzy routing algorithm is compared with a mathematical solution which is considered to be optimal for some parameters. To make algorithms comparable, most link-specific parameters are kept constant for each link, as seen above. So the fuzzy algorithm cannot gain advantage by using parameters for which the other algorithms were not developed.

Our investigations show the comparison of the RIP algorithm and the fuzzy algorithm. With a load of 50 kbit/s generated at each node, the fuzzy algorithm has significant advantages. The mean total end-to-end delay of a packet decreases by a factor of 2.4. The variance of the end-to-end delay decreases by a factor of 10.6.

If the load is raised to an amount of 100 kbit/s, the RIP algorithm is about 17% better in end-to-end delay than the fuzzy algorithm. This can be explained by the fact that this load causes a relative service rate of 179% on the links which connect the two four-node clusters. The fuzzy algorithm tries to save packets from getting lost and buffers them in other links. Indeed, the fuzzy algorithm loses fewer packets than the RIP algorithm. This buffering results in congested queues at other nodes and therefore a higher waiting time for packets in these nodes. However, this behavior cannot be corrected, since the fuzzy algorithm has to know more about the topological structure of the network. The RIP algorithm does not save any packets at all, so they just get lost and will not prevent other packets from travelling through the network.

The implementation of the Boorstyne solution showed the effect that a very simple implementation of the first stage, which divides the links in good and bad paths, is highly dependent on the topological presumptions. When the first stage does not care about these facts, a good routing performance is a mere coincidence and cannot react on dynamic changes of the load flow through the network; this also holds for the RIP algorithm.

A mathematical analysis of the given network leads to an optimum solution of the global end-to-end delay. It is given by the bifurcated routing scheme which leads to a linear program for the optimal load distribution in the network. In the given network the optimum load distribution leads to the following total load flows. The links which connect the four-node clusters will henceforth be called type-i links. They all have a load flow of $\lambda_i = 8/7\gamma$. The other links connecting nodes within these clusters are called type-ii links. Each of these links have a total load flow of $\lambda_{ii} = 5/7\gamma$. The total network wide load flow is then given by $\lambda_{tot} = 16 \cdot \dfrac{5}{7}\gamma + 4 \cdot \dfrac{8}{7}\gamma = 16\gamma$. The total network wide generated load is $\gamma_{tot} = 8\gamma$. The mean number of hops a packet takes from the source to the sink node is $hop = \dfrac{\lambda_{tot}}{\gamma_{tot}}$. The average percentage of packets travelling from nodes with two links h_2 and nodes with three links h_3 is

$$h_2 = \frac{8 \cdot (5/7)\gamma}{\lambda_{tot}} = 0.357, \quad h_3 = 1 - h_2 = 0.643.$$

Every solution leading to these average load flows is an optimum solution to the problem. Now the first stage of the Boorstyne algorithm becomes clear. Only minimum hop paths are 'good paths'. If two paths exist with a minimum hop number, both paths are treated as 'good paths'. This scheme provides the above load distribution over the network and it is indeed a very simple scheme for the first stage. But this depends on the fact that the offered load at each node above corresponds to the made assumptions. If the load situation changes, the routing scheme is no longer optimal.

Node-internal parameters can be derived from these values; therefore, the restriction for the queue length is removed. Then, the waiting queues behave in the model like M/M/1-queues, with the interarrival times of the incoming traffic being assumed as exponential-distributed. The calculation is performed for a $\gamma = 50$ kbit/s. The packet arrival rate at a node with two outgoing links is given by

$$\lambda_{in,2} = \gamma + (10/7)\gamma = 121.429$$

expressed in packets per second. In this formula, the first γ is the load the node offers to the network. The second γ denotes the remaining load the network routes through this node. Then the mean delay in the routing algorithm and the incoming queue is given by

$$t_{w,in,2} = \frac{1}{\lambda_{in} - \lambda_{in,2}} = 0.007.$$

Similarly, for a node with three links, the incoming waiting queue behaves as follows: $\lambda_{in,3} = 178.571$ and $t_{w,in,3} = 0.013$.

Then the mean time delay it takes the packets through the incoming queues and the routing algorithm is given by $t_{w,in} = t_{w,in,2} \cdot h_2 + t_{w,in,3} \cdot h_3 = 0.011$.

For the outgoing queues it is necessary to divide the two types of links. For both types the following values are obtained $\lambda_{out,i} = 57.143$ and $t_{w,out,i} = 0.146$ for the first type and $\lambda_{out,ii} = 37.714$ and $t_{w,out,ii} = 0.035$ for the second type.

Then the mean time delay which it takes the packets to get through the waiting queues at the outgoing links and the connected servers is

$$t_{w,out} = \frac{16 \cdot \lambda_{out,ii} \cdot t_{w,out,ii} + 4 \cdot \lambda_{out,i} \cdot t_{w,out,i}}{16 \cdot \lambda_{out,ii} + 4 \cdot \lambda_{out,i}} = 0.067.$$

At last the mean global end-to-end delay is given by

$$t_{ete} = t_{w,in} + hop \cdot (t_{w,in} + t_{w,out}) = 0.167.$$

During the simulations the fuzzy algorithm resulted in a mean global end-to-end delay of 0.222 s; this is 32.93% more than the optimum value. This is definitely not optimal but for an algorithm which does not know anything about the topology this is a pretty good result. Another point for the fuzzy algorithm is that the bifurcated routing strategy is difficult to implement and causes too much overhead on the network which is not taken into consideration in the above calculation. It is significant to note that no implementation of a bifurcated routing strategy has been reported up to now.

5 Traffic Management in ATM Networks

5.1 Call Admission Control and Usage Parameter Control

In cases of congestion the network performance or the quality of service (QoS) may quickly degrade and might result in queuing delay and cell loss. Thus, it is a necessary traffic management task to avoid congestions. In ATM networks this is done by two basic functions: CAC (call admission control) and UPC (usage parameter control).

To establish a new end-to-end connection it may be necessary to set up a path through several nodes (ATM-switches). As the average congestion situation of each node may differ, each node has to perform the CAC algorithm and to decide whether to accept or reject the requested connection and an exception occurs only if there are sufficient network resources to establish this connection with the required QoS and maintain the agreed QoS of the existing connections.

There are various proposed CAC-algorithms which are based on different approaches of traffic description. Some algorithms, e.g., the *IBM algorithm*, use a set of parameters including a description for *peak cell rate* (PCR), *mean cell rate* (MCR), and *burst size* (BS) of a traffic load. The definitions of these concepts differ widely.

In addition to CAC UPC provides a mechanism which monitors the established connections to ensure that the negotiated parameters are kept. Therefore the aim of UPC is to detect a violating traffic source and to carry out distinct measures to prevent an overloading of the network. The UPC is located between the traffic source at the first node which manipulates the ATM cell stream. As UPC works online, it must satisfy a strictly real time demand.

To recognize a violating cell stream, some parameters have to be inspected. These parameters should be a subset of the CAC-controlled parameters. Many possible algorithms are proposed. The most famous one is the so-called *Leaky Bucket algorithm.*

An ATM connection may be characterized by some traffic parameters, which build the so-called traffic descriptor.

- The *sustainable cell rate* (SCR) is defined as the quotient of cells that were sent and the connection time. The upper limit of the SCR is the bandwidth of the medium.
- The *peak cell rate* (PCR) is defined as the reciprocal of the minimum arrival time T between two generated cells.
- The *maximum burst size* (MBS) is defined as the maximum number of cells that are being sent during a PCR phase.
- The *burst tolerance* defines the minimum time between sending two bursts of MBS that SCR is not exceeded.
- The *burstiness* is a measure of the changes in the cell transfer and the time between these changes.

5.2 Common Call Admission Control

A number of CAC algorithms are described in the literature. Two source classes are usually classified by the algorithm: *constant bit rate* (CBR) and *variable bit rate* (VBR). Others classify sources with regard to the ratio between *peak cell rate* (PCR) and *sustainable cell rate* (SCR). The IBM algorithm also uses the parameter *middle cell rate.*

The *COST algorithm* separates between connections that can be statistically multiplexed and those that cannot. Connections in this last category are assigned to the *peak cell rate*, the most pessimistic value. The other connections have to satisfy

$$0.005 \le \frac{SCR_i}{PCR_i} \le 0.5 \text{ and } 15 \le \frac{C_0}{PCR_i} \le 1000.$$

C_0 is the so-called net link capacity. This value denotes which part of the present bandwidth can be assigned to the user because a certain part of the bandwidth has to be used for network management. The effective bandwidth of a connection appropriate for multiplexing can be calculated with the following empirically derived formula:

$$C_i = \begin{cases} 1.2 \cdot SCR_i + 60 \cdot \dfrac{\sigma_i^2}{C_0} & if \quad P_{Loss} = 10^{-9} \\[3mm] 1.1 \cdot SCR_i + 35 \cdot \dfrac{\sigma_i^2}{C_0} & if \quad P_{Loss} = 10^{-5} \end{cases}.$$

P_{Loss} denotes the probability of cell losses. The variance σ_i^2 can according to [16] be estimated by $\sigma_i^2 = SCR_i \cdot (PCR_i - SCR_i)$.

The *Sigma Rule algorithm* also suggests a division into two classes. Class I includes connections with constant bit rate and those connections that cannot be statistically multiplexed. All other connections belong to Class II. Like above, connections in Class I are assigned to the *peak cell rate*. In Class II statistical multiplexing only takes place when the bandwidth c for this class is greater than a predefined constant C_{II}. If $c < C_{II}$ the system also reserves *peak cell rate*. Connections in Class II have to satisfy several properties that depend on the kind of sigma-rule that is used. The example in [16] is restricted as follows:

$$0.1 \le \frac{SCR_i}{PCR_i} \le 0.5 \quad and \quad 64\frac{kbit}{s} \le PCR_i \le 6.144\frac{Mbit}{s}.$$

A new connection can be accepted if either the sum of the *peak cell rates* from all N connections is less than or equal to a parameter depending on the probability of a cell loss $\sum_{i=1}^{N} PCR_i \le C(P_{Loss})$ or the bit rate that is available for Class II connections allows statistical multiplexing, i.e., in case of $c \le C_{II}$ and the required bandwidth for multiplexing is less than c:

$$q(c) \cdot \sqrt{\sum_{ClassII} \sigma_i^2} + \sum_{ClassII} SCR_i + \max_{ClassII} PCR_i \le c.$$

The values for C_{II} and q(c) have to be calculated in a rather complex iterative process [19] . Like in the COST-algorithm the parameter σ_i^2 can be estimated.

The *IBM algorithm* uses two different analytical approaches to calculate the effective bit rate. The first approach uses fluid flow models. The sum of the bit rates of the multiplexed connections can be considered as a continuous bit stream. The distribution function of the buffer content is a function of the connection parameters and the service rate of the buffer. This function is used to determine the equivalent bit rate C^*. The following equation shows an approximation to calculate C^* iteratively [13]:

$$C_i^* = \frac{\alpha\beta_i(1-\rho_i)PCR_i - x + \sqrt{D}}{2\alpha\beta_i(1-\rho_i)}$$

$$D = [\alpha\beta_i(1-\rho_i)PCR_i - x]^2 + 4x\alpha\beta\rho_i(1-\rho_i)PCR_i$$

The following parameters are used in this equation: $\alpha = \ln(\frac{1}{P_{Loss}})$, P_{Loss} and PCR_i like above, x is the buffer size, $\rho_i = \frac{m_i}{p_i}$ is the source utilization, and β_i is the MBS of the source. The *equivalent bit rate* of the total traffic can be calculated by

$$C^* = \sum_{i=1}^{N} C_i^*$$

This approximation gives a too optimistic estimation of the equivalent bit rate. Therefore, a second approach uses statistical multiplexing. It is based on a stationary bit distribution of the arrival process. The equivalent bit rate C^{**} is determined in such a way that the stationary sums of the bit rates of all the connections will exceed the value C^{**} by a probability P_{Loss} only. An approximation of C^{**} is

$$C^{**} = \overline{SCR} + \alpha' \text{ with } \alpha' = \sqrt{-2\ln(P_{Loss}) - \ln(2\pi)}.$$

Here $\overline{SCR}$ denotes the average sum of the bit rates and σ denotes the standard deviation of the sum of the bit rates. The minimum of the two results presented above gives us the final result $C = \min\{C^*, C^{**}\}$.

5.3 Fuzzy Call Admission Control

Our solution suggested for a fuzzy CAC system is based on an integrated fuzzy system performing the following functions:

- The estimation of the bandwidth that has to be reserved for a single connection (we call this assumed required bandwidth *effective bandwidth* (EffBw)). Refer Figure 9.
- The correction of the estimated effective bandwidth by measuring the actual network load.
- The correction of the estimated effective bandwidth by estimating the suitability of the whole set of existing connections with regard to statistical multiplexing.
- The comparison of the corrected effective bandwidth with the available link capacity.

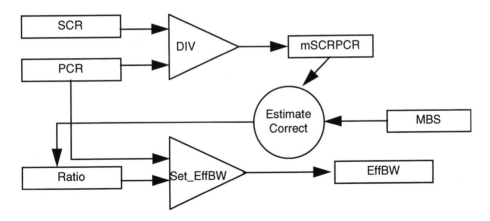

Figure 9: Fuzzy system to estimate the effective bandwidth

As in ATM networks burstiness of connections is an essential criterion to define the effective bandwidth; the *burst factor* (respectively its reciprocal value) together with the *maximum burst size* (MBS) are used as inputs for the fuzzy rule base. The burst factor is determined by the ratio of the parameters SCR and PCR as defined by the ATM forum in [2]. The fuzzy rule base basically defines that connections are expected to perform badly with regard to statistical multiplexing if they have a large MBS and a SCR-PCR-ratio close to 1, i.e., these connections probably behave almost like a constant bit rate connection with an effective bandwidth close to PCR.

To avoid overload situations, which is a main goal of the CAC, this procedure proves to be good. However, network providers have to maximize the traffic that can be put onto a network without violating quality requirements. So, the CAC has to reach a maximum capacity utilization and can therefore be enhanced by the following ideas:

- Often there are some accepted connections which do not use the complete bandwidth that was specified in the traffic contract and therefore do not need to be reserved to the effective bandwidth calculated above. Assuming a sufficient number of such sources, one can use the difference between negotiated and used bandwidth to correct the estimation of the effective bandwidth.

- Moreover we increased the accuracy of the CAC by estimating the suitability of the accepted connections with regard to the gain of statistical multiplexing.

These two enhancements have been built in a fuzzy rule base that estimates how to correct the effective bandwidth based on the measured load difference, the number of established connections and the average ratio between SCR and PCR.

As simulation of very rare events takes too much time, CAC algorithms are often shown to work correctly by using analytical estimations. These estimations are based on assumptions about the load distribution. The assumptions are often derived from worst case analyses of the used CAC algorithm. In case of a fuzzy CAC this is unfortunately very hard to do. So far, we can present some plausibility checks to prove that our CAC works correctly as far as quality is concerned.

In call admission control, the parameters from the traffic descriptor are used: PCR, SCR, and MBS. As a result we calculate the *effective bandwidth* (EffBW) that has to be available when the connection has to be accepted. It can be regarded as a function of three input parameters: EffBW = f (PCR, SCR, MBS) and should be in the interval [SCR, PCR].

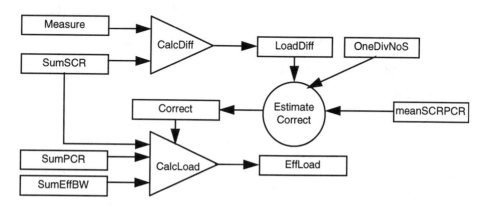

Figure 10: Structure of the fuzzy system to calculate the effective bandwidth

What kind of value definitely has to be selected within this interval depends on other parameters than those described above. The smaller the cell loss probability within the node has to be set, the closer will the EffBW value be to the PCR. If maximum load is the top priority, the value is shifted toward the lower bound of the interval, i.e., towards the SCR. An increase of the load and reduction of the cell loss probability are competitive objectives. Figure 10 shows the structure of the designed fuzzy controller.

If an upper limit for the PCR is set which is clearly smaller than the maximum bandwidth available, the controller as described above can already be used. The used membership functions however are not definite but are to be understood as default setting for the controller. A 'tuning' of the controller can finally adapt it to the required performance parameter such as the *cell loss probability*. An environment could be assumed, for example, using specifically set parameters for each traffic class. For admission control, the required service quality class would have to be indicated at first. Based on this class, the decision about accepting the connection would then have to be taken by the corresponding part of the controller. This version is more advantageous compared to the service quality class used as an input for the fuzzy controller, since any additional variable used as an input for the rule base would mean additional rules and thus a higher processing time. The CAC algorithm is based on a comparison between the calculated effective bandwidth and the free bandwidth.

If the number of connections to be multiplexed is very small, the required bandwidth can be underestimated. This is extremely critical if no other upper limit than the maximum available bandwidth is set for PCR. These drawbacks are now to be compensated by another controller *Capacity* which corrects the calculated sum of all the connections *SumEffBW*, i.e., also that of the potentially new connection, according to the given situation to evaluate the actually assumed load.

A very small number of connections with a large bandwidth (in relation to the maximum bandwidth) is less suitable for statistical multiplexing than a large number of connections with a correspondingly small bandwidth. The exception is a situation with only one connection whose peak cell rate is within the maximum bandwidth. In this case, almost the peak cell rate of the connection would have to be reserved.

For calculating the *effective bandwidth,* sigma algorithm and IBM algorithm use the variance of the cell arrival distribution. The value $\sigma = \sqrt{\sum_{i=1}^{N} \sigma_i^2}$ is thus an indicator for the quality of statistical multiplexing. If σ is high, statistical multiplexing is insufficient. A deviation from this value thus improves the quality of multiplexing. If a weighted average V of all the connections is built, a conclusion can be drawn about the consequences of statistical multiplexing on the total stream.

With the controller *Capacity* used as an extension to controller *Consumption*, the situation of the network at the time of admission control can be evaluated much better. Compared to the exclusive use of the controller *Consumption* (on the precondition that the two controllers are adapted to each other) the results are much more accurate and allow a higher flexibility when selecting the input values.

5.4 CAC Simulation

New sources are accepted as long as the variable *EffLoad* calculated by the system *capacity* is smaller than the maximum bandwidth. The corresponding simulation environments were then created from the sources accepted this way using OPNET. Despite the very small number of simulated cells within a simulation run, the simulation results show that the fuzzy CAC principally works correctly.

In a first simulation, exclusively 2-Mbit block data sources with an MBS of 54 cells were used. These sources were initialized one after the other. Cell losses did not occur at the beginning of the simulation. Based on the low load of the queue (1.04 cells on average) it can be assumed that the controller - with pre-given setting - strongly underestimates this source type as far as its bandwidth requirement is concerned. If this is the case, the load of the line (for this simulation 51.76%) can also be improved.

For the next simulation with these block data sources different probability density functions were assigned; the values for the average queue load were similar and no cell losses occurred.

During another simulation, two different bandwidths (2 and 10 Mbit) were used besides different probability density functions. In this simulation, the load of the queue (average 2.37 cells) is clearly higher than that of the preceding ones despite the low sum of all SCR_i. This confirms that a higher source number with a small bandwidth is more suitable for multiplexing than a smaller number of sources at a correspondingly higher bandwidth. An overflow of the queue could not be detected either during this simulation.

Simulations with the same simulation environment but ten times the simulation sequence using only MPEG video sources having a much higher MBS than the block data sources yielded an average queue load of 10.3 cells. The average number of cells in the queue is reduced during the simulation of 400 seconds; it can therefore be assumed that the starting phase is also critical. Moreover, a clear peak could be detected during the average delay at the beginning of the simulation. In this case, no cell losses were detected, either.

During the simulation of a traffic comprising 14 MPEG Video PAL TV sources, the load of the line became smaller than 40% and thus very small since the PAL TV sources have a comparably high cell rate and a large BS on the other. However, the average number of cells in the queue with 2.94 cells is clearly smaller than that during the simulation of video sources. This might imply an overestimation of the MBS compared to video sources. Cell losses could not be detected.

During the next simulation equal bandwidth parts are used for MPEG video PAL TV and MPEG video sources. As expected, the attained load lies between the loads attained by the two preceding sources.

The traffic mixtures of the last simulation were identical. The simulations differ as far as the length of the simulated time is concerned. The simulation environment encompasses three groups of source models: video, audio, as well as block data sources. Due to the admission of audio sources generating a nearly constant cell stream, the load of the line was very high compared to the other simulations. However, simulation shows that such a traffic mixture causes a very high load of the queue. The average number of cells in the queue was approx. 64 cells for these simulations which corresponds to an average delay of the cells in the queue of approx. $2.55 \cdot 10^{-4}$ s. It has to be considered whether constant traffic streams such as the audio source used can be operated independent of the bursty traffic streams.

5.5 Common Usage Parameter Control

In addition to the CAC the UPC provides a mechanism which monitors the established connections to ensure that the negotiated parameters are kept. The aim of the UPC is therefore to detect a violating traffic source and to carry out distinct measures to prevent an overloading of the network. The UPC is located between the traffic source and the first node which manipulates the ATM cell stream. As the UPC works online, it must satisfy a strict real time demand.

In principle, the method marks incoming cells of a connection as *conform*, if they match with the bandwidth of negotiated parameters. They are marked as non-conform, if they exceed the defined frame of a connection. Conform cells can be sent. Non-conform cells may be treated in different ways:

1. Delay of a cell: as long as the parameter again fit into the negotiated limits.
2. Marking a cell: for marking a cell as a candidate to be replaced by another network element at a later time.
3. Deleting a cell: this is the easiest way.
4. Informing the source: this active measure would be a slow and clumsy method in a WAN.

It is often useful to mix these methods to obtain an efficient monitoring instrument.

Many possible algorithms are suggested. The most famous one is the so called *Leaky Bucket algorithm* defined in the I. 371 recommendation of ITU-T (International Telecommunications Union - Telecommunication Standardization) [9]. The leaky bucket method 'monitors' the SCR and the PCR after a corresponding change of the input values of the method. Figure 11 shows a simple model for the algorithm. The cell stream from the user goes into a bucket with a hole from which the contents are dripping at constant speed. If the bucket is not filled, the cell stream is passed on. If the bucket overflows, the part having caused the overflow is lost.

Figure 11: Model of the leaky bucket method

5.6 Fuzzy Usage Parameter Control

To recognize a violating cell stream some parameters have to be inspected. These parameters should be a subset of the CAC-controlled parameters. Our fuzzy UPC is based on the parameters SCR, PCR and MBS; these are exactly the parameters the CAC algorithm is based on. The main idea is based on the fact that the number of ATM cells wanting to enter the network has to be limited to a specified amount reflecting the average cell rate. The critical point is the size of the time window which is used to enforce an average rate. To enable the fuzzy system to 'remember' the amount of cells having passed the UPC, a token pool mechanism like that of the leaky bucket model is used. Every cell wanting to pass the UPC to enter the network obtains a token - the token is erased when a cell uses it to pass on. The tokens are generated in a specified rate which depends on the SCR. Depending on the number of tokens in the token pool and the time distance between two cell arrivals the fuzzy system classifies every cell as *non-violating*, *partially violating*, and *violating*. Non-violating cells simply pass the UPC; partially violating cells are tagged so that they can be eliminated in a node in case of congestion. Violating cells are immediately eliminated.

The *peak cell rate* is strictly controlled. If the time between two cell arrivals is lower than the minimum time allowed by the PCR, the cells are removed. The PCR is interpreted here as an absolutely strict border which cannot be exceeded. The amount of tokens which can be stored in the token pool is directly connected to the degree of burstiness of the traffic. The burstiness is computed by a fuzzy system using the parameters SCR, PCR and MBS; the computed value specifies the amount of tokens which can be stored by the token pool.

5.7 UPC Simulation

The functionality of this fuzzy UPC system was proved by simulating the system using the network simulation tool OPNET. A variety of different traffic types and sources was used.

The simulated network only consists of a single node, which is the actual load source, and the UPC mechanism. The necessity to simulate several nodes is omitted, since, in reality, the UPC should be positioned as close as possible to the load source, i.e., in the same node, if possible. The node consists of a load source; the available source types were described above. The cells generated by the source are duplicated and treated by two different UPC mechanisms. Thus, two fully identical cell streams can be considered that are tested for their conformity with the traffic parameters by two different methods: our Fuzzy UPC controller and a method implemented as a leaky bucket. A simple model was used for the processor representing the leaky bucket UPC. It monitors the SCR and operates with a token quantity, whose tokens are generated in the SCR rhythm. If the bucket (token quantity) contains a token, an arriving cell is sent; if no token is available the cell is deleted. The size of the bucket can be defined by the user like the initial filler state of the token quantity.

Table 2: Parameters and results of the UPC simulation; the simulation time was 15 minutes. SCR = 4765 bit/s, PCR = 23590 bit/s, MBS = 54

Nr.	Real time	Received cells	Fuzzy-UPC Sent/Marked/Rejected	LB-UPC Sent/Rejected
1	8h12m	4.663.137	9.99%/81.75%/8.26%	91.86%/2.14%
2	7h49m	4.240.583	85.31%/14.68%/0.01%	99.97%/0.03%
3	8h12m	4.663.114	33.31%/58.44%/8.25%	91.84%/8.16%
4	8h26m	5.124.315	2.17%/81.32%/16.51%	83.59%/16.41%
5	7h38m	4.240.605	74.86%/24.02%/1.12%	97.21%/2.39%
6	8h24m	5.124.336	27.60%/55.88%/16.52%	83.57%/16.43%
7	7h22m	4.240.596	50.91%/0.0%/19.09%	99.99%/0.01%
8	9h27m	6.023.331	0.01%/71.01%/28.98%	71.11%/28.89%
9	9h24m	6.023.324	8.90%/62.06%/29.04%	71.11%/28.89%
10	7h48m	4.240.595	60.59%/29.36%/10.05%	86.87%/13.13%

Variable MBS, SCR and PCR were again given and the probability density function of the burst length during the calculation of the average was required as additional parameter for the simulation. *The source model for block data* (simulations 1-4) serves for generating cell streams, corresponding to typical traffic in modern computer networks such as Inter-LAN-communication, file-transfer or telnet. The second source models the behaviour of a *video source* (simulations 5-8), coded according to the MPEG method. *Audio data* as specified in the MPEG standard are to be simulated by a third source model. Simulations 9-11 are with reference to mixed data.

The chosen simulations offered the possibility to compare the fuzzy system with a UPC based on a simple leaky bucket mechanism. The simulation showed that the fuzzy UPC is always at least as good as the simple UPC; in special cases the fuzzy system showed slight advantages. The real advantages have to be shown in a larger network environment with multitudes of nodes and different traffic sources. But this would be a subject for further studies.

Reference and Further Reading

[1]   W. Arnold, H. Hellendoorn, R. Seising, C. Thomas, A. Weitzel, (1997), Fuzzy Routing, *Fuzzy Sets and Systems*, 85, pp. 131-153.

[2]   ATM-Forum, (1995), Traffic Management Specification, Version 4.0/5.0.

[3]   P.R. Bell, J. Kamal, (1986), Review of Point-to-Point Network Routing Algorithms, *IEEE Comm. Magazine*, 24, 1, pp. 34-38.

[4]   R.R. Boorstyne, A. Livne, (1981), A technique for adaptive routing in networks, *IEEE Trans. Comm.*, 29, pp. 474-480.

[5]   G.A. Cope, P.B. Key, (1990), Distributed Routing Schemes, *IEEE Comm. Magazine*, 28, 10, pp. 54-64.

[6]   E. Dijkstra, (1959), A note on two problems in connection with graphs, *Numer. Math.*,1, pp. 269-271.

[7]   L.R. Ford, Jr., D.R. Fulkerson, (1962), *Flows in Networks*, Princeton: Princeton University Press.

[8]   H. Hellendoorn, R. Seising, W. Metternich, M. Nissel, C. Thomas, (1997), Verkehrslastregelung in ATM-Netzwerken mit Fuzzy-Methoden, *Informatik Forschung und Entwicklung*, 12, 1, pp. 23-29.

[9]   International Telecommunication Union, (1993), *Integrated Services Digital Networks (ISDN), Overall Network Aspects and Functions, Traffic Control and Congestion Control in B-ISDN*. ITU-T Recommendation I.371.

[10] A. Khanna, J. Zinky, (1989), The Revised ARPANET Routing Metric, *Sigcomm '89 Symp. Comm. Arch. & Protocols*, Austin: ACM Press, pp. 45-56.

[11] O. Kyas (1993), *ATM-Netzwerke*: Aufbau, Funktion, Performance, Bergheim: Datacom.

[12] J.M. McQuillian, I. Richer, E.C. Rosen, (1980), The New Routing Algorithm for the ARPANET, *IEEE Transactions on Communications*, 28, 5, pp. 711-719.

[13] M. Naghshineh, R. Guerin, H. Ahmadi, (1991), Equivalent capacity and its applications to bandwidth allocation in high-speed networks, *IEEE J. Selected Areas Commun*, 9, 7.

[14] OPNET MODELLER: MIL3, Inc., 3400 International Drive NW, Washington, DC 20008, USA.

[15] M. de Prycker, (1994), *Asynchronous transfer mode*. Die Lösung für Breitband-ISDN. London: Prentice Hall.

[16] R. Siebenhaar, T. Bauschert, (1993), *Vergleich von Algorithmen zur Verbindungsaufnahme in ATM-Netzen*. Lehrstuhl für Kommunikationsnetze, Technische Universität München, 1993.

[17] SieFuzzy User Manual Version 2.0a, Siemens ANL A4, Postfach 3240, D-91050 Erlangen.

[18] A.S. Tanenbaum, (1989), *Computer Networks*, Prentice Hall, Englewood Cliffs, NJ.

[19] E. Wallmeier, C. M. Hauber, (1991), Blocking probabilities in ATM pipes controlled by a connection acceptance algorithm based on mean and peak rates. Queueing, Performance and Control in ATM (ITC-13 Workshops), pp. 131-142. Amsterdam: North Holland.

[20] L.A. Zadeh, (1965), Fuzzy Sets, *Inform. Control*, 8, pp. 338-353.

Chapter 5:

Fuzzy Logic in
Power Supply Applications

FUZZY LOGIC IN POWER SUPPLY APPLICATIONS

Alberto Bellini, Riccardo Rovatti
DEIS
Università degli studi di Bologna, Bologna
Italy

Michael Scheffler
Electronics Lab
ETH Zurich
Switzerland

In modern microelectronics technology, a high-performance power supply is one of the key factors. Very small steady-state error and fast settling time have to be coupled with short-circuit protection and soft start-up to avoid current and voltage overshoot.

To achieve the above goals a two-stage power supply is needed. A DC/DC power-conversion stage is necessary after a coarse AC/DC rectifier, in order to eliminate disturbance, and obtain a precise supply voltage needed to ensure correct operation.

Complex integrated circuits have been developed to realize this second DC/DC stage. However in these circuits, more sophisticated features are added to conventional control laws by means of additional circuitry, e.g., external capacitive elements.

Nevertheless, we can expect this additional complexity to be reduced if we design the control law with a more sophisticated technique, like a fuzzy control, which can take articulated input-output correspondence into account while keeping computational complexity to a reasonable level. As fuzzy logic relies more on the understanding of the system's behavior than on precise mathematical modelling, we may foresee not only a reduction in the implementation complexity, but also an increase in the sophistication and robustness of the control policies.

In this chapter we will discuss the application of fuzzy logic to some implementations of DC/DC converters.

1 Introduction

The evolution of the consumer electronics market allows users to get cheap but sophisticated electronic appliances for home, office and entertainment. Often these small devices require a well-regulated DC power supply between 5 and 15 Volts,

0-8493-9803-7/99/$0.00+$.50

while the network delivers an AC voltage of 125 or 220 Volts. Therefore AC/DC converters are mandatory to produce a stable DC supply. The power system must be small, efficient, cheap and must keep a very stable DC voltage even when abrupt changes in the current absorption of the load occur to support high performance devices such as modern microprocessors. A modern AC/DC converter can be roughly schematized as divided in two parts. The first rectifying stage transforms external AC power into a DC operating voltage. Then, a further DC/DC conversion stage is necessary to eliminate disturbance and obtain a controlled supply. Most of the "intelligence" of power supply systems resides in this last stage whose design may involve sophisticated control, dealing with intrinsically non-linear phenomena and with safety and conversion efficiency constraints often difficult to accommodate with simple and cheap control circuits.

Fuzzy logic may help to tackle this problem as it gives methods to deal with complex and non-linear systems and to analyze their behavior exploiting intuitive as well as more formalized information. The existence of well-studied automatic implementation flows for fuzzy analog controllers makes the fuzzy paradigm even more attractive. These flows, in fact, may provide extremely cheap analog realizations of the synthesized fuzzy controller, which can be directly interfaced to the power system without additional circuitry devoted to analog-to-digital and digital-to-analog conversion.

In this chapter we will review some fundamentals of switching DC/DC power conversion as well as the classical control strategies with their limitations. Then, we will discuss some proposals (e.g., [1]-[11]) addressing the application of fuzzy logic to the control of switching DC/DC converters.

A more complete analysis of the design of a fuzzy controller for a DC/DC conversion stage will be then carried out referring to a power supply for high-performance microprocessors. In that framework the availability of a smart and performing power supply is one of the key points. In fact, very small steady-state error and fast settling times have to be coupled with short-circuit protection and soft start-up which avoids current and voltage overshoot. The DC/DC stage converts the rectified voltage in the range 15V-20V to a very accurate 3.3V supply and controls it to ensure proper operation of the microprocessor and of the other components of the board. This problem will give us the opportunity to delve into some details of the power supply design such as soft start-up and general current limitation as well as to consider some implementation issues that are rarely examined. Actually, complex integrated circuits have been developed to realize this kind of DC/DC stages, e.g., the L296 and L4992 Power Switching Regulators from SGS-THOMSON MICROELECTRONICS [12]. In these circuits more sophisticated behaviors are added to the conventional control laws at the cost of additional circuitry, so that external capacitive elements are necessary to obtain, for example, a soft start-up.

Nevertheless, we might expect this additional complexity to vanish if we design the control law with a non-linear technique. Moreover, the application of the fuzzy paradigm is promising, as it may allow to incorporate informal understanding of the system's behavior in the control policy, and let us foresee not only a reduction in the implementation complexity, but also an increase in the system performance.

At the end we will present a fuzzy controller causing the DC/DC stage to feature small settling time, no voltage overshoot, soft start-up, and automatic current limitation at the cost of no additional circuitry.

The controller will be implemented with the fuzzy analog processor AFE, designed at the University of Bologna, using a CMOS 0.7µm technology compatible with the silicon technology supporting the power device, provided by SGS-THOMSON MICROELECTRONICS.

This analog implementation makes A/D and D/A converters no longer necessary and allows an operating frequency of 300kHz. Hence, smaller reactive elements may be used in the filtering part of the converter, thus reducing the cost of the whole system. The resulting performance fulfills the electrical specifications for a power supply driving INTEL Pentium microprocessors from 75MHz to 120MHz [13].

A comparative analysis of the classical control strategies and those based on fuzzy logic is finally sketched in the final section.

2   Switch Mode Power Conversion

2.1   Fundamentals

The DC/DC power conversion stage is an important component in any sophisticated power supply system converting AC power supply lines into a DC voltage supply satisfying the requirements of modern electrical and electronic devices. Its task is to provide regulated DC supply starting from the unregulated output of the rectifier, and most of the "intelligence" of the power supply system in terms of automatic control mechanisms is devoted to the fine regulation of the output voltage.

DC/DC conversion stages are traditionally classified into two main categories: linear regulator and switching regulators. In linear regulators, the control gate of a power semiconductor device is driven with continuity by a linear feedback, which tries to regulate the output voltage. These regulators feature very good performance in rejecting disturbances on the input line and in following steep load changes. Regrettably, they are characterized by often non-negligible output ripple and, worst of all, a high internal power dissipation and poor conversion efficiency which can be accepted only when very low power levels are handled or no efficiency issue has to be considered. As these two conditions are rarely met in the growing world of complex systems, but preferably in power-efficient digital systems, the application of alternative power conversion strategies is becoming mandatory.

Switching DC/DC stages is a step in this direction. In these schemes, the power semiconductor devices are operated either in the ON or OFF state to convert unregulated DC into a high frequency pulse of modulated width which is then filtered back to DC.

In ideal conditions the switch and the reactive components of the subsequent filter do not dissipate power, and so lossless power conversion could be achieved. Obviously, real-world power semiconductor devices and reactive components do have a power dissipation but, even so, the conversion efficiency of most switching DC/DC stages outperform that of linear regulators.

The main drawback of the switching schemes is a slower transient response as control actions produce their effect only after the filtering action. A more sophisticated control mechanism is then needed to achieve acceptable performance. As switching systems are inherently non-linear, the design and implementation of control circuitry cannot rely on the wide corpus of linear system theory without an often-disturbing degree of approximation.

Actually, a great effort has been devoted to provide the designers with analytical tools for Switch Mode Power converters (SMP) planning. Surely, the most widely exploited outcome of such efforts is the so-called state-space average method which transforms the intrinsic non-linear model of the circuit in an averaged linear model weighting the ON and the OFF models according to their duration. Though this approach takes the SMP control problem back into the framework of linear systems, the inherent approximation obviously leads to sub-optimal results paving the way to the application of real non-linear controllers coping with the switching phenomenon.

SMP converters are directly or indirectly derived from three main topology, called Buck (step-down), Boost (step-up) and Buck-Boost, schematically represented in Figure 1 [14][15]. More sophisticated topologies are recently being introduced to overcome discontinuities in energy transfer (the Cuk converter topology [16]) and loss of efficiency when raising the switching frequency to few hundreds kHz (the resonant converter scheme).

2.2 Basic Configurations

Some features are common to the three classical SMP topology. They store charge on an output capacitor to maintain a regulated output voltage. This voltage is the result of averaging a train of pulses through an inductance which acts as a low-pass filter. This train of pulses is produced by a switch, setting the pulse value during ON phases, and one or more diodes setting the pulse value when the switch is OFF.

The three topologies are the answer to three basic needs in power conversion: obtaining a regulated output voltage which is lower than the rectified one, obtaining a regulated voltage which is higher, and controlling whether the regulated voltage is lower or higher than the rectified one.

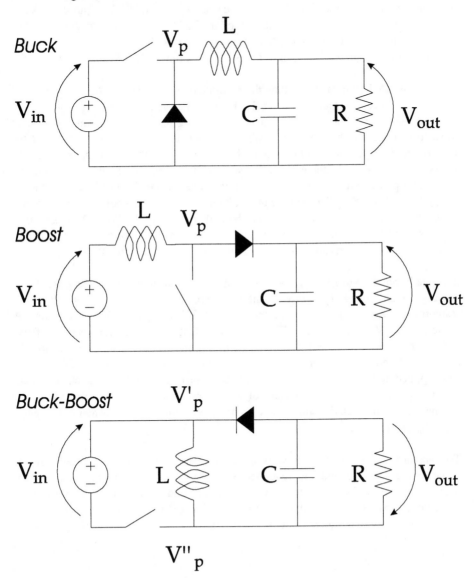

Figure 1 Common schemes for DC-DC converters: *Buck*, *Boost* and *Buck-Boost*

When a regulated voltage lower than the rectified one is needed the *Buck* converter is employed (the first circuit in Figure 1). Its operation can be easily understood assuming an ideal switch and neglecting the voltage across a diode whenever current is forced through it. In this case the voltage V_p is equal to V_{in} during the ON phase and is brought down to zero during the OFF phase.

With an appropriate design of the switching frequency $1/(T_{ON}+T_{OFF})$ and of the inductance value only the time average value of the train of voltage pulses at V_p is propagated to V_{out} and stored on the capacitor. Such average value depends on the ratio between the duration of the ON phase and the switching period, i.e., on the duty cycle δ, and the steady state output of the *Buck* converter is $V_{out}=\delta V_{in}$.

When a regulated voltage higher than the rectified one is needed the *Boost* topology is adopted (the second circuit in Figure 1). If the switch and the diode are once more assumed ideal the voltage V_p is equal to V_{out} during the OFF phase and is brought down to zero during the ON phase. With a proper design, the average value of the train of voltage pulses V_p must equal the DC value at the left-hand side of the inductance, i.e., V_{in}. As such average value depends on the ratio between the duration of the OFF phase and the switching period, we have the steady state relationships $(1-\delta)V_{out}=V_{in}$ and $V_{out}\geq V_{in}$. To see how this voltage boosting is possible note that even if the switch is never operated, V_{out} gets charged to V_{in} by the diode. Voltage boost happens when the switch is turned ON and OFF again as inductor current increases in the ON phase and pumps additional charge into the capacitor during the OFF phase.

It is finally possible to select voltage boosting or voltage reduction if the *Buck-Boost* topology is employed (the third circuit in Figure 1). In this case, under the usual assumptions, the voltage across the inductor $V'_p-V''_p$ is equal to V_{in} during the ON phase and to $-V_{out}$ during the OFF phase. This situation can be thought of as if two separate trains of voltage pulses at V'_p (V_{in} during the ON phase and zero during the OFF phase) and at V''_{up} (zero during the ON phase and V_{out} during the OFF phase) were applied at the two sides of the inductance. A properly designed inductance forces the average values of these two trains of voltage pulses to be equal so that we finally get the steady-state relationship $(1-\delta)V_{out}=\delta V_{in}$. With this, $V_{out}>V_{in}$ when $\delta>0.5$ while $V_{out}<V_{in}$ when $\delta<0.5$.

To transform these schemes into working DC/DC stages, isolation has to be provided between the rectified and the regulated voltages. This is commonly achieved by introducing a transformer instead of a single coil inductance. Though transformer design becomes a key part of the power conversion, it is well beyond the scope of this chapter, and shall be ignored in the following discussion.

2.3   Modeling of the *Buck* Converter

In this section we discuss some modeling issues concerning the *Buck* converter. All the following considerations can be straightforwardly extended to the other configuration described in Section 2.2.

A more detailed scheme of the *Buck* is shown in Figure 2. The switch is handled by a pulse width modulator (PWM) whose control voltage is derived from the output of the converter; parasite resistors are also shown.

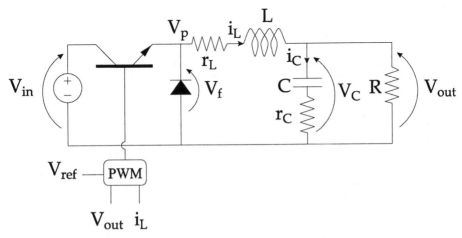

Figure 2 A more realistic model of a *Buck* converter

The operation of this circuit is as follows [14]. The transistor acts as a switch at frequency f_{switch} and the ON and OFF times are controlled by the PWM circuit. When the transistor is ON it is saturated, energy is absorbed from the input and transferred to the output through L. The emitter voltage of the transistor (V_p) is V_{in}-V_{sat}.

During the OFF phase the current flows through L and D and V_p=-V_f, where V_f is the forward voltage across diode D. Consequently, a rectangular shaped voltage appears at the emitter of the transistor and is then filtered and converted into a continuous mean value across capacitor C and therefore across the load.

Figure 3 shows the waveforms of some important quantities characterizing the circuit behavior and helps us to understand the operation of the regulator. For the sake of simplicity r_L is neglected in the following considerations.
- Figure 3-a) shows the emitter voltage V_p (taking into account the saturation voltage V_{CEsat}), where V_f is the forward voltage.
- Figure 3-b) shows the coil current i_L assuming that both the transistor and the diode dynamics are ideal. Such a current is the sum of the transistor current and the current through the clamping diode, and $\left|\Delta i_L^+\right| = \left|\Delta i_L^-\right|$.

- Figure 3-c) shows the current i_C flowing through C which is i_L-i_R. This current is responsible for the output voltage ripple.
- Figure 3-d) shows the output voltage ripple ΔV_{out} which consists of two components: the capacitive one $\Delta V_c = \frac{1}{C}\int i_c dt = \frac{\Delta Q}{C}$, and the resistive one $\Delta V_{r_c} = \Delta i_L r_c$.

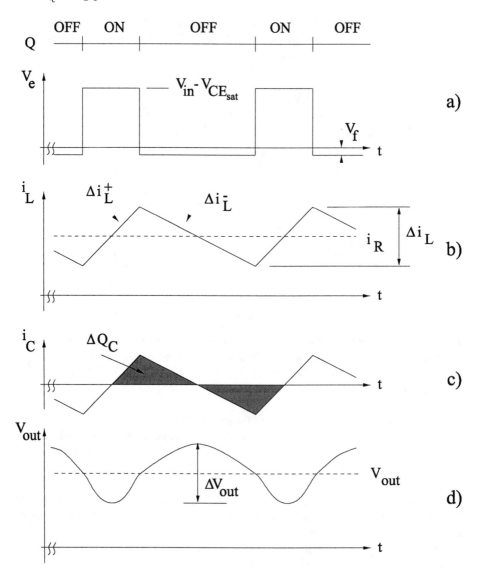

Figure 3 Main waveforms of a buck converter

As the aim of control strategies is to maintain the nominal steady-state characteristic $V_{out} = \delta V_{in}$ when external conditions change (e.g., at startup or when the load changes), their synthesis depends on the availability of a suitable dynamic model of the circuit. Obviously, the time domain behavior of a switching regulator can be divided into two phases, the ON state and the OFF state, which are sketched in Figure 4, taking the switch and the diode as ideal components.

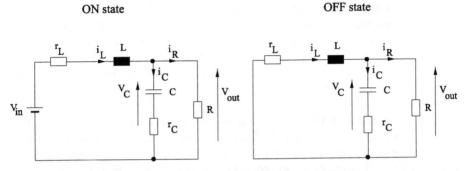

Figure 4 Equivalent circuit of ON state and OFF state

The individual networks, which are shown above, are linear, but the switching between the two phases makes the converter non-linear [14]. Nevertheless a linear model exists for each phase.

If we denote the state vector as:

$$x = \begin{pmatrix} i_L \\ v_C \end{pmatrix}$$

and $\dot{x}$ as its derivative, we can arrange the state space matrix model according to the general model [17]:

$$\dot{x} = \underline{A}x + \underline{b}\,V_{in}$$
$$V_{out} = \underline{c}^T x$$

where $\underline{A}$ is the state space matrix, $\underline{b}$ is the input vector and $\underline{c}^T$ the transposed output vector. Assuming $R \gg r_C, r_L$ we have

$$\underline{A} = \begin{pmatrix} -\dfrac{1}{L}(r_C + r_L) & -\dfrac{1}{L} \\ \dfrac{1}{C} & -\dfrac{1}{RC} \end{pmatrix} \quad \underline{b} = \begin{pmatrix} \dfrac{1}{L} \\ 0 \end{pmatrix}$$

$$\underline{c}^T = \begin{pmatrix} r_C & 1 \end{pmatrix}$$

for the ON state, while $\underline{b} = \begin{pmatrix} 0 \\ 0 \end{pmatrix}$ in the OFF state.

The correct analysis of the global behavior implies the integration of the differential equations corresponding to each state using the last state of the previous phase as the initial condition for the analysis in the subsequent phase. Regrettably this approach does not allow the application of classical control synthesis methodologies which depend on the availability of a global linear model. A common workaround to this problem is the application of the so-called "state space averaging model" which obtains a unique linear model as an affine combination of the ON and OFF models weighted by the duty cycle.

Though clever and fruitful, this approximation can be reasonably expected to lead to poorer results with respect to a truly non-linear control strategy considering the non-linear nature of the circuit. This is what can be tried by means of fuzzy logic which may give a sound methodology to cope with inherent model complexity and devise a more effective truly non-linear control policy.

2.4   Classical Control Strategies

Integrated circuits for the automatic control of DC/DC switching strategies are available from several manufacturers. These chips can be usually adapted to the different circuit topologies described above and provide the switching signal for the power device. They include a PWM module and some control logic implementing at least one of the two most common strategies: voltage control and current control. Both strategies rely on the sensing of both output voltage and a current which can be the output current or the coil current.

In the voltage control scheme V_{out} is compared with its nominal value and δ is adjusted correspondingly by means of a suitable error amplifier (e.g., δ is increased when V_{out} is below its nominal value in a *Buck* converter). To avoid overcurrents, either the output currents or the coil current is sensed and if a threshold is reached the voltage control loop is disabled and δ driven to quickly limit energy transfer (typically switching OFF the power device).

If a more sophisticated control of the current behavior is needed, a different strategy may be adopted. In the current control scheme the output of the voltage error amplifier does not directly operate on the PWM. Instead, it provides the reference input to a second error amplifier in which the sensed current also enters. Safety threshold considerations can still be incorporated in this control strategy if the output of the voltage error amplifier is clamped to a maximum value corresponding to the maximum acceptable current in the system.

A practical scheme to achieve a pulse width modulation obeying a current control policy is illustrated in Figure 5. A clock generator provides pulses at the switching frequency and exploits the S input of the set-reset flip-flop to turn ON the power device at the beginning of each clock cycle. The same power device is then turned OFF when the R input of the flip-flop goes high. This happens when the output of the digital comparator rises, i.e., when the sensed current overcomes a threshold. Such athreshold is set by a voltage error amplifier comparing the nominal value of V_{out} with the actual one. With this scheme, for higher and positive errors, the higher the current flowing to the load before turning on the power device while voltage overshoots implies no current transferred to the load.

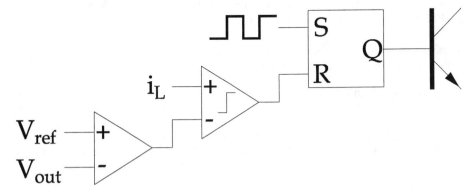

Figure 5 Scheme of a classical current control loop

While this classical control scheme is a good regulator for a circuit operating close to the steady state nominal conditions, it fails to provide the regulated output voltage with some often desirable features. One common example of such a feature is the so-called soft start-up. In fact policies based on linear feedback cannot freely address the trade-off between the speed with which, at system startup, V_{out} rises to its steady state value and the overshoot of the resulting behavior. In particular, systems which are designed to be extremely reactive (e.g., to achieve quick stabilization after a load change) result in a step-like startup, extremely high currents and high overshoot. Some sort of gain scheduling is the obvious countermeasure to this problem, which is a kind of non-linear regulation easily accomplished by fuzzy controllers.

3   Fuzzy Control for DC/DC Power Switching Regulators

Power systems are ideal candidates for the application of fuzzy logic-based control as they may benefit from the non-linearity of such an approach as well as from its ability to cope with imprecisely modeled systems whose behavior can be partially unpredictable (think of a power system start-up with no load instead of the nominal one).

For these reasons, fuzzy control has been applied in this field since 1990 and not only for regulation of switching power converters but also for motor control, current regulation in inverters and uninterruptible power supply systems [18]. In these cases enhanced functionality is almost always achieved as a fuzzy controller has more degrees of freedom than, say, a classical PID controller. On the other hand fuzzy controllers do not usually result in significantly improved performance with respect to linear regulators when small-signal conditions hold, i.e., when well known optimal control techniques can be applied.

When these observations are brought into the field of switching DC/DC converter regulation, they give rise to two classes of fuzzy controllers:

- "pure" fuzzy controllers;
- "hybrid" controllers which combine classical and fuzzy control strategies.

In the following, some examples of both approaches will be briefly discussed. The "hybrid" one will be discussed first, to highlight possible enhancements due to the introduction of fuzzy logic but without detailing the underlying classical control theory.

3.1   Hybrid Control Solutions

One of the first "hybrids" was presented in [7] where a conventional sliding-mode controller is enhanced introducing fuzzy logic. This enhancement is needed as the switching characteristic of sliding mode controllers is an efficient way of driving the systems close to the set point but generates undesirable output chattering when a neighbourhood of the steady-state condition is reached.

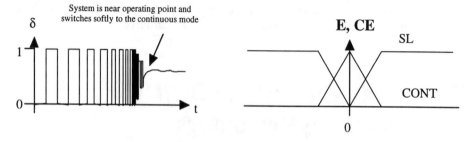

Figure 6 Duty cycle (left) while reaching target (right) Membership functions of the fuzzy controller.

The proposed solution is to switch to a continuous controller whenever such a neighbourhood is reached. In fact, the ideal behaviour of the duty cycle is shown in Figure 6 (left side).

Fuzzy control is introduced for smoothly passing from the discontinuous sliding-mode control u_s to the continuous control u_c as the steady state condition is approached. In fact, the duty cycle is defined as

$$\delta = \frac{h_c \cdot u_c + h_s \cdot u_s}{h_c + h_s}$$

where h_c and h_s are the truth values of the preconditions:

IF E = SL AND CE = SL   THEN u_s
IF E = CONT AND CE = CONT   THEN u_c

The membership functions are shown in Figure 6 (right side) where **E** is the error of the output voltage and **CE** is the change of error. Notwithstanding its simplicity, this approach achieves a significant reduction in the output voltage chattering.

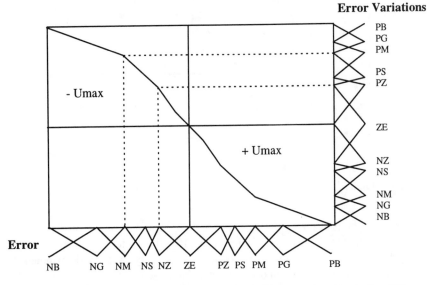

Figure 7 Phase plane of the Fuzzy Optimal Commutation Controller [1]

In [1], an optimal non-linear switching manifold in the **E-CE** plane is proposed. The manifold (see Figure 7) is smoothed using fuzzy switching to reduce chattering. A digital implementation of this controller is also proposed consisting of an analog-to-digital (A/D) and a digital-to-analog (D/A) interface as well as a computation core realised by means of a field-programmable gate array (FPGA). The controller performance is compared with one of two PID controllers and a classical sliding mode controller for V_{in}=50V and f_{switch}=50KHz. The results showed improved performance in the response to step input and load change.

In [8] the fuzzy interpolation was used to implement a classical optimal controller designed with a cell-state space algorithm. To do so, the **E-CE** state space was partitioned into a finite number of regions. For each region the optimal control action is computed obtaining a piecewise-constant map from state to controller output. Such a discontinuous control law would produce chattering and steady-state error. Thus, a neuro-fuzzy system was trained to reproduce a smoothed version of the rough control law managing transition between different control actions which are optimal in different regions. Again, a digital implementation was considered with A/D and D/A interfaces and an FPGA computation core relying on a EPROM to store the control surface data. This implementation is claimed to produce an inference computation, and thus a control action, every 15μs.

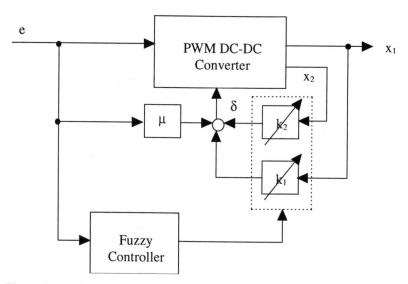

Figure 8 Quasi-Linear Model with Fuzzy Controller for Gain Scheduling [10]

In [9] fuzzy logic is used to improve a classical approach based on "quasi-linear modelling". With the "quasi-linear" approach [10], the system is linearized in the neighbourhood of a *varying* operating point and the duty cycle is determined as a linear combination of the state and the input voltage (see upper part of Figure 8). A simple gain scheduling strategy allows the system to react quickly to input disturbance (in that case, sinusoidal signal with 3V amplitude).

In [9], a more intelligent gain scheduling can be achieved by means of a fuzzy controller monitoring input disturbance and relocating the operating, point i.e., modifying the feedback gains (lower part Figure 8). This approach can be compared with the classical "quasi-linear" control showing a further improvement of performance for load change and input disturbance (allowing an increased 5V amplitude of the sinusoidal perturbation).

3.2   Fuzzy Inference Control

In the following we will try to sketch the state of the art of "pure" fuzzy controllers for switching DC/DC converters.

In our classification, "pure" controllers are those relying exclusively on fuzzy inference to decide the appropriate control action. In all the discussed examples, the system architecture can be derived from the general structure of a Mamdani-type fuzzy controller (see Figure 9) consisting of a fuzzification interface, of an inference mechanism or decision logic, and of a defuzzification interface generating the crisp controller output.

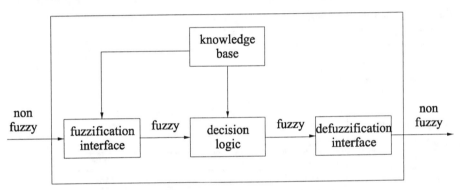

Figure 9 General structure of a Mamdani Controller

These systems are purely non-linear and offer higher degrees of freedom than "hybrid" solutions. Objectives are correspondingly more ambitious and, though every proposal we will discuss is designed and applied to a special converter type, we will report the following performance indexes for all of them:

- start-up time (if possible compared to clock cycle),
- overshoot during settling,
- time for load change response (if possible compared to clock cycle),
- stability of output voltage during load change.

To the best of the authors' knowledge, the first known approach was presented in 1991 by Ueno et al. [5]. The converter to be controlled is a Cuk converter (4th order system), and the inputs are again the error of the output voltage (E) and the change of error (CE). The controller output is the relative change of the duty cycle $\Delta\delta$, limited to maximum of ±5% in one clock cycle. This choice eases the analogy with a PID controller, as the error **E** is related to the proportional component that brings the system near the target, while the change of error **CE** is related to the derivative input improving the dynamics. Moreover, the integral action of a PID has a strict counterpart in the fact that the controller emits changes of duty cycle $\Delta\delta$ which have to be integrated to obtain the PWM control.

The rule table is shown in Table 1. The choice of a 5×5 rule-set is justified by noting that a 3×3 rule-set leads to unsatisfactory control action granularity while an increase to a 7×7 rule-set is not worth the measured improvements.

The input membership functions (MSFs) are triangular, rule consequences are singletons, and the centre-of-gravity (COG) method is used for defuzzification. Singletons simplify the inference computation, thus diminishing implementation cost.

The system was simulated for f_{switch}=50KHz, V_{in}=10V and a target output voltage of V_{out}=5V. Results were benchmarked against a classical PID controller. The comparison shows that the proposed fuzzy controller results in a better performance in most cases of input or load change. At start-up, an overshoot of about 50% of the reference value is simulated, while during load change the signal remains in a tolerance band of ±10% of the same set point. Start-up settling as well as load change reaction lasts about 4ms.

Table 1 Rule table of the controller proposed in [5]

CE E	NB	NS	ZO	PS	PB
NB	1.00	0.75	0.50	0.25	0.10
NS	0.50	0.20	0.10	0.00	0.00
ZO	0.25	0.10	0.00	-0.10	-0.25
PS	0.00	0.00	-0.10	-0.20	-0.50
PB	-0.10	-0.25	-0.50	-0.75	-1.00

Another solution was presented by Lin and Hua for a *Buck-Boost* converter (2nd order) [2], and for a *Buck* converter [11]. In both cases, the rule table is very regular and similar to the one of the previous approach. The same input and output variables (**E**, **CE**, $\Delta\delta$) are used, while V_{in}=50V and a target V_{out}=25V is considered in simulations. Clock frequency is not specified. Again, the input MSFs are triangular, rule consequences are singletons, and the COG method is used for defuzzification.

The controller was simulated using the state-space averaging model for a *Buck* converter and has been compared to a sliding mode control method. For the fuzzy controller, the settling took about 7ms with a slight overshoot of 2% which was 2ms faster compared to the sliding mode solution. Also, the maximum current absorbed at start-up is only 6A instead of 11A. During load change (about 1.5ms), the output voltage remained in a tolerance band of ±5% of the reference value.

In 1994, So et al. [3] publishd a fuzzy controller applicable to all second order converters. The rule table is based on some very intuitive criteria:

- When the output is far from the set point, the change of duty cycle must be large so as to quickly bring the output to the set point.
- When the set point is reached and the output is still changing, the duty cycle must be changed a little to prevent the output from moving away.

Again, MSFs used are triangular and symmetric. The controller was simulated for $V_{in}=15V$ and a target $V_{out}=5V$. Overshoot during start-up is totally prevented; the settling time is about 3ms. During load change the output signal remains in a ±15% tolerance band, and returns to its steady state values after 2ms.

In that paper, the effects of changing the input and output scaling factors (β_e, β_{ce} and η in Table 2) are also considered. In general, these factors are used to ensure that good control action are defined over the whole input space, thus providing maximum solution and sensitivity, but they can also be used to fine-tune the controller.

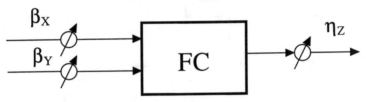

Figure 10 Scaling factors of a Fuzzy Controller

The effects of these factors on the dynamics of the system are summarised in Table 2 where "⇑" stands for an increase, "⇓" for a decrease, "°" denotes a weak effect while "•" a strong one.

Table 2 Effects of changing the scaling factors [3]

Scaling	parameters	rise time	ringing	damping
η	⇑	decrease •	encourage	light °
	⇓	increase •	discourage	heavy °
β_e	⇑	increase	discourage	heavy
	⇓	decrease	encourage	light
β_{ce}	⇑	decrease °	encourage •	light •
	⇓	increase °	discourage •	heavy •

A digital implementation of the above proposed controller was presented in [4], consisting of A/D and D/A converters, a MOSFET switch, and a digital signal processor (DSP), leading to 10μs of computation time. The controller has been tested for a clock frequency of 100KHz, so the converter could be regulated with only one sampling delay. This limits the number of instructions and therefore the complexity of the rule table. The measurements of the real system corroborate the results of the simulations.

The next milestone was reached by Mattavelli et al. in 1995 [6]. They introduced a general-purpose fuzzy controller with a new approach, a parallel structure consisting of the two controllers Fuzzy P and Fuzzy I (see Figure 11).

To improve the dynamics of the Fuzzy controller, not only the error but also the inductor current and its error (defined as the difference between the instantaneous current value and its DC value obtained from a low-pass filter) have been used as controller inputs. Increased information is used to provide simultaneous control of the supplied voltage and current. This may be crucial as most of the supplied circuits have a maximum input current limit enforcing this constraint on supply device.

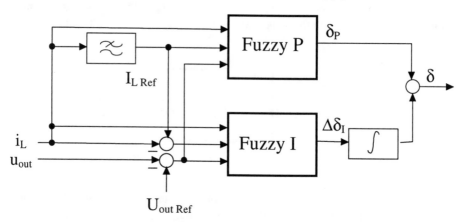

Figure 11 Structure of the fuzzy controller proposed in [6]

The controller output is the absolute value of the duty cycle δ, a combination of the output of both the controllers. The Fuzzy-P controller gives the proportional part δ_P; the Fuzzy-I gives the increment $\Delta\delta_I$ that is integrated afterwards. The membership functions of the inputs are shown in Figure 12.

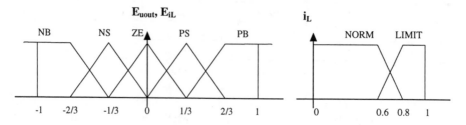

Figure 12 Membership functions of the inputs [6]

The control methodology is presented in the human-like IF…THEN scheme:

- When the output voltage is far from the set point, the correction must be strong in order to have a fast response, but obeying the current limit specifications. Under these conditions the output of the Fuzzy-I will be zero.
- If the output voltage is close to the target, the current error should be taken into account properly in order to ensure stability around the set point. Here, the Fuzzy-I comes into play driving the output voltage slowly to the set point avoiding overshoot and steady-state error.
- When the current approaches the limit value, suitable rules have to be employed to respect the limit while preventing large overshoot.
- An emergency rule depending on the sensed current will deactivate both the Fuzzy P and Fuzzy I, setting δ to zero in case the safety threshold is reached.

The controller described above has been implemented digitally, using 3 A/D interfaces for the inputs, a look-up table on an EPROM as a controller and 2 D/A interfaces for the outputs. The DC/DC stage under test is a *Buck-Boost* converter operating at f_{switch}=50KHz and with a target output voltage of V_{out}=20V. In these conditions start-up terminates after 1.6ms respecting fully the current limit of 10A and showing an overshoot voltage of only 2% of the final value. Reaction to load change lasts 2ms keeping the output within 5% of its nominal value.

4   Analog Fuzzy Control of a Buck DC/DC Converter: Application to a Microprocessor Power Supply

In this section we will present both the design and the implementation of a fuzzy controller for a DC/DC converter based on the *Buck* topology and specialized to supply a digital board hosting a modern microprocessor. In particular, we will refer to a power supply for an Intel Pentium processor which are summarized in Table 3.

Table 3 Power supply requirements for Intel Pentium electrical specifications.

	Intel Pentium	
	75MHz	120MHz
Rising time	$\leq$ 2ms	
Maximum inductor current (i_L)	4A	5A
Voltage overshoot	none	
Steady state supply	V_{out}=V_{ref} ±5%	
Steady state max absorption (i_R)	2.65A	3.7A
Load change response time	$\leq$ 66µs	

As usual we define the rising time as the delay needed to bring the output voltage from 0V to V_{ref} at start-up, while the load change response time is the delay in which the output voltage resumes steady-state conditions, after an abrupt change of the current absorbed by the load. The adopted converter can be characterized by its parameters assuming the values listed in Table 4.

Table 4 Parameters of the Buck converter

F_{switch}	300kHz
C	600µF
r_C	58 Ω
L	26 µH
r_L	25 mΩ
V_{in}	10 V
V_{ref}	3.3 V
I_{load}	[1.2-2.7] A

Speed is the major concern of this kind of power supply system. In fact, the complexity and the increased parallelism of modern microprocessors make their current absorption highly dependent on the task they are performing and on the need of driving large capacitive signal buses. Moreover the high clock speed results in very steep current transients both at start-up and during normal system operation.

Normally, bulk storage capacitors in the 10 to 100 µF range with a low series resistance are required around the processor to maintain a regulated supply voltage during the interval between the time the current load changes and the time the power supply device can react to such a change. Thus for faster DC/DC converters, smaller and fewer storage capacitors are required [13]. This is a great advantage as they are large in size, expensive and toxic.

Control of the current levels is another concern as microprocessor boards are often complex and expensive and may be extremely sensitive to overcurrents. This simultaneous accommodation of performance and safety requirements calls for a non-trivial control policy which can be hopefully synthesized in the fuzzy framework.

In our case reactivity is partially achieved decreasing the switching period to 3.3µs. Yet, this choice implies a very fast implementation of the non-trivial control law and makes the analog option favored against the digital one.

Actually, though often adopted, the digital approach is best suited in applications where precision is a basic requirement, or when the chip must work in a microcontroller-based system as a coprocessor. On the contrary, the analog solution is able to satisfy low-cost constraints even when high speed is needed but accuracy is not the main issue. In fact, a direct interfacing to input and output continuous variables is possible, thus making A/D and D/A interfacing unnecessary. This improves speed since the translation processes may take up to several microseconds, but lowers noise immunity margins, encoding more than one bit of information with the same physical quantity.

In 1994 the analog fuzzy controller AFE was presented. It has been designed using a CMOS n-well 0.7μm technology and features a maximum propagation delay between input and outputs of about 600ns [19][20]. Its input/output relationship can be programmed to synthesize various control functions. The values of the programmable parameters are automatically computed by a development tool, provided with the chip [21][22][23]. The starting point is the controller expected behavior, given by means of linguistic and/or numerical information. The result of the automatic implementation flow is either a bit string configuring a field-programmable version of the analog inference circuit or the mask-level description of a dedicated circuit featuring the assigned input/output relationship and ready for mass production in a foundry. All the measures that will be reported are obtained from the field-programmable version suitably mounted on a measurement board.

Hereafter we will show how fuzzy control policies can be coupled with a dedicated analog implementation to produce an effective and low-cost control structure for high-performance DC/DC converter.

4.1   The Fuzzy Control Strategy

The fuzzy control solution exploits the idea of combining two controllers [6] to obtain a higher flexibility. Namely, the proposed structure contains:

- a "Large signal controller" (LSC) which is responsible only for current managing at start-up, and takes care of the current limit.
- a "Small signal controller" (SSC) which is active when the system is close to the target, and avoids voltage overshoot while controlling response to sudden variations like load current change.

In the following paragraphs the design criteria for the two controllers will be described.

4.1.1   Large Signal Controller

During start-up there are two problems to deal with: the capacitor C should be charged as fast as possible, while the inductor current must not exceed the current limitation. In fact the inductor current in steady state is equal to the current drawn by the load, the current on the capacitor being null. Therefore the ideal control should make the duty cycle very high at the beginning to increase the current which charges the capacitor. Then, δ has to be reduced just before the current limitation is reached, trying to keep the inductor current as high as possible until the voltage set point is approached (Figure 13).

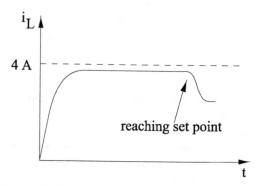

Figure 13 Ideal behavior of the inductor current i_L.

As fine settling and handling of load changes are in charge of the SSC, the output of the LSC should be zero when the error is small and the inductor current is well below the limit. Thus, the LSC needs two inputs: the error of output voltage V_{out} -V_{ref} and the inductor current. These two inputs are normalized in [-1, 1] and [0, 1] respectively, with proper scaling factors β_{el} and β_{cc}, depending on the particular application specifications. The normalized inputs are defined as EL and CC. The corresponding membership functions are shown in Figure 14 and Figure 15 while the rules are arranged in Table 5.

Table 5 Normalized rule table for the LSC (EL: voltage error, CC: inductor current)

		CC					
		ZE	SM	ME	LA	NL	LIM
	NB	0.15	0	-0.11	0	0	-0.15
	NS	0	0	0	0.017	0	-0.15
EL	ZE	0	0	0	0	0	-0.15
	PS	0	0	0	0	0	-0.15
	PB	-0.15	-0.15	-0.15	-0.15	-0.15	-0.15

A large reduction in the duty cycle will occur for a big error, or for high current, as shown in Table 5. The latter is used to prevent the current from exceeding the limit, the former to avoid large voltage overshoot during settling.

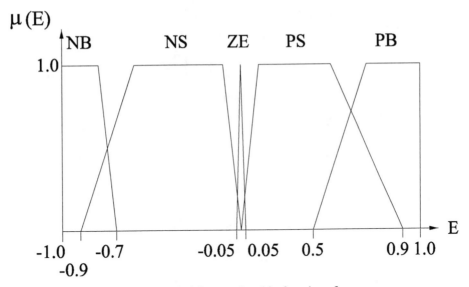

Figure 14 Shape of the membership functions for error

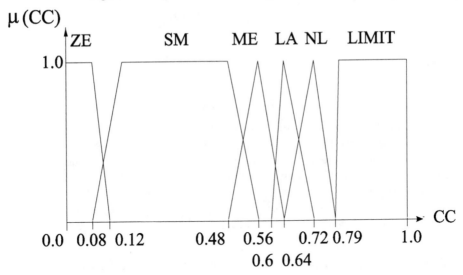

Figure 15 Shape of the membership functions for Inductor Current.

4.1.2 Small Signal Controller

To handle the sudden system variations such as load changes and input voltage ripples, a second more reactive controller is needed. Therefore the change of error has to be monitored, and the inputs of SSC are: the error of output voltage, the change of error from one clock cycle to the next assuming V_{ref} constant. Both inputs are normalized in [-1, 1] with scaling factors named β_{es} and β_{ce}. The normalized inputs are defined as ES and CE. Fuzzy sets are defined as in Figure 18 and Figure 19.

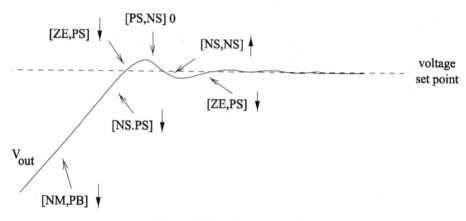

Figure 16 Overshoot protection.

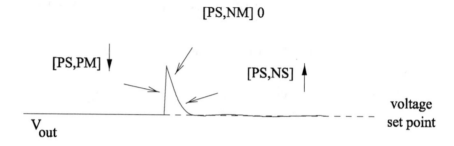

Figure 17 Load change response.

Figure 16 and Figure 17 show how the SSC should act to prevent voltage overshoot and how a quick control reaction to a change of load current could be achieved. The expressions in brackets represent linguistic values of the error ES and the change of error CE, respectively. The arrows or the number zero represent the consequences of rules, i.e., whether the duty cycle should increase or decrease. The SSC should be active only when the system is close to the target. Thus, its output should be zero for large errors. Table 6 shows the necessary rules.

Table 6 Normalized rule table for the SSC (ES: voltage error, CE: change of error)

		CE				
		NM	NS	ZE	PS	PM
	NB	0	0	0	0	0
	NM	0.09	0.09	0.06	0	0
	NS	0.09	0.09	0.03	-0.06	0
ES	ZE	0	0.03	0	-0.03	0
	PS	0	0.06	-0.03	-0.09	-0.09
	PM	0	0	-0.06	-0.09	-0.09
	PB	0	0	0	0	0

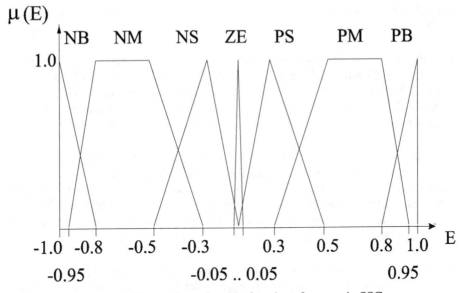

Figure 18 Shape of membership functions for error in SSC.

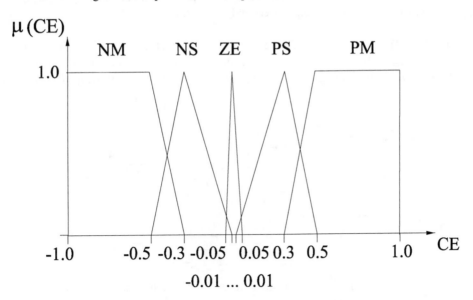

Figure 19 Shape of membership functions for change of error in SSC.

To evaluate the proposed controller, time domain simulations are used with the program MATLAB and its SIMULINK toolbox, using the Runge-Kutta 2nd order method to solve the ordinal differential equations. This method is applied to the state space matrices models obtained in Section 2.3. The two state-space matrix models are solved separately for the ON and OFF state, respectively in the time-domain. Thus, a higher accuracy is obtained, which is required to address output ringing problems and steady-state error.

Starting with the initial conditions: $\underline{x}=0$, $y=0$, and $\delta=0$ the simulation is done as follows: The ON state model is solved for the time interval between kT and kT+δT (where T is the clock period), then $\underline{x}$ and y are given as initial conditions to the OFF model which has to be solved for the time interval between kT+δT and (k+1)T, again afterwards giving $\underline{x}$ and y to the ON model at (k+1) clock cycle and so on.

The Fuzzy controller is described in MATLAB code too, using singletons as rule consequences and MAX-MIN inference. After every clock cycle the output voltage and the inductor current are taken, and the values for error, change of error and coil current are computed and normalized in the suitable intervals to obtain ES, EL, CE, and CC which are fed into the controller subroutine. The two outputs are merged considering the incremental control action weighted by a factor η.

The simulated closed loop system is shown in Figure 20. The control part is discrete-time as the control action computed in each switching period is applied in the next one. As the implementation we are thinking of produces an inference every 600ns, this leaves plenty of time for driving buffers and amplifiers.

To satisfy specifications for Pentium 120MHz we set $\beta_{el}=3.3$, $\beta_{cc}=4.5$, $\eta_L=0.1$, $\beta_{es}=0.08$, $\beta_{ce}=0.01$, $\eta_S=0.475$. The same rule-set can be applied to the supply of Pentium 75, by choosing: $\beta_{el}=3.0$, $\beta_{cc}=3.55$, $\eta_L=0.1$, $\beta_{es}=0.08$, $\beta_{ce}=0.01$, $\eta_S=0.435$.

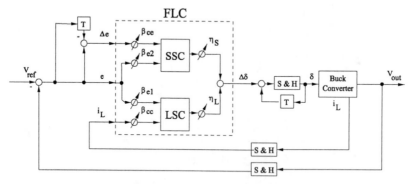

Figure 20 Schematic fuzzy controller system.

At t=0 the converter is switched on, and the whole startup behavior is simulated. After 520 clock cycles, the current absorption is suddenly changed from the worst case 2.7A to the typical 1.2A, in order to evaluate the capability of the designed control to adapt to a sudden change of the load. A quantitative evaluation of the achieved performance is shown in Table 7.

Table 7 Theoretical results with the fuzzy control.

Parameters	Values
Settling time t_s (ms)	1.4
Settling overshoot (% of final value)	< 0.5
maximum current	3.7
steady state error	none
load change response [µs]	90
load change output stability	< 1

According to these parameter values, the proposed control strategy fulfills specifications better than the other recent fuzzy-related proposals discussed in Section 3. Simulations also revealed that the achievable performance is robust against parameter variations. Yet, the overall system may seem quite complex and the implementation issue shall be discussed in detail.

4.2   The Implementation Phase

The implementation phase for the fuzzy controller AFE can be divided in two steps: the design of a minimum abstract system and the hardware mapping. The first design step involves the use of both classical and fuzzy techniques for the synthesis of the control and the minimization of the number of rules required to describe the resulting control actions. The synthesis of the control can be performed either in a linguistic way (and this is the case in our example application) or by synthesizing a non-linear static surface obtained, for instance, through sliding-mode theory.

Once the control law is decided and described in terms of input-output samples or linguistic information, an equivalent fuzzy system is determined with a minimal set of rules. Linguistic specifications are accepted as fuzzy IF...THEN rules involving membership functions of either Gaussian or trapezoidal shape. Missing rules are induced from the available numerical evidence.

Rule induction considers all the possible combinations of conjunctive preconditions accounting for the system inputs and consequences. A weight ranging from 0 to 1 is associated with each potential rule. The heavier a rule the greater its influence on the behavior of the fuzzy system. The best set of rule weights is found minimizing a cost function accounting for the mismatch with the given examples as well as the complexity of the resulting rule-set. A last step picks the heaviest rules and constructs the rule-set which is assigned to the system [24].

The rule minimization mechanism [24], [25] is loosely inspired to multi-level minimization procedures in the Boolean context. The hardware mapping of the resulting minimal fuzzy system requires minimum area and, to some extent, features maximum speed.

Additional hardware resources, if available, can be spent to improve the accuracy of the reproduction of the specified behavior. If this is the case, rules are iteratively added and a gradient-based optimization step places each new rule in a position allowing maximum error reduction.

The hardware mapping phase takes the abstract fuzzy system and searches a library of analog pre-designed cells to be aligned in a regular circuit layout implementing the controller. The same regular structure, corresponding to 15 rules, is also the processing core of a programmable version of AFE whose input-output relationship depends on a sequence of digital values stored in the chip. To allow fast validation of the control law on a prototype board the implementation flow may also produce the bit string encoding the quantized voltages needed to bias the re-configurable controller so that it features the desired I/O characteristic. Such bit string can be stored in a commercial EEPROM to be automatically loaded by the controller at start-up.

4.3   Simulations of the Implemented Controller

The implementation flow described above was applied to the fuzzy controller described in Subsection 4.1 The two minimized fuzzy systems equivalent to the LSC and to the SSC featured respectively 12 instead of 30 and 13 instead of 35 rules. As 15 rules are available on the field-programmable version of AFE, some rules could be added to improve reproduction accuracy as already sketched.

Measurements of the circuits were implemented as an equivalent lookup table relying on bilinear interpolation was inserted in the feedback loop for simulation using the model of the DC/DC converter. The results of these new closed-loop simulations are presented in Figure 21, Figure 22 and Figure 23.

From Figure 21 it is evident that the rising time of the proposed converter is around 1.2ms, i.e., well under the maximum 2ms. Looking at the magnitude of the inductor current i_L (Figure 22), we can realize that limitation boundary is satisfied and that the ideal behavior in Figure 13 is roughly approximated as i_L is kept as high as possible until the target is not approached. Note also the load change at k=520, corresponding to 1.716 ms.

It is easy to see that V_{out} never overcomes V_{ref} by more than 0.5%, so that no overshoot actually exists. Finally, one can observe Figure 23 to note that $V_{out} < V_{ref} + 5\%$ even when the absorbed current changes from 3.7A to 1.2A and that the actual load change response time is very low. In fact, even if the accuracy requirement is enforced to 1% of the target value, only 60µs are necessary to revert to normal operation conditions. This time delay does not consider the dead beat occurring soon after abrupt load change.

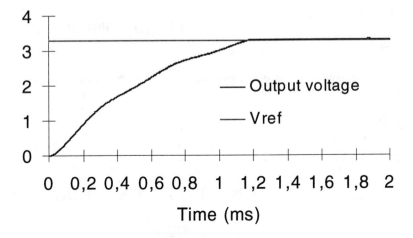

Figure 21 Step response of the implemented fuzzy controlled DC/DC Buck converter

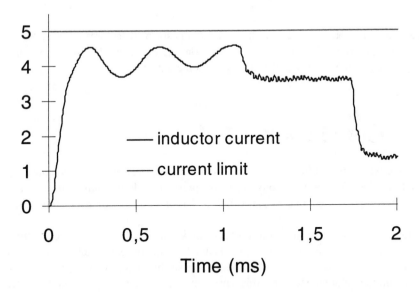

Figure 22 Inductor current of the implemented fuzzy controlled DC/DC Buck converter

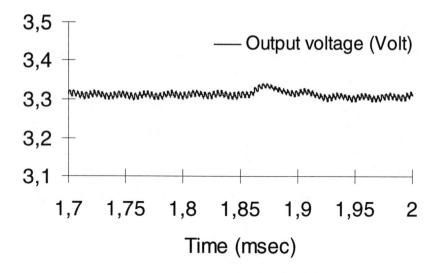

Figure 23 Load change response of the implemented fuzzy controlled DC/DC Buck
converter

Finally a dedicated circuit layout has been synthesized. It features an area occupancy
of about $3.18mm^2$ for the set of two controllers. This demonstrates also the
compactness achievable with the analog implementation.

5   Conclusion

In this chapter an outline of the state of the art application of fuzzy controllers to
switching DC/DC power converters is presented, highlighting the achievable
advantages with respect to classical solutions based on linear control techniques.

A final comparison of the solutions is shown in Table 8, in which percentage
tolerances are referred to the nominal steady state output. Each of the reported
solutions is dedicated to a specific application so that a common merit factor cannot
be elaborated. Notwithstanding this apparent non-homogeneity it can be perceived
how each proposal presents an improvement or at least one new feature with respect to
the previous approaches (in chronological order) and that fuzzy controlled DC/DC
often behave better than our reference industrial controller without sharing its
complexity.

Table 8 Performance of conventional (shaded) and fuzzy controllers of DC/DC stages in chronological order

	[1]	[5]	[10]	[3][4]	[6]	[26]
Inputs and	E, i_L,	E, CE,	E, CE,	E, CE,	E_{uout}, i_L, E_{iL}	E, CE, i_L
Outputs	δ	Δδ	Δδ	Δδ	Δδ, δ	Δδ, δ
Switching frequency	100KHz	50KHz	?	100KHz	50KHz	300KHz
Start-up — Overshoot	no	50%	2%	no	2%	no
Start-up — Time	9.6ms	4ms	7ms	3ms	1.6ms	1.2ms
Load change — max V_{out} deviation	±5%	±10%	±5%	±15%	±5%	±5%
Load change — reaction time	10ms	4ms	1.5ms	2ms	2ms	60µs
Current limitation	yes	no	no	no	yes	yes
Implementation	mixed	no	no	digital	digital	analog
Computation Time	10µs			10µs	(given by A/D and D/A)	2µs

A few points are worth noting, namely:

• Our expectations on the application of non-linear control laws are fulfilled as fuzzy controllers perform sensibly better than the conventional approaches when managing input voltage variations as well as load current changes.

• The Fuzzy controllers are easy to design (IF...THEN scheme) and may be easy to implement even in the analog case if precision is not the main issue.

• No attempt has been made to exploit special membership functions so that the optimization of such profiles can be reasonably expected to lead to further improvement.

References

[1] Gateau G., Maussion P. and Faucher J. (1994), Fuzzy Controller Based on Optimal Control Commutation Principle for a DC/DC Converter in Current Mode, *Proc. of IECON '94*, pp. 1320-1324.

[2] Lin B.-R. and Hua C. (1993), Buck/Boost Converter Control with Fuzzy Logic Approach, *Proc. of the IECON '93*, pp. 1342-1346.

[3] So W.C., Tse C.K. and Lee Y.S. (1994), A Fuzzy Controller for DC/DC Converters, *Proc. on PESC '94*, pp. 315-320.

[4] So W.C., Tse C.K. and Lee Y.S. (1995), An Experimental Fuzzy Controller for DC/DC Converters, *Proc. on PESC '95*, pp. 1339-1345.

[5] Ueno F., Inoue T., Oota L. and Sasaki M. (1991), Regulation of Cuk Converters using Fuzzy Controllers, *Proc. on INTELEC '91*, pp. 261-267.

[6] Mattavelli P., Rossetto L., Spiazzi G. and Tenti P. (1995), General Purpose Fuzzy Controller for DC/DC Converters, *Proc. on APEC '95*, pp. 723-730.

[7] Ishigame, A. et al., (1993), Sliding Mode Controller Design Based on Fuzzy Inference for Nonlinear Systems, *IEEE Trans. Industrial Electronics*, Vol. 40, No. 1, pp. 64-69.

[8] Carrasco J.M. et al. (1994), A Fuzzy Logic Control for Power Converters using a Cell State Algorithm, *Proc. IECON 1994*, pp. 1325-1330.

[9] Li C.K. et al. (1995), Fuzzy control of power converters based on quasi-linear modeling, *Electronics Letters*, vol. 31, No. 7, pp. 594-595.

[10] Tse C.K. et al. (1992), Quasi-Linear Modeling and Control of DC-DC Converters, *IEEE Trans. on Power Electr.*, Vol. 7, No. 2, pp. 315-323.

[11] Lin B.R. (1993), Analysis of Fuzzy Control Method Applied to DC/DC Converters, *Proc. APEC 1993*, pp. 22-28.

[12] "L296 Monolithic Power Switching Regulator -- Application Note" (1988), SGS-THOMSON MICROELECTRONICS, 1988.

[13] Pentium Processor 75MHz, 90MHz, 100MHz, 120MHz, Intel, 1995.

[14] Sum K.K. (1984), *Switch Mode Power Conversion - Basic Theory and Design*, Dekker Inc., New York/Basel.

[15] Mohan N., Undeland T.M. and Robbins W.P. (1989), *Power Electronics: Converters, Applications, and Design*, John Wiley & Sons, New York.

[16] Middlebrook R.D. and Cuk S. (1981), *Advances in Switched-Mode Power Conversion*, vol. I and II, TESLAco, Pasadena, CA.

[17] Kuo B. (1995), *Automatic Control Systems*, 7th edition, Prentice Hall.

[18] Lin B.R. and Hoft, R.G. (1994), Neural networks and Fuzzy Logic in Power Electronics, *Control Eng. Practice*, vol. 2., No. 1, pp. 113-121.

[19] Manaresi N., Franchi E., Guerrieri R., Baccarani G. and Poluzzi R. (1994), A Modular Analog Architecture for Fuzzy Controllers, *Proc. of ESSCIRC '94*.

[20] Manaresi N., Franchi E. and Baccarani G. (1996), A Field-programmable Analog Fuzzy Processor with Enhanced Temperature Performance, *Proc. of ESSCIRC '96*, pp. 152-155.

[21] Manaresi N., Rovatti R., Franchi E., Guerrieri R. and Baccarani G. (1996), Automatic Synthesis of Analog Fuzzy Controllers: A Hardware and Software Approach, *IEEE Transaction on Industrial Electronics*, vol. 43, pp. 217-225.

[22] Manaresi N., Rovatti R., Franchi E., Guerrieri R. and Baccarani G. (1996), Silicon Compiler of Analog Fuzzy Controllers: from Behavioral Specifications to Layout, *IEEE Transactions on Fuzzy Sets and Systems, special issue on Hardware Implementations*.

[23] Rovatti R., Bellini A., Scheffler M., Franchi E., Manaresi N. and Travaglia F. (1997), A Development Tool for Analog Fuzzy Controllers: Features and Applications, *Proc. of Fuzzy-Neuro Systems '97*.

[24] Rovatti R., Guerrieri R. and Baccarani G. (1995), An Enhanced Two-Level Boolean Synthesis Methodology for Fuzzy Rules Minimization, *IEEE Trans. on Fuzzy Systems*, vol. 3, no. 3, pp. 288-299.

[25] Rovatti R. (1996), Logical Optimization of Rule-Based Models in *Fuzzy Modelling, Paradigms and Practice* Ed. W. Pedrycz, Kluwer Academic, Boston.

[26] Scheffler M., Bellini A., Rovatti R., Zafarana A. and Diazzi C. (1996), Fuzzy Analog Controller for High-Performance Microprocessor Power Supply, *Proc. of Fourth European Congress on Intelligent Techniques and Soft Computing (EUFIT)*, pp. 1000-1004.

Chapter 6:

Intelligent Motor Fault Detection

INTELLIGENT MOTOR FAULT DETECTION

Mo-Yuen Chow, Bo Li, and Gregory Goddu
Electrical and Computer Engineering
North Carolina State University, Raleigh, NC 27695
U.S.A.

Motor fault detection is an extremely important topic that is often difficult to tackle. Since motors are highly complex devices, their fault detection is equally intricate. Given their non-linearity, it is difficult to find a simple detection technique which yields the highly accurate results that are desired. Seemingly, the best way to accomplish this fault detection is by hiring an experienced engineer with a deep understanding of motors. However, since experienced engineers are expensive and not generally given to tasks like staring at motors all day, it is necessary to find another method to carry out this procedure. Our objective therefore is to design an inexpensive automated fault detection methodology capable of non-linear mapping. The most efficient way to accomplish this is through the use of intelligent fault detection. However, from the research experience of the authors, it is determined that the conventional intelligent motor fault detection methodology has some inherent limitations, including accuracy performance. This drawback is mainly due to the highly non-linear mapping between the measured input data and the motor conditions. In this chapter, the authors introduce a novel knowledge-based approach to improve the detection accuracy of the intelligent motor fault detector. The method introduced in this chapter is accomplished through the use of data filters to process the measured data before it enters the system and thereby transform the original highly non-linear input-output mapping into two simpler mappings. This approach can greatly improve the accuracy of the designed intelligent motor fault detector.

1 Introduction to Motor Fault Detection

Motors have a large number of applications spread over numerous different fields, such as the power and manufacturing areas. Many of these applications are extremely important and require that the motors be kept in excellent condition. There are two common forms of maintenance in order to ensure this constant high caliber of performance. Reactive maintenance entails recognizing equipment that has failed and fixing it. Preventative maintenance involves continually monitoring the performance of the equipment in order to detect faults before they occur [2-6, 9]. This second procedure, fault detection, is an extremely important and often studied topic.

0-8493-9803-7/99/$0.00+$.50

1.1 Importance of Motor Fault Detection

The use of motors in modern industry is extensive, and many of these motors are exposed to different hostile environments. Both internal and external motor faults are inevitable over time [2,19,22-24,33]. Motor fault detection is the process of detecting potential failures before they can occur. Although rotating machines are usually well constructed and robust, the possibility of incipient faults is inherent due to the stresses involved in the conversion of electrical energy to mechanical energy [11,12]. By detecting faults before they can significantly impair the performance of the motor, many possible problems can be avoided.

One predicament which can be averted by effective preventative fault detection is a financial one. When a motor breaks down, it must be taken off-line for a period of time in order to fix the problem. Such unplanned downtime can significantly hurt production. When a motor's production is reduced, the companies' profits may be similarly affected. Early fault detection allows preventative maintenance to be arranged for machines during scheduled downtime, avoiding extensive motor failure and the resultant extended period of inactivity.

Sometimes, a fault may not be significant enough to stop production, but still serious enough to affect safety or product quality. An example of a loss of safety could be the production of high current sparks as a result of a faulty winding [14,21,22,25,28]. By preventing motors from reaching states of disrepair, potentially hazardous situations may be avoided. Also, when items are not satisfactory and have to be discarded, both money and time are lost.

Motor problems often lead to situations which can be irritating, especially if the problems could have been avoided. Reliability demands for electric motors are constantly increasing due to the importance of motor applications and the advancement in technologies[36,37]. Motor fault detection is therefore becoming an ever-increasing area of interest and consequence.

1.2 Current Approaches to Motor Fault Detection

One of the most important issues in motor fault detection is whether the method being used is *invasive* or *non-invasive*. Invasive methods may adversely effect the performance of the motor, while non-invasive schemes use easily accessible measurements to predict conditions [9,11-15]. Since non-invasive techniques avoid the possibly negative ramifications of the invasive detector, they are very suitable for use in on-line monitoring and fault detection scenarios [2,7,9-13].

There are currently two major classes of motor fault detection techniques. One of these methods is referred to as *model-based* and the other as *human-based* [7,11,12].

1.2.1   Model-Based Methods

Model-based methods of fault detection are based on mathematical models of the system of interest. Unfortunately, since most machines of interest exhibit non-linear dynamics [8,16,17,19,33,40-44], many assumptions must be made before a simple mathematical model of the machine may be derived. Generally, the model of the system results in a fault detection system which is not robust enough in the presence of noise and other perturbations [12,14,49].

Parameter estimation is one of the most popular model-based methods of fault detection [8,44,48]. This methodology is based on knowledge of an accurate mathematical model, the dynamics of the system, and the relation between the two. An example of this relation is that as the friction condition worsens, the damping coefficient will increase. Knowing this relation, the damping coefficient can be calculated from the mechanical equations and motor measurements and then used to predict the condition of the bearing [1,18,19,40]. The major weakness to this approach is the fact that it requires an accurate mathematical model.

1.2.2   Human-Based Methods

Human-based methods of fault detection are where most of the interests in this field currently lies. Since experienced engineers are often able to detect motor faults without knowing the specific dynamics of the system, the uncertainty of non-linear modeling can be circumvented. A problem with using engineers for fault detection is that this experience is gained over a period of many years and is very expensive. Therefore, the goal of this method is to teach a machine to mimic human knowledge and intuition in order to make informed decisions.

1.3 Intelligent Fault Detection

Due to the high complexity of motors and motor fault detection, engineers are usually required to devote a large amount of time to the study of the specific motor in which they are interested. Only after this initial gathering of knowledge can they discern which variables will supply the information that will be relevant to their task and the appropriate way to obtain the correct data. The eventual fault detection scheme is often a highly complex, motor specific procedure that may not be understandable to anyone other than the designer.

The high complexity of some systems is just one example of the shortcomings that are prevalent in many different fault detection procedures. Examples of other fault detection methods with inherent disadvantages are techniques that require expensive measurement devices and techniques in which faults are determined using off-line analysis [9,11,13,14].

Ideally, we would like a fault detection scheme which can be performed on-line by a computer with minimal cost for diagnostic equipment. This can be accomplished using intelligent fault detection. Several common forms of intelligent fault detection are based on *artificial neural networks, fuzzy logic*, and the combination of the two [1, 6-16]. The method of intelligent fault detection concentrated on in this chapter is the artificial neural network.

1.3.1 Application of Feedforward Artificial Neural Networks to Fault Detection

Artificial neural networks were developed based upon the study of the human brain [13,14,29,50,53]. The brain is made up of millions of interconnected neurons - special cells that process electrical signals. An example of a typical neuron used in feedforward artificial neural networks is shown in Figure 1. It consists of n inputs $X = [x_1, \cdots, x_n]^T$ with weights $W = [w_1, \cdots, w_n]^T$ and an offset bias b. These $n+1$ inputs are then summed to form the activation value s, defined as:

$$s = \sum_{i=1}^{n} (w_i x_i) + b = w^T x + b$$

(1)

and passed through an *activation function f*, resulting in an output o. The activation function{ XE "activation function" } is usually chosen as a monotonically non-decreasing and differentiable function such as a *sigmoid* function:

$$o(s) = \frac{e^s - e^{-s}}{e^s + e^{-s}},$$

(2)

which is shown in Figure 2. Although independently they have fairly weak computing power, by connecting several of these artificial neurons together a computationally powerful artificial neural network is created [55].

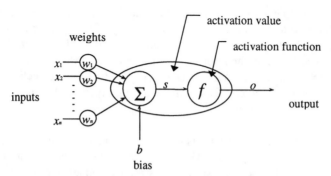

Figure 1. Basic structure of an artificial neuron model.

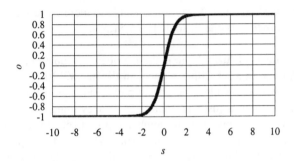

Figure 2. A typical bi-polar sigmoid activation function.

Artificial neural networks have been successfully applied to many areas. Some of these areas include fault detection [9,12-15,47,50,53], control [10,28,29,31,53], and signal processing [50,53]. Thanks to several breakthroughs in the field of artificial neural networks and given the limitations of many of the other existing methods currently employed, the demand for the use of artificial neural networks to solve engineering problems is expected to increase significantly in the next ten years [55]. Results to date have demonstrated the significant performance advantages of artificial neural networks relative to other currently available methods.

Neural networks exist in many different forms. Some of the most popular models are multi-layer feedforward networks, Kohonen networks, and Hopfield networks[55]. By far the most popular neural network architecture [55], the multi-layer feedforward network consists of an input layer of neurons, a variable number of hidden layers, and an output layer. The term feedforward comes from the fact that data flows through the network in one direction only.

The capacity of artificial neural networks to mimic and automate human expertise is what makes them ideal for handling non-linear systems. Neural networks are able to learn expert knowledge by being trained using a representative set of data [7,53]. The training session uses the error in the output values to update the weights of the neural network, thereby improving the accuracy. Once the network is sufficiently trained, the network weights should be saved. They now contain all the necessary knowledge to perform the fault detection.

1.3.2   Application of Fuzzy Logic to Fault Detection

Dr. Lotfi A Zadeh first presented fuzzy sets and fuzzy logic to the world in 1965 [7, 25,51,52]. Fuzzy logic is based on the idea that the real world is not crisp, not all yes and no, right and wrong, 1 and 0. While with classic logic an object is either a member of set A or not, fuzzy logic allows the object to have a degree membership in

A ranging from 0 to 1 [7,25,51,52]. You don't have to be at point *A* or not; you can be *"near"* point *A* or other relative, linguistic terms. Because of these added regions of closeness to a desired value, fuzzy logic is able to more closely emulate the way in which humans think than is classic logic [7,25,51,52].

One of the basic ideas of fuzzy logic is the membership function. It is a function that associates each point in a set with a number in the interval [0,1]. A membership of 0 indicates no membership, while a membership of 1 indicates full membership in a set. In this way, classic logic is just a special case of fuzzy logic. The additional terms of fuzzy logic allow you to have partial membership in a set. An example could be the membership function of the set of tall men. While 7 feet would definitely be considered tall (membership of 1) and 5 feet would definitely be not tall (membership of 0), a height of 6 feet is not clearly in either set. In this case, you may assign to 6 feet a membership value of 0.8 in the set *"tall"*. A possible membership function for this set is shown in Figure 3. Membership values can vary based on the situation and who assigns them.

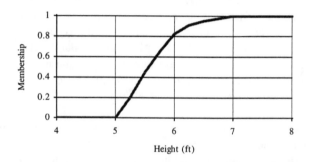

Figure 3. Membership function for the set "tall".

There are many different ways to assign membership functions. Several of the most common methods are intuition, inference, rank ordering, and neural networks [7,25, 51,52]. The intuition method is based upon human common sense. Inference uses a knowledge base to deduce values. Rank ordering is used when several different intuitive sets exist, in order to choose one. Although each of these methods have their own pluses and minuses, the neural network method is the one in which we are most interested, as we have already learned that neural nets are ideal for non-linear fault detection.

Due to its linguistic base, fuzzy logic has the freedom to completely define a decision surface without the use of complex mathematical analysis. As an example, fuzzy fault detection is performed using fuzzy rules of the form:

IF (a set of conditions is satisfied), THEN (a certain action is taken).

While fuzzy rules are quite good at simulating human response, they are not mathematically precise [7]. This imprecision can often cause problems when applied to motor fault detection. For this reason, we seek to find a way to combine the precision of neural networks with the human decision capabilities of fuzzy logic.

1.3.3 Application of Combined Neural/Fuzzy Systems to Fault Detection

Both neural networks and fuzzy logic have their own individual drawbacks when considered for use in fault detection systems. Neural networks, in general, cannot do *heuristic reasoning*. This means that the neural network is not capable of explaining the qualitative details of the fault. Although fuzzy logic can easily translate linguistic and qualitative knowledge to quantitative knowledge, it provides solutions that are not exact without much fine tuning of the membership functions and fuzzy rules. Given the complementary strengths of these two methods, it is possible to construct a hybrid neural/fuzzy system that minimizes the weaknesses of each while enhancing their strengths [9,29].

In a hybrid neural/fuzzy system, fuzzy rule-base modeling is used to create a desired input/output mapping. Neural networks "learn" the best membership function through training. This membership function is then used to create the if-then rule base. The neural network has the learning ability to implement a highly precise fuzzy system that simulates human reasoning and intuition.

2 Motor System Simulation

Motor faults can occur anywhere in a motor - the rotors, stators, or bearings [2,3,5,7,16,18-22,26,27,30,32-35,41-43,46-49]. Generally, motor fault detection approaches are problem- and motor-dependent. Factors such as the proper set of measurements, sensors, and fault detection algorithm are very important for successful motor fault detection. For example, using a *vibration signal* collected from an accelerometer mounted on a motor has long been a common practice for detecting faults in motor bearings[7,21,27,41,42,46]. Another example is the use of motor speed and current to detect the motor friction situation[30]. However, without the knowledge of more detailed information, such as the motor type and the operating and load conditions, merely using the fault detection algorithm and expecting to obtain accurate fault detection results is near impossible.

To design a practical motor fault detection scheme, the characteristics of the motor should be studied carefully. The Fast Prototype Motor System Simulation software, MotorSIM, provides this capability and is used by the authors to assist in designing the proper intelligent motor fault detection schemes.

2.1 MotorSIM - Motor Simulation Software

The *Fast Prototype Motor Simulation* (MotorSIM) software [8] is a MATLAB-SIMULINK based program that provides a framework for in-depth simulation of motor dynamics. The simulation capabilities of MotorSIM include: time-domain simulation (transient and steady-state), non-linear effects of motors (e.g., saturation and temperature), fault injection, constant or variable load effects, and magnetic and mechanical vibration measurements. MotorSIM can be used to generate the appropriate motor data, with different operating and loading conditions, in a cost effective and time efficient manner.

Although motor simulation software cannot completely model all real-world situations, a computer simulation can provide more control of several aspects of motor operation such as what variables to use, the range of motor operating conditions to investigate, the types of faults to study, and the kind of data to generate. These are very important factors for the intelligent motor fault detection algorithm design. Computer simulations are one of the best ways to show the feasibility of new algorithms and methodologies. From the research experience of the authors, MotorSIM is a feasible tool. It allows full control of different fault conditions and can help to ease the understanding of the rationale behind the different fault situations.

2.2 MotorSIM Structure and Features

MotorSIM is a well-structured motor simulation program composed of several different blocks and modules having distinct inputs and outputs. Each of these modules can be used separately in different scenarios and for different purposes with the appropriate connections of inputs and outputs. MotorSIM also provides database ability to allow the user to store and retrieve different sets of parameters for each module through a graphical user interface (GUI) module. Moreover, different factors at the system level, such as the ambient temperature, load conditions, input noises, motor system configurations and control algorithms, can be added to the software package as interactive modules when needed. The schematic diagram of the MotorSIM software package is shown in Figure 4.

MotorSIM has an Input Module, the Motor System Module and an Output Module. Each of these modules has a unique library that contains sub-modules with modeling and simulation properties. The Motor System Module includes the motor module and the load module. The assumptions are a sinusoidal input voltage and a constant torque load.

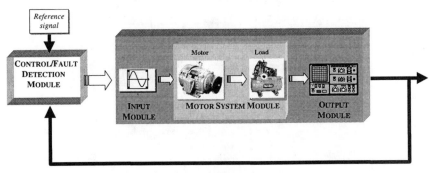

Figure 4. Overall structure of MotorSIM software.

The motor module can contain different sub-modules, such as the base module (including the electrical module and the mechanical module), the saturation module, the temperature module, and the vibration module.

The base module simulates a motor based on the current-flux relationship. However, in the real world, ideal situations are not always encountered and the motor may not always operate within specified operating conditions. For example, the motor operating conditions can be driven into the saturation region due to temporary overload conditions, or into unusually hot ambient conditions due to unexpected hot weather [8]. In these cases, the motor performance with saturation effect and temperature effect needs to be considered. Including the saturation module along with the base module provides the simulation results for a motor with saturation effect considered. Likewise, including the temperature module along with the base module simulates the motor dynamics with temperature effects considered.

Insulation failure, friction fault, and bearing wear can also be simulated in MotorSIM. Other motor effects can be added to the library as the need arises.

The MotorSIM software was developed with a user-friendly interface. A setup wizard, which is shown in Figure 5, can help the user to build his/her own specific motor system with different block and module combinations. The resultant output can be displayed immediately or stored into different formats for further study and application.

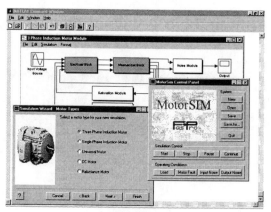

Figure 5. MotorSIM setup wizard.

A good motor fault detection algorithm is based on the careful study of motor measurements under different operation conditions. For different motor fault detection and protection algorithm designs, it is important to know the motor response subject to different fault conditions. MotorSIM can easily model and simulate different types of motor faults by including motor fault sub-modules in the motor base module.

A significant amount of motor research has focused on vibration analysis to detect motor bearing conditions [29]. MotorSIM can generate time-domain vibration signals for different conditions of bearing failure by incorporating the bearing wear sub-module in the motor base module.

2.3 Application to Motor Fault Detection

To illustrate the intelligent motor fault detection methodology, we will use MotorSIM to generate two types of incipient faults: winding faults and friction-related faults.

Winding faults can be determined by the winding condition. The winding condition is assumed to reflect the equivalent number of turns of the winding. By this, it is meant the number of turns that the motor sees after taking into account short circuits. The winding condition can affect the magnetic inductance of the motor windings [7]. Based on the equivalent number of turns of the motor winding, the motor winding condition can be classified into three categories: *good*, *fair*, and *bad*. If we use 1,0, and -1, respectively, to represent these three conditions, the winding conditions can be defined as:

$$W_c \in W = \{1, 0, -1\}, \tag{3}$$

where W_c indicates the motor winding condition and W is the universe of motor winding conditions.

Friction-related faults are reflected in the friction coefficient B (also known as the damping coefficient) in equation (4) for motor mechanical dynamics:

$$\dot{\omega}_e = \frac{P}{2J}\left(-B\omega_e + T_e - T_l\right),$$

(4)

where ω_e is the rotor's electric angular velocity, P is the number of poles in the motor, J is the moment of inertia of the rotor, B is the friction (damping) coefficient of the rotor, T_e is the electric torque of the motor ,and T_l is the load torque of the motor.

The result of friction-related faults is an increase of the overall power loss[7]. Similar to the winding condition, the friction condition of the motor can be classified into three categories for different friction coefficient B: *good, fair,* and *bad.* If we once again use 1,0, and -1 to represent these three conditions respectively, the friction conditions can be defined as:

$$F_c \in F = \{1,0,-1\},$$

(5)

where F_c indicates the motor friction condition and F is the universe of motor friction conditions.

When there is deterioration of the motor winding condition or the motor friction condition, the effect can be reflected by the variation of motor stator current and the motor angular speed. The steady-state stator current I and the average rotor angular speed ω can be considered as a nonlinear function g of the equivalent number of windings N and the damping coefficient B as shown in equation (6).

$$g(I,\omega,N,B) = 0.$$

(6)

The relations of I and ω to the winding condition and friction condition of a 3 HP three-phase induction motor are plotted in Figure 6 and Figure 7, respectively.

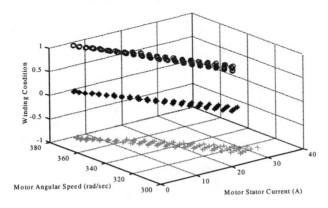

Figure 6. Plot of winding condition over the measurement space of stator current I and rotor speed ω.

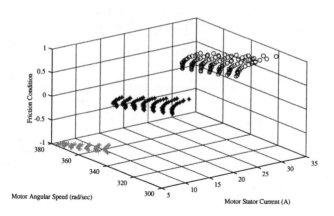

Figure 7. Plot of friction condition over the measurement space of stator current I and rotor speed ω.

The measurements of motor stator current I and motor angular speed ω can be obtained easily during motor operation. Equation (6) shows that there is a mapping between (I, ω) and (N, B). Now we can use MotorSIM to generate I and ω under different conditions of N and B, and train the neural network to learn the relation of (I, ω) to (N, B). After the network has been sufficiently trained, it has the ability to identify different friction condition and winding condition from the measured data of I and ω.

3 Conventional Approach of Using Feedforward Neural Networks for Motor Fault Detection

Motor faults can often be detected by examining the performance of certain motor measurements. Thus, if we can sample some selected variables, and use expert knowledge to build and *train* a neural network, we should be able to detect faults from the sampled data. By training a neural network to *learn* the fault detection based solely on input-output examples without the need of mathematical models, the complexity of the modeling needed in parameter estimation can be avoided. This approach to fault detection is called a *neural fault detector*.

3.1 Problem and Data Set Description

3.1.1   What is a Neural Network?

Artificial neural networks, which can simulate and automate human expertise, can be trained to perform motor fault detection by using a representative set of data to learn expert knowledge [7]. Figure 8 depicts this process. At the beginning of a neural network's *learning* (or *training*) *session*, the neural network fault detector's detection and diagnosis of the motor's condition will not be accurate. An *error quantity*, based on the difference between the correct decision made by the expert and the one made by the neural network, is generated and used to adjust the neural network's internal parameters (called *network weights*) in order to produce a more accurate output decision. After being trained, the network stores the knowledge of many experts and can easily apply it for motor fault detection (Figure 9).

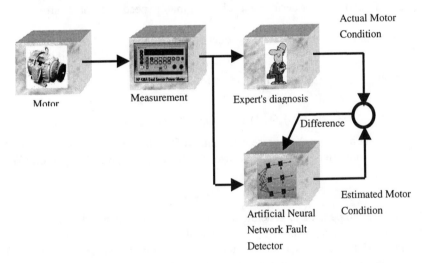

Figure 8. Schematic diagram of the training of the artificial neural network fault detector.

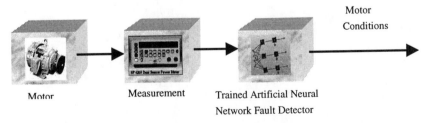

Figure 9. Artificial neural network motor fault detection and diagnosis process.

3.1.2　Definition of the Problem Studied

In the motor fault detection problem presented here, we use the angular speed ω and stator current I of the motor to detect the motor friction condition F_c and the motor winding condition W_c. Therefore, our neural network will have two input measurements (current and speed) and two output fault detectors (friction condition and winding condition).

3.1.3　Description of the Data Set Generated by MotorSIM

For the problem discussed, we train a neural network to detect the conditions of winding and friction. The input data for the network are actual measurements of speed ω and current I taken from MotorSIM. The output data, however, is a linguistic variable which describes the condition of interest. It comes from the set {good, fair, bad}, which is represented by {1, 0, -1}. Different conditions of winding and friction should affect the motor performance, both in motor speed and stator current.

Let us define X as the Cartesian product of I and ω.

$$X = I \times \omega. \tag{7}$$

Similarly, Y is the Cartesian product of F and W.

$$Y = F \times W$$
$$= \{(1,1), (1,0), (1,-1), (0,1), (0,0), (0,-1), (-1,1), (-1,0), (-1,-1)\} \tag{8}$$

The nine members in Y represent the nine different operating conditions created by different conditions of winding and friction. Now, the relation in equation (6) can be redefined as:

$$f : X \to Y. \tag{9}$$

MotorSIM can be used to generate a data set to be applied in order to train the neural network to learn this mapping. The results of this MotorSIM simulation are shown in the plots of the current and speed data for the different cases for winding and friction conditions that are shown in Figures 10 and 11, respectively.

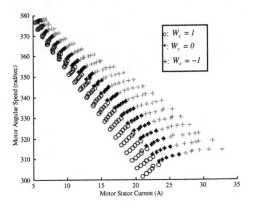

Figure 10. The distribution of winding condition for various values of current and speed.

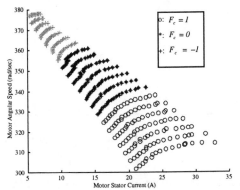

Figure 11. The distribution of friction condition for various values of current and speed.

3.2 Construction of the Neural Network

3.2.1 Multi-layer Feedforward Artificial Neural Networks

The basic multi-layer feedforward net contains three components: an input layer, one or more hidden layers, and an output layer, as shown in Figure 12. Each network layer contains a set of processing units called *nodes* or *neurons*, as described in Section (1.3.1). Every node in a network layer sends its output to all the nodes of the next layer uni-directionally, but has no connection to the nodes in its own layer. In the input layer, the nodes receive external signals from the outside world, such as motor current and motor speed measurements (using current transducers and tachometers, respectively) for our motor fault detection application. The input layer of the neural network serves as an interface that takes information from the outside world and transmits it to the internal processing units of the network, analogous to human interface parts such as our eyes' retina and our fingers' sensing cells. Similarly, the output layer of the neural network serves as an interface that sends information from the neural network's internal processing units to the external world. The nodes in the hidden layers are the neural network's internal processing units.

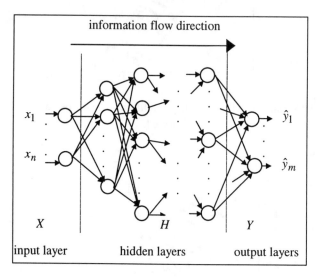

Figure 12. Basic structure of a multi-layer feedforward artificial neural network.

All the nodes in the hidden and output layers have the structure shown in Figure 1. Each node j in the hidden and output layer receives signals $v = [v_1, v_2,..., v_k]^T$ from the nodes of the previous layer, scaled by the weights $w_j = [w_{j1}, w_{j2}, ..., w_{jk}]^T$. The j-th node in layer l computes the following quantity:

$$s_j = \sum_{i=1}^{k} w_{ji}v_i + b_j = w_j^T v + b_j, \tag{10}$$

where b_j is the bias term of the j-th neuron. The quantity s_j will be processed by an activation function (usually nonlinear) to give the output o_j of the j-th neuron.

Unlike the hidden and output layer nodes, the input layer nodes conventionally use a linear activation function and each input layer node j receives only one input signal, $v = [x_j]$, as shown in Figure 12, representing each measured signal from the outside world. The inputs to the neural network are conventionally normalized between [0, 1] for numerical stability reasons.

It has been proven that three-layer feedforward nets (one input layer, one hidden layer and one output layer) are able to learn any complex continuous input-output mapping [17]. A three-layer network can be denoted as N_{n_X, n_H, n_Y}, where n_X is the number of input nodes, n_H the number of hidden nodes, and n_Y the number of output nodes, respectively. Although researchers and engineers sometimes use different network configurations, the three-layer network configuration is the most popular and will be illustrated here.

3.2.2 Mathematical Formulation

Let us define a system (Figure 13), such as a motor, with inputs $x = [x_1, x_2, \cdots, x_n]^T$, such as motor measurements, and corresponding outputs $y(x) = [y_1, y_2, \cdots, y_m]^T$, such as motor conditions. It is convenient to represent the system as the relationship M between the input space $X: \{x \in X \mid x \text{ is the input to the system}\}$ and the output space $Y: \{y(x) \in Y \mid y \text{ is the output of the system with input } x\}$, as expressed in Equation (11):

$$M: X \to Y. \tag{11}$$

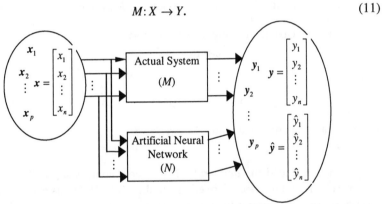

Figure 13. Schematic diagram of the input-output relation of an actual system and an artificial neural network.

The network training process can be thought of as training the network to represent M through the input-output relation as close as possible by adjusting the network internal parameters (or weights) w, represented mathematically as:

$$\min_{w \in W} \left\| \hat{y}(x|w) - y(x) \right\|, \text{ for all } x \in X. \tag{12}$$

Let us define e_p as the training error of training pattern p, i.e., the difference between the output of the network and the output of the system with input x_p and current network weight w:

$$e_p = e(x_p, w) = \left\| \hat{y}(x_p, w) - y(x_p) \right\|. \tag{13}$$

During network training, we would like to minimize the error for all training patterns (rather than minimizing the error for a single training pattern). Therefore we define the training error of the network as a quantity E as:

$$E(w) = \frac{1}{P} \sum_{p=1}^{P} e(x_p, w). \tag{14}$$

Methods of training multi-layer feedforward nets by minimizing E in Equation (14) include the *backpropagation* algorithm[39] and *simulated annealing*[1,45]. These methods train the network by iteratively adjusting the network weights to minimize E. The *backpropagation* algorithm is by far the most popular training algorithm for feedforward nets and will be briefly presented in the next section.

3.2.3   Backpropagation

The backpropagation training algorithm is a commonly used steepest descent method of training[55] that searches for an optimal w to minimize the error E in Equation (14). The general procedure is:

(i)   Find $\dfrac{\partial E}{\partial w}$, which is the slope of E with respect to w.

(ii)   Update the weight w^q to w^{q+1} as:

$$w^{q+1} = w^q + \Delta w^q, \tag{15}$$

where

$$\Delta w_{ji}^{q+1} = \eta \, \delta_j \, o_j + \alpha \, \Delta w_{ji}^{q}. \tag{16}$$

These steps are then repeated until $\dfrac{\partial E}{\partial w} \approx 0$.

Equation (16) is called the *delta rule*. It is a commonly used method to adapt the network weights and has been derived in detail in [37,53]. In this equation, η is called the *learning rate* (equivalent to step size in the steepest descent algorithm) and α is called the *momentum rate*. The $\alpha \, \Delta w_{ji}^{q}$ term is called the *momentum term* and is included in the weight update equation to try to avoid a local minimum[37,53]. Choosing proper values for the rates η and α is an important part of the design step.

3.2.4   Design Issues Specific to the Motor Fault Detection Problem

For the induction motor fault detection application,

$$x = [I, \omega]^{\mathrm{T}} \in X, \tag{17}$$

and

$$y = [F_c, W_c]^{\mathrm{T}} \in Y. \tag{18}$$

The training data set will consist of 54 current and speed data pairs. This number was arrived at rather arbitrarily in order to keep the training set small while still covering the full range of input values. From each of the nine possible output combinations, six input data pairs will be chosen.

A three-layer network is used for the motor fault detector. The optimal number of hidden nodes is determined to be 10, a number that was arrived at after many different trial attempts. A learning rate of 0.01 and momentum of 0.4 were chosen, also after much experimentation. Hence, the form of the neural network is $N_{2,10,2}$, with $\eta = 0.01$ and $\alpha = 0.4$.

3.3 Motor Fault Detector Performance

3.3.1 Definition of Network Performance

In motor fault detection design and study, we need to identify if the designed fault detection algorithm is able to correctly classify different motor fault conditions. The important issues when applying artificial neural networks to a motor fault detection problem are the performance accuracy of the results and the training speed of the network [7]. These two issues are affected by the network design and the training data chosen.

Accuracy is the percentage of data points that were correctly trained by the network. In other words, this is the percentage of time that the network correctly identifies the fault of interest for the testing data set.

Training speed is the number of *epochs* that are required in order to sufficiently train the neural network. An epoch is one training cycle of the neural network. Therefore, the number of epochs is the number of times that the weights of the network have to be updated before an acceptable error measure is reached.

3.3.2 Network Performance

The performance of the conventional motor fault detector was tested using the data generated by MotorSIM. Several smaller training data sets were selected from the original testing data set and used to train the designed conventional intelligent motor fault detector. From the testing results, it was determined that the choice of the training data set can significantly affect the performance of the designed motor fault detector based on how representative this data is of the full data set. If the training data set is lacking in some crucial data, the performance of the fault detector may be less than adequate. An increase in the included information of the training data set should result in a corresponding increase in performance of the fault detector. In practice, it is very difficult to correctly choose the training data set in order to satisfy the above-mentioned requirement. This is a large limitation of the conventional intelligent motor fault detector.

The performance of the conventional feedforward neural network motor fault detector is shown in Table 1.

Table 1. The performance of the conventional motor fault detector.

Training Data Set	Testing Data Set	Detection Accuracy for W_c	Detection Accuracy for F_c	Training time (epochs)
54 Randomly Selected Pairs of (I, ω)	357 Pairs of (I, ω)	65.83%	95.52%	100000
54 Carefully Selected Pairs of (I, ω)	357 Pairs of (I, ω)	93.28%	98.04%	100000

3.4 Drawbacks of this Approach

As can be seen from the previous section, this approach to motor fault detection does have several weaknesses. Among these deficiencies are low accuracy, long training time, and effect of selection of data points.

3.4.1 Accuracy

As was mentioned very early in the chapter, undetected motor faults can cause significant problems. Therefore, the single most important factor for our fault detector is its accuracy. Although the values which we achieved for accuracy (93.28% for winding and 98.04% for friction) may seem to be acceptable, and in fact commendable, they may not be for some applications. If we were to attempt to use an actual motor fault detector with these performance values, we would still find ourselves very disappointed with the number of undetected faults which continued to cause breakdown or injury.

3.4.2 Training Time

We do not have much of a base of comparison in order to determine what qualifies as a long training time. However, while running several earlier trials we did find various instances in which we were able to attain a lower training time, albeit at the cost of an inferior accuracy. We therefore believe that there must be multiple ways to achieve faster training times.

3.4.3 Effect of Selection of Training Data

A third, though possibly less important, drawback is the effect that the selection of training data has on the accuracy of the fault detector. We have shown results from two different cases in this section. The same number of training data points was used for each example and in each instance there were six data pairs chosen from each of the nine different operating conditions given in equation (8). In the first case, the data points were chosen randomly. The second trial used carefully selected data points designed to be representative of the entire operating region. It was clear from the results that by spending extra time to carefully choose the training data, we can improve our performance. However, ideally we would like to design a fault detector where the choice of training data is not important, thus saving a considerable amount of time in the data selection stage.

4 Knowledge-Based Error Band Reduction Motor Fault Detector

4.1 Correlation of Motor Measurements

Problem areas for the input-output mapping exist in the form of bands along the speed and current axes in which data points do not clearly fall into one output condition category. We define these bands as *error bands* in the input data distribution area. These error bands are wider, and thus more of a problem, for the case of winding condition. This fact is demonstrated by noting that the accuracy for friction is much greater than that for winding. Therefore, what we want to do is find a way to reduce, and possibly even eliminate, the error bands for the winding case. This will be done by pre-filtering the data in order to create a visible separation of output data sets.

The error bands can be seen in Figures 14 and 15. Note how, for instance, over the current range [6,23] (Error Band 3 in Figure 15) the value for W_c (winding condition) can fall into either the case of 1 or 0. This is almost the entire range of each condition. On the other hand, the F_c value seems to bear a strong relation to the speed data. Error Band 2 (of Figure 14), between $F_c = 1$ and $F_c = 0$, is only approximately 15% of the entire spread of either condition.

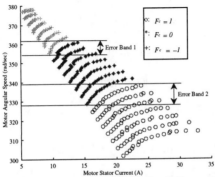

Figure 14. The distribution of measured data for different friction conditions with error bands illustrated.

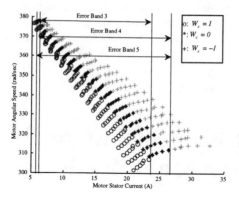

Figure 15. The distribution of measured data for different winding conditions with error bands illustrated.

We will apply an approach termed *Error Band Reduction* in order to reduce the W_c error bands to a level closer to those of F_c.

4.2   Mechanism of Error Band Reduction Approach

In Equations (7) to (9), we have defined the universe of inputs X, the universe of outputs Y, and the mapping from inputs to outputs $f : X \rightarrow Y$.
Let us define sets:

$$X_{F1} = \{(I, \omega) | F_c = 1\}, \tag{19}$$

$$X_{F2} = \{(I, \omega) | F_c = 0\}, \tag{20}$$

$$X_{F3} = \{(I, \omega) | F_c = -1\}, \tag{21}$$

$$X_{W1} = \{(I, \omega) | W_c = 1\}, \tag{22}$$

$$X_{W2} = \{(I, \omega) | W_c = 0\}, \tag{23}$$

$$X_{W3} = \{(I, \omega) | W_c = -1\}. \tag{24}$$

From Figures 14 and 15, we can see that under the mapping of $f : X \rightarrow Y$, we have:

$$X_{Wi} \cap X_{Wj} \neq \phi, \text{ where } i,j = 1,2,3 \text{ and } i \neq j, \tag{25}$$

$$X_{Fi} \cap X_{Fj} \approx \phi, \text{ where } i,j = 1,2,3 \text{ and } i \neq j. \tag{26}$$

The non-empty interaction of Equation (25) is caused by the nonlinear mapping of $f : X \rightarrow Y$. From the network training experience of the authors, the conventional feedforward neural network motor fault detector has demonstrated better performance for F_c than for W_c. The reason for this difference of performance is because of the relations that can be seen from Equations (25) and (26). For the input data sets under different F_c, the interaction between them is almost an empty set. However, the input data sets under different W_c exhibit a large interaction resulting in cross-over data sets with many members.

The approach presented in this section is to train the network to first identify the correct F_c value from the input measurement $(I, \omega) \in X$, as before due to equation (26). Then, another mapping value I^* is created from the input I under different F_c. This new mapping will help to reduce the error band for the new input data (I^*, ω), i.e.:

$$f_1 : (I, \omega) \rightarrow (I^*, \omega) \quad \text{for } F_c = 1, 0, -1 \text{ respectively,} \tag{27}$$

in order to create:

$$Z_{Wi} \cap Z_{Wj} \approx \phi, \quad \text{where } i, j = 1, 2, 3 \text{ and } i \neq j, \tag{28}$$

where:

$$Z_{W1} = \{(I^*, \omega) | W_c = 1, \text{ for } F_c = 1, 0, -1 \text{ respectively}\}, \tag{29}$$

$$Z_{W2} = \{(I^*, \omega) | W_c = 0, \text{ for } F_c = 1, 0, -1 \text{ respectively}\}, \tag{30}$$

$$Z_{W3} = \{(I^*, \omega) | W_c = -1, \text{ for } F_c = 1, 0, -1 \text{ respectively}\}. \tag{31}$$

This will greatly improve the neural network performance for motor fault detection.

Let us define Z as the Cartesian product of I^* and ω:

$$Z = I^* \times \omega. \tag{32}$$

Thus the problem for motor fault detection can be described as:

$$f = f_1 \circ f_2, \tag{33}$$

where

$$f_1 = (I, \omega) \in X \rightarrow (I^*, \omega) \in Z, \tag{34}$$

$$f_2 = (I^*, \omega) \in Z \rightarrow (F_c, W_c) \in Y. \tag{35}$$

To build the mapping f_1 in equation (27), filters are used to process the input data.

4.3   Design of the New Motor Fault Detector

As we have mentioned previously, one reason for the subpar performance for the conventional neural network motor fault detector is that the mapping $f : X \rightarrow Y$ is highly nonlinear due to the large W_c error band for the measured data. In this section, we will discuss in detail how to apply the Error Band Reduction approach to improve the fault detection accuracy of the intelligent motor fault detector.

4.3.1   Data Filter Design

The essence of the Error Band Reduction approach is that the original mapping is replaced by two simpler mappings as shown in equation (33). In this equation, the mapping of f_1 is accomplished using a data filter. It is clear that this mapping is very non-linear and, therefore, is difficult to achieve by conventional linear or nonlinear mapping functions. Another methodology must be used to get the mapping shown in equation (27) and the function shown in equation (28). The neural network is an ideal candidate because it has the ability to classify highly nonlinear patterns[55].

From equations (25) and (26), we can see that for the two motor conditions F_c and W_c, the measured data for F_c has a relatively small error band. Therefore, if we allow the system to focus only on F_c, the motor fault detector can be expected to identify the motor condition at an accuracy of nearly 100% correct.

In the *Error Band Reduction* approach, a neural network is first used to identify the motor friction condition F_c. This neural network will be called the friction filter. It can be implemented as before by a three-layer conventional feedforward neural network with 2 inputs and 10 hidden neurons, but only 1 output. Based on the detected value of F_c, the system chooses one of three different filters to process the measured data. These *Current Filters* are also three-layer conventional feedforward neural networks with 2 inputs, 10 hidden neurons and 1 output. The output of these filters is W_c under different F_c. As the output of a network is in the range of $[-1,1]$, to distinguish the filtered measured current data for different F_c value, the output of a network is used to multiply the original measured current data, i.e.:

$$I^* |_{F_c=1} = g_1(I, \omega) \cdot I + C_1, \tag{36}$$

$$I^* |_{F_c=0} = g_2(I, \omega) \cdot I + C_2, \tag{37}$$

$$I^* |_{F_c=-1} = g_3(I, \omega) \cdot I + C_3. \tag{38}$$

Equations (36) to (38) show that the mapped data I^* contains some a priori knowledge about W_c; thus this approach will be called *Knowledge-Based Error Band Reduction*.

If we focus on the mapped results illustrated in equations (36) to (38), we can see that the motor fault detection problem can be simplified from the original nine output combinations as shown in equation (8) to only three output combinations for each current filter. Thus, the Knowledge-Based Error Band Reduction approach can significantly reduce the complexity of the mapping by replacing the original $X \xrightarrow{\ f\ } Y$ mapping seen in equation (9) by the two more linear mappings $X \xrightarrow{\ f_1\ } Z \xrightarrow{\ f_2\ } Y$ seen in equation (33).

4.3.2   Filter Performance

The relation of (I^*, ω) with (F_c, W_c) is shown in Figures 16 and 17. As compared with Figures 14 and 15, we can see the error bands in Figures 16 and 17 are reduced, especially for (I^*, ω) distribution under different W_c. Due to mapping of $f_1 : X \rightarrow Z$, the distribution of (I^*, ω) under different F_c now has a clear boundary under different W_c and vice versa. This illustrates the new, closer-to-linear relationship described in equation (33) to (35).

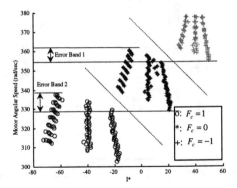

Figure 16. The distribution of mapped data for different friction conditions with error bands illustrated.

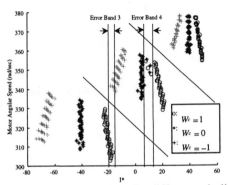

Figure 17. The distribution of mapped data for different winding conditions with error bands illustrated.

4.3.3 Overall System of Knowledge-Based Error Band Reduction Motor Fault Detector

From the discussion of filter design we already have a general idea of what the structure of the *Knowledge-Based Error Band Reduction* approach looks like. The overall structure is shown in Figure 18. First, the measured data (I, ω) are passed through the Friction Condition Filter. Then, based on the value of F_c, one of three Current Filters will be applied to the same measured data (I, ω). These filters implement the mapping of $f_1 : (I, \omega) \in X \rightarrow (I^*, \omega) \in Z$. After the filter processing, we get (I^*, ω). These transformed data have a much more linear relationship with (F_c, W_c) than did the original measured data (I, ω). Finally, a standard feedforward neural network is used to fulfill the mapping of $f_2 : (I^*, \omega) \in Z \rightarrow (F_c, W_c) \in Y$. All neural networks used in this system consist of two inputs, ten hidden neurons, and either one or two outputs, as necessary.

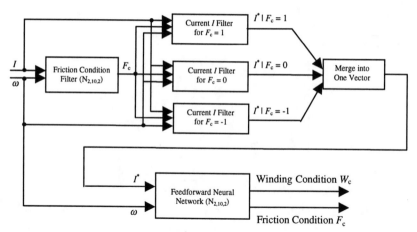

Figure 18. The overall structure of *Knowledge-Based Error Band Reduction* Motor Fault Detector.

4.4 Performance

The performance of the knowledge-based error band reduction motor fault detector is shown in Table 2.

Table 2. Performance of the knowledge-based error band reduction motor fault detector.

Training Data Set	Testing Data Set	Detection Accuracy for W_c	Detection Accuracy for F_c	Training time (epochs)
54 Randomly Selected Pairs of (I, ω)	357 Pairs of (I, ω)	99.13%	100%	7305
54 Carefully Selected Pairs of (I, ω)	357 Pairs of (I, ω)	99.13%	100%	6850

4.5   Improvements Over Conventional Method

The *Knowledge-Based Error Band Reduction* Motor Fault Detector showed vast improvements in both accuracy and training time when compared to the conventional approach of neural network fault detection. The dependency on a "good" choice of training data has also been removed. We now have a motor fault detector which would be more welcomed for real-world industrial applications. Our accuracy is at or near 100% for both winding and friction condition with a reasonable training time. Also, since the detector was implemented via an artificial neural network, which is capable of processing data extremely quickly, we can expect nearly instant recognition of faults once the network is trained. Perhaps most significantly, we now have a fully realized intelligent motor fault detector capable of reaching experienced engineer levels of detection for a much more reasonable price.

5 Summary

This chapter has introduced the concept of intelligent fault detection and shown its application within the field of motors. The concepts of both fuzzy logic and artificial neural networks were discussed briefly, along with their combined procedure, the neural/fuzzy system. All three of these concepts are currently very popular. For further information on these three topics, see [7,36,53], respectively. The utilization of artificial neural networks for motor fault detection was discussed in great depth in the third section. Both the strengths and the weaknesses of this approach were presented. A method of improving upon the conventional neural network fault detector was provided in Section 4. Given the importance of industrial motors and their applications, and the often high incipient fault rates for said machines, it is important to be able to detect faults before they can do serious damage. Therefore, intelligent motor fault detection is presently an important and popular research topic.

Acknowledgment
The authors would like to acknowledge the support of the National Science Foundation, for Grant ECS-9521609.

References

[1] G. L. Bilbro, W. E. Snyder, S. J. Garnier, and J. W. Gault (1992), Mean Field Annealing: A Formalism for Constructing GNC-Like Algorithms, *IEEE Transaction on Neural Networks*, vol. 3, no. 1, pp. 131-138.

[2] A. H. Bonnett and G. Soukup (1988), Analysis of Rotor Failures in Squirrel-Cage Induction Motors, *IEEE Transactions on Industry Applications*, vol. 24, no. 6, pp. 1124-1130.

[3] D. R. Boothman and E. C. Elgar (1974), Thermal Tracking — A Rational Approach to Motor Protection, *IEEE Transactions on Power Engineering Systems*, pp.1335-1344.

[4] J. J. Burke, D. A. Douglass, and D. J. Lawrence (1983), Distribution Fault Current Analysis, EPRI, Research Project 1209-1 EL-3085, May.

[5] S. R. Campbell, G. C. Stone, H. G. Sedding, G. S. Klempner, W. McDermid, and R. G. Bussey (1994), Practical On-Line Partial Discharge Tests for Turbine Generators and Motors, *IEEE Transactions on Energy Conversion*, vol. 9, no. 2.

[6] M.-y. Chow (1997), Fuzzy Logic Based Control, in *CRC Press Industrial Electronics Handbook*, D. Irwin, Ed., CRC Press.

[7] M.-y. Chow (1997), *Methodologies of Using Neural Network and Fuzzy Logic Technologies for Motor Incipient Fault Detection*: World Scientific Publisher.

[8] M.-y. Chow, S. Altug, and B. Li (1997), Motor System Time Domain Fast Prototype Software Simulation, *Proceedings of Navy Symposium on Electric Machine*, Newport, RI, pp. 183-187.

[9] M.-y. Chow, R. N. Sharpe, and J. C. Hung (1993), On the Application and Design Consideration of Artificial Neural Network Fault Detectors, *IEEE Transactions on Industrial Electronics*, vol. 40, no. 2, pp. 181-198.

[10] M.-y. Chow and J. Teeter (1995), A Knowledge-Based Approach for Improved Neural Network Control of a Servomotor System with Nonlinear Friction Characteristics, *Mechatronics*, vol. 5, no. 8, pp. 949-962.

[11] M.-y. Chow and S.-O. Yee (1991), Methodology For On-Line Incipient Fault Detection in Single-Phase Squirrel-Cage Induction Motors Using Artificial Neural Networks, *IEEE Transactions on Energy Conversion*, vol. 6, no. 3, pp. 536-545.

[12] M.-y. Chow and S.-O. Yee (1991), Robustness Test of an Incipient Fault Detector Artificial Neural Network, *Proceedings of IJCNN-91-Seattle*.

[13] M.-y. Chow and S.-O. Yee (1991), Using Neural Networks to Detect Incipient Faults in Induction Motors, *Journal of Neural Network Computing*, vol. 2, no. 3, pp. 26-32.

[14] M.-y. Chow and S. O. Yee (1990), Real Time Application of Artificial Neural Networks for Incipient Fault Detection of Induction Machines, *Proceedings of The Third International Conference of Industrial and Engineering Applications of Artificial Intelligence and Expert Systems*.

[15] M.-y. Chow, S. O. Yee, and L. S. Taylor (1993), Recognizing Animal-Caused Faults in Power Distribution Systems Using Artificial Neural Networks, *IEEE Transactions on Power Delivery*, vol. 8, no. 3, pp. 1268-1274.

[16] M. J. Costello (1994), Shaft Voltages and Rotating Machinery, *IEEE Transactions on Industry Applications*, vol. 29, no. 2, pp. 419-426.

[17] G. Cybenko (1989), Approximation by Superpositions of a Sigmoidal Function, *Mathematics of Control, Signals, and Systems*, vol. 2, pp. 303-314.

[18] J. C. Das (1990), Effects of Momentary Voltage Dips on the Operation of Induction and Synchronous Motors, *IEEE Transactions on Industry Applications*, vol. 26, no. 4, pp. 711-718.

[19] J. Douglas, J. Edmonds, and J. C. White (1988), Early Warning for Hydro Generator Failure, *EPRI Journal*, pp. 31–35.

[20] R. E. Fenton, B. E. B. Gott, and C. V. Maughan (1992), Preventative Maintenance of Turbine-Generator Stator Windings, *IEEE Transactions on Energy Conversion*, vol. 7, no. 1, pp. 216-222.

[21] W. R. Finley and R. R. Burke (1994), Troubleshooting Motor Problems, *IEEE Transactions on Industry Applications*, vol. 30, no. 5, pp. 1383-1397.

[22] B. K. Gupta and I. M. Culbert (1992), Assessment of Insulation Condition in Rotating Machine Stators, *IEEE Transactions on Energy Conversion*, vol. 7, no. 3.

[23] R. Isermann and B. Freyermuth (1991), Process Fault Diagnosis Based on Process Model Knowledge — Part I : Principles for Fault Diagnosis with Parameter Estimation, *Journal of Dynamic Systems, Measurement, and Control*, vol. 113, pp. 620-626.

[24] R. Isermann and B. Freyermuth (1991), Process fault Diagnosis Based on Process Model Knowledge — Part II: Case Study Experiments, *Journal of Dynamic Systems, Measurement, and Control*, vol. 113, pp. 627-633.

[25] G. J. Klir and T. A. Folger (1988), *Fuzzy Sets, Uncertainty, and Information*: Prentice-Hall, Englewood Cliffs, New Jersey.

[26] J. T. LaForte, R. M. McCoy, and D. K. Sharma (1988), Impulse Voltage Withstand Capability of Rotating Machine Insulation as Determined from Model Specimens, *IEEE Transactions on Energy Conversion*, vol. 3, no. 1.

[27] G. F. Lang (1994), Of Cages, Induction, Deduction, Bars, Vars and Squirrels, *Sound and Vibration*, vol. 12, pp. 8-20.

[28] T. H. Lee, W. K. Tan, and J. M.H. Ang (1994), A Neural Network Control System with Parallel Adaptive Enhancements Applicable to Nonlinear Servomechanisms, *IEEE Transactions on Industrial Electronics*, vol. 41, no. 3, pp. 269-277.

[29] B. Li, G. Goddu, and M.-y. Chow (1998), Detection of Common Motor Bearing Faults Using Frequency-Domain Vibration Signals and a Neural Network Based Approach, *Proceedings of American Control Conference*, Philadephia, PA, June 24-26, 1998.

[30] B. Li, G. Goddu, and M.-y. Chow (1997), Knowledge Based Technique to Enhance the Performance of Neural Network Based Motor Fault Detectors, *Proceedings of IECon'97*, New Orleans, LA, November 9-14, 1997.

[31] C. Lin and C. S. G. Lee (1991), Neural-Network-Based Fuzzy Logic Control and Decision System, *IEEE Transactions on Computers*, vol. 40, no. 12, pp. 1320-1336.

[32] R. Maier (1992), Protection of Squirrel-Cage Induction Motor Utilizing Instantaneous Power and Phase Information, *IEEE Transactions on Industry Applications*, vol. 28, no. 2, pp. 376-380.

[33] K. S. Narendra and K. Parthasarathy (1990), Identification and Control of Dynamical Systems Using Neural Networks, *IEEE Transactions on Neural Networks*, vol. 1.

[34] O. M. Nassar (1987), The Use of Partial Discharge and Impulse Voltage Testing in the Evaluation of Interturn Insulation Failure of Large Motors, *IEEE Transactions on Energy Conversion*, vol. 2, no. 4.

[35] R. Natarajan (1989), Failure Identification of Induction Motors by Sensing Unbalanced Stator Currents, *IEEE Transactions on Energy Conversion*, vol. 4, no. 4, pp. 585-590.

[36] G. J. Pailetti and A. Rose (1989), Improving Existing Motor Protection for Medium Voltage Motors, *IEEE Transactions on Industry Applications*, vol. 25, no. 3, pp. 456-464.

[37] J. Reason (1988), Boost Availability with Up-to-Date Maintenance Techniques, in *Electrical World*.

[38] T. J. Ross (1995), *Fuzzy Logic with Engineering Applications*: McGraw Hill, New York.

[39] D. E. Rumelhart and J. L. McClelland (1986), *Parallel Distributed Processing: Explorations in the Microstructure of Cognition*, vol. 1&2, Cambridge, Massachusetts: The MIT Press.

[40] D. E. Schump (1989), Reliability Testing of Electric Motor, *IEEE Transactions on Industry Applications*, vol. 25, no. 3.

[41] D. J. T. Siyambalapitiya and P. G. Mclaren (1990), Reliability Improvement and Economic Benefits of On-Line Monitoring Systems for Large Induction Machines, *IEEE Transactions on Industry Applications*, vol. 26, no. 6, pp. 1018-1025.

[42] R. W. Smeaton (1987), *Motor Application and Maintenance Handbook*: McGraw-Hill Book Company, New York.

[43] A. K. Sood, A. A. Fahs, and N. A. Henein (1985), Engine Fault Analysis Part I : Statistical Methods, *IEEE Transactions on Industrial Electronics*, vol. 32, no. 4.

[44] A. K. Sood, A. A. Fahs, and N. A. Henein (1985), Engine Fault Analysis Part II: Parameter Estimation Approach, *IEEE Transactions on Industrial Electronics*, vol. 32, no. 4.

[45] J. Sottile, Jr. and J. L. Kohler (1993), An On-Line Method to Detect Incipient Failure of Turn Insulation in Random-Wound Motors, *IEEE Transactions on Energy Conversion*, vol. 8, no. 4, pp. 762-768.

[46] G. C. Soukup (1989), Determination of Motor Quality Through Routine Electrical Tests, *IEEE Transactions on Industry Applications*, vol. 25, no. 5, pp. 873-880.

[47] H. Szu and K. Scheff (1990), Simulated Annealing Feature Extraction from Occluded and Cluttered Objects, *Proceedings of International Joint Conference on Neural Networks*.

[48] P. J. Tavner and J. Penman (1989), *Condition Monitoring of Electrical Machines*: Research Studies Press Ltd. John Wiley & Sons Inc., New York.

[49] J. E. Timperley (1983), Incipient Fault Identification Through Neutral RF Monitoring of Large Rotating Machines, *IEEE Transactions on Power Apparatus and Systems*, vol. 102, no. 3.

[50] J. E. Timperley and J. R. Michalec (1994), Estimating the Remaining Service Life of Asphalt-Mica Stator Insulation, *IEEE Transactions on Energy Conversion*, vol. 9, no. 4, pp. 686-693.

[51] F. C. Trutt, C. S. Cruz, J. L. Kohler, and J. Sittuke (1993), Prediction of Electrical Behavior in Deteriorating Induction Motors, *IEEE Transactions on Industry Applications*, vol. 29, no. 4, pp. 1239-1243.

[52] B. Widrow and R. Winter (1988), Neural Nets for Adaptive Filtering and Adaptive Pattern Recognition, in *Computer Magazine*.

[53] L. A. Zadeh (1965), Fuzzy Sets, in *Information and Control*, vol. 8, New York: Academic Press, pp. 338-353.

[54] H.-J. Zimmermann (1991), *Fuzzy Set Theory - and Its Applications*, Kluwer Academic Publishers.

[55] J. M. Zurada (1992), *Introduction to Artificial Neural Systems*, West Publishing Company, St. Paul, MN.

Chapter 7:

Self-Organizing Manufacturing Systems Using Genetic Algorithms

SELF-ORGANIZING MANUFACTURING SYSTEMS USING GENETIC ALGORITHMS

T. Fukuda
Center for Cooperative Research in Advanced Science and Technology,
Dept. of Mechano-Informatics and Systems and Dept. of Micro System Engineering
Nagoya University
Furo-cho, Chikusa-ku, Nagoya 464-8603, Japan

N. Kubota
Dept. of Mechanical Engineering
Osaka Institute of Technology
5-16-1 Omiya, Asahi-ku, Osaka 535-8585, Japan

This chapter deals with self-organizing manufacturing systems (SOMS), in which each module self-organizes effectively according to other modules. A module is defined as a process for decision making concerning manufacturing systems. Each module decides outputs through the interaction among modules. There are, however, various combinatorial optimization problems in manufacturing systems. We have applied genetic algorithms to combinatorial optimization problems such as scheduling problems, path planning problems and resource allocation problems. In addition, each module of the SOMS has a close relation with other modules, but the module does not share complete information concerning other modules. Furthermore, the information received from other modules often includes ambiguous and incomplete information. We therefore apply fuzzy theory to represent incomplete information concerning other modules. We have used virus-evolutionary genetic algorithms to fuzzy flow shop scheduling problems with fuzzy transportation time as an example of the SOMS. Computer simulation results indicate that the fuzzified information is effective when a module has incomplete information in the SOMS.

1 Introduction

A number of optimization techniques have been reported for solving complicated optimization problems. Especially, operations research provides various types of techniques for production systems [34]. Furthermore, artificial intelligence also provides expert systems and decision support systems [14]. The new manufacturing systems of the next generation have been recently reported [1-7]. Intelligent manufacturing system (IMS) comprises a new concept for coping with a large number of products and manufacturing processes [7]. The concept of IMS is based on self-organization, distributed autonomous system and social biology. In general, a manufacturing system is composed of numerically controlled machines, machining centers, assembling stations, manipulation robots and so on. Furthermore, automatic transportation systems such as belt conveyors, transportation vehicles and monorail cars are part of the manufacturing system. In addition, it has been easy to manage various information concerning the manufacturing system through a computer network. The purpose of the IMS is to perform the processes such as design, machining, control and management automatically by integrating flexible machines and computerized control. However, manufacturing systems have very difficult optimization problems which are ill-defined and ill-structured. The manufacturing systems have lots of various constraints such as space capacity, machining ability and time restriction. To deal with these kinds of difficult problems in the real world, soft computing and computational intelligence techniques have been often applied.

Soft computing was proposed by Zadeh as a new concept for information processing. The objective is to realize a new approach for analyzing and creating flexible information processing of humans such as sensing, understanding, learning, recognizing and thinking [18,28]. Computational intelligence aims to describe intelligence from the viewpoints of biology, evolution and self-organization, and tries to construct intelligence numerically by internal description, while classical artificial intelligence tries to construct intelligence logically by external (explicit) description. Therefore, information and knowledge of a system in computational intelligence should be learned or acquired by the system itself. Other recent research fields concerning intelligence and life include brain science and artificial life [15-19]. The brain science aims to understand the biochemical and physical mechanism of the human brain and to construct a highly interconnected neural network like the human brain [15-17]. Artificial life (A-life) means 'life made by humans rather than nature' [19]. A-life has three types of approaches: 1) wetware system from the molecular level, 2) software system from the cellular level and 3) hardware system from the organism level [19].

These research fields, however, use neural network (NN), fuzzy system (FS), genetic algorithm (GA), reinforcement learning and others to realize their aims [9,11-18]. These techniques play the roles in intelligent systems. The NN simulates physiological features of the human brain, and has been applied for non-linear mapping by the numerical approach [9,28]. The FS simulates psychological features of human brain, and has been applied for linguistic translating by membership functions [9,28]. On the other hand, the GA simulates evolution on a computer [11-13], and has been applied for solving combinatorial optimization problems. In fact, NN and FS are used for the learning and inference in the manufacturing system, and GA is used for approximately solving the combinatorial optimization problems in the manufacturing systems [8,28,32,33].

A machine scheduling problem is one of the most important problems in the manufacturing system [2-5, 29-31]. In general, a scheduling problem is to order n operations on m machines for minimizing cost functions. However, there are many restrictions concerning transportation methods and the location of machining centers in the real manufacturing systems. The optimization problems with these restrictions are known as path planning problems and optimal location problems, respectively. It is very difficult to solve the scheduling problems including the path planning problem and the optimal location problem. Furthermore, it is difficult to globally control the large size of the manufacturing system. To deal with these problems effectively, we have proposed a self-organizing manufacturing system (SOMS), in which each module self-organizes effectively according to other modules [7]. Here each module plays the specific role concerning machine scheduling, path planning, machine locating, manufacturing managing, and so on. Consequently, the SOMS is composed of distributed multiple modules. Each module decides outputs through the interaction with other modules, but the module does not share all information concerning other modules because of the limitations such as information storage. In addition, the information received from other modules often includes ambiguous and incomplete information. Consequently, each module must decide outputs based on the incomplete information concerning other modules. In this chapter, we apply fuzzy theory [8,9,18] to represent incomplete information received from other modules. We consider a fuzzy flow shop scheduling problem with fuzzy transportation time, and then apply a virus-evolutionary genetic algorithm (VE-GA) for solving the fuzzy flow shop scheduling problem [35]. The VE-GA is a stochastic optimization method simulating coevolution of a host population and a virus population.

This chapter is organized as follows. Section 2 presents the concept of the SOMS and a typical manufacturing line. Section 3 presents the VE-GA in detail. The virus infection operators are defined and incorporated into GA. Section 4 formulates a fuzzy flow shop scheduling problem with fuzzy transportation time, and applies the VE-GA to the fuzzy flow shop scheduling problem. Furthermore, several computer simulation results and the effectiveness of the proposed method are shown.

2 Self-Organizing Manufacturing System

2.1 Optimization Problems in Manufacturing System

The manufacturing system has various optimization problems such as optimal location problems, resource allocation problems, scheduling problems, path planning problems (Figure 1). Each optimization problem has a close relation with other optimization problems. The optimal location problem is to determine the location of machining centers, belt conveyors, manipulation robots and so on. The productivity of the manufacturing system mainly depends on the plant layout by the optimal location problem. The scheduling problem is one of the most important issues in the manufacturing system. There is, for example, a job-shop scheduling problem, a flow-shop scheduling problem, and an open-shop scheduling problem. The job shop scheduling problem is a typical machine scheduling problem. However, most of the machining lines are controlled under a flow shop scheduling. If machining centers are sequentially located according to given jobs, the path planning of automated guided vehicles (AGV) or the locations of belt conveyers become easier to design. The path planning problem is to generate a path of AGVs between two or several points in the work space for avoiding a collision with obstacles. This problem has been investigated in the field of autonomous mobile robots. Thus, the actual manufacturing systems have complicated optimization problems.

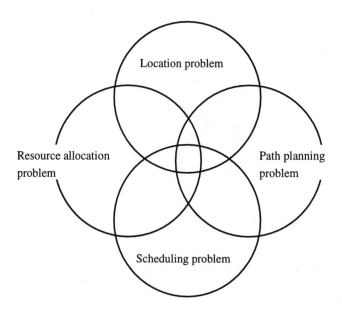

Figure 1: Optimization problems in manufacturing systems

2.2 Self-Organizing Manufacturing System

To create an ideal manufacturing environment, we have proposed a self-organizing manufacturing system (SOMS) that a module self-organizes according to other modules (Figure 2). A module in Figure 2 represents a process in the manufacturing system such as product design, resource allocation, plant location and manufacturing scheduling. Each module self-organizes which is based on outputs from other modules. The SOMS is capable of reorganizing hardware as well as software of the manufacturing system. We have shown that a module can self-organize through computer simulations [7,25].

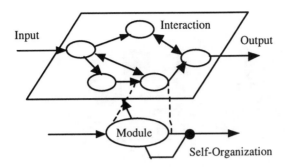

Figure 2: Self-organizing manufacturing system

We consider a manufacturing line composed of a number of conveyor units, tool storages and machining centers as an example of the SOMS (Figure 3). A machining center has the capability of performing a variety of operations with exchangeable tools. Furthermore, the machining center can produce various types of products without exchanging tools. The machining center includes redundancy in its operation. Here a redundancy means that a machining center can equip with tools more than required. For example, when a machining center has three tools, the machining center can perform three types of processing. A tool storage provides exchangeable tools which are required in the machining centers. A conveyor unit transports not only materials/products but also exchangeable tools. The machining information about a material is kept by the bucket holding the material. Therefore, the conveyor can transport a bucket to the machining center according to its machining information. In this case, the required modules are a machine scheduling module, a path planning module, a tool locating module, a resource allocation module, and so on.

The flow of the machining process is generally summarized as follows: (1) design of the machining center, (2) planning of a machine schedule, and (3) output products according to the planned schedule. Figure 4 shows the flow of the machining process of this manufacturing line. The machining centers are designed by the tool locating module based on the local information from the machine scheduling module and path planning module. After tool locating, the machine schedule is optimized according to the tool location and transportation time from the path planning module. The tool location and machine schedule are determined before machining, but the path planning includes the preplanning before machining and the replanning in the actual machining. The replanning of transportation can reduce the machining delay. This kind of local replanning is performed by decision making between some conveyor units. In general, it is important to optimize all modules in order to reduce the manufacturing cost. However, the simultaneous optimization of all modules is very difficult because the optimization problem has a very large solution space. In addition, the optimized modules are vulnerable to breakdowns of the modules, sudden changes and delays of the planned schedules, and so on. Therefore, the self-organization according to other modules is required with regard to the flexibility of the whole manufacturing system.

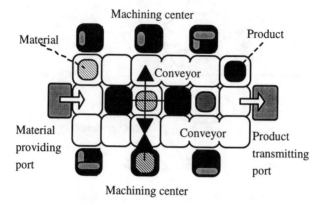

Figure 3: Typical manufacturing line with conveyor units, tool storages and
machining centers

In addition, as the system size increases, it becomes difficult for each module to keep
complete information concerning other modules. Consequently, each module must
decide its output based on the incomplete information concerning other modules. In
this case, the actual transportation time by conveyor units is not clear, since the
transportation time is dependent on the buckets with materials. Consequently, the
scheduling module must decide the schedule based on the incomplete transportation
time, since it is difficult to estimate transportation time actually required. The actual
transportation time is decided by the conveyor units according to the planned
schedule.

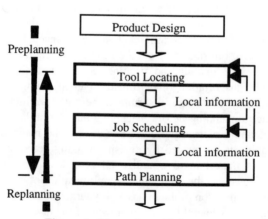

Figure 4: Flow of machining process

3 Virus-Evolutionary Genetic Algorithm

3.1 Evolutionary Computation for Optimization Problems

Various new optimization methods have been proposed so far in the last few decades. The optimization methods can be divided into two categories of exact and approximate methods. The exact methods can obtain optimal solutions using local information peculiar to the optimization problem, but are computationally intensive. On the other hand, the approximate methods can obtain near or approximately optimal solutions with less computational cost. The evolutionary computation techniques fundamentally belong to the latter method.

From the historical point of view, the evolutionary optimization methods are divided into three main categories, genetic algorithm (GA), evolutionary programming (EP) and evolution strategy [11-13]. These methods are fundamentally iterative generation and alternation processes operating on a set of candidate solutions, which is called a population. All the population evolves toward better candidate solutions by selection operation and genetic operators such as crossover and mutation. The selection decides candidate solutions into the next generation, which limits the search space. The crossover and mutation generate new solution candidates from the search space. The evolutionary optimization methods can be divided into some categories from various points of view. This chapter divides the evolutionary optimization methods into *genetic algorithm* (GA) and *evolutionary algorithm* (EA) (Figure 5).

EAs use numerical operations from the viewpoint of phenotype, but EAs also use symbolic operation such as mutation and crossover. EAs including EP and ES have been applied for solving numerical optimization problems such as function optimization problems, and weight optimization of neural networks. The important feature of EAs is self-adaptation, especially self-adaptive mutation which is a very useful operation, and can self-tune the search range according to the success records [13]. In the EAs, tournament selection and deterministic selection are often applied as the selection scheme.

GAs use simple symbolic operations from the viewpoint of genotype. GAs are often applied to combinatorial optimization problems such as traveling salesman problems and job shop problems. It is well established that the GAs can obtain near or approximately optimal solutions with less computational cost. In general, a candidate solution is encoded into binary string or several characters. Schema theorem is well known as a fundamental theorem of the GA [12]. A scheme is defined as a substring of a candidate solution. The increase of good schemata enables the effective search, and makes all the population evolve toward better solutions. Thus the GA can find better solutions with less computation cost, but there is a trade-off between the convergence of a population and the maintenance of genetic diversity. To generate various candidate solutions, a population should maintain the solution subspace (search space) as large as possible, but the population evolves slowly. Therefore, we propose virus-evolutionary genetic algorithms (VE-GA) to improve the search ability of the GA.

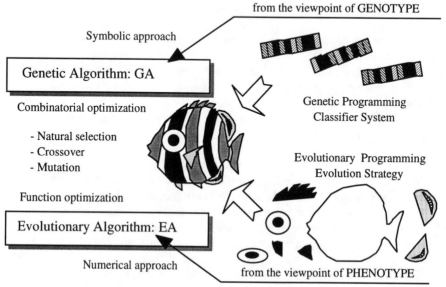

Figure 5: Evolutionary computation: genetic algorithm and evolutionary algorithm

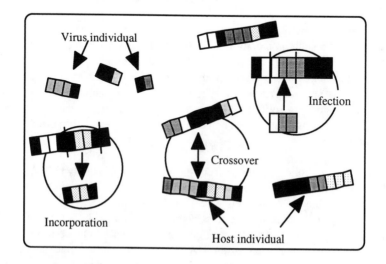

Figure 6: Virus-evolutionary genetic algorithm

3.2 Virus-Evolutionary Genetic Algorithm Architecture

GA methods simulating various evolutionary models have been widely reported. Virus theory of evolution is based on the view that virus incorporation is a key mechanism for transporting segments of DNA across species [22,23]. A virus-evolutionary genetic algorithm (VE-GA) simulates co-evolution based on the virus theory of evolution. VE-GA has two populations: a host population and a virus population (Figure 6). The host population and the virus population are defined as a set of candidate solutions and a substring set of the host population, respectively. We assume that the virus population enables the horizontal propagation in the host population, while the crossover and selection enables the vertical inheritance from parents to children. The VE-GA has two virus infection operators:

(a) Reverse transcription operator (infection): A virus overwrites its substring on the string of a host individual for generating new host individuals (Figure 7.a).
(b) Incorporation operator: A virus takes out a substring from the string of a host individual for generating new virus individuals (Figure 7.b).

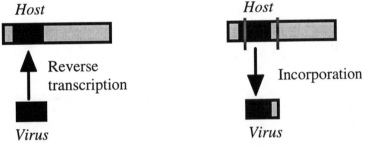

(a) Reverse transcription operator   (b) Incorporation operator

Figure 7: Virus infection operators

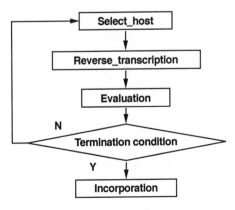

Figure 8: The operation of virus infection

The operation of a virus infection is shown in Figure 8. First, a virus performs the reverse transcription to a host individual randomly selected out of the host population. The number of infections is controlled under its virus infection rate. Each virus has *fitvirus_i*, as a strength about the virus infection. We assume that *fithost_j* and *fithost'_j* are the fitness value of a host individual *j* before and after the infection, respectively. The *fitvirus_{i,j}* denotes the difference between *fithost_j* and *fithost'_j*, which is equal to the improvement value obtained by infecting to the host individual:

$$fitvirus_{i, j} = fithost'_j - fithost_j \qquad (1)$$

$$fitvirus_i = \sum_{j \in S} fitvirus_{i, j} \qquad (2)$$

where *i* is the virus number and *S* is a set of the host individuals which are infected by the virus *i*. After infections, each virus evolves by incorporation according to *fitvirus_i*. If *fitvirus_i* is larger than zero, the virus performs incorporation by taking out a partially new substring from one of the infected host individuals. Otherwise, a virus shortens the genotype by removing some genes. Actually, the virus length shortens/extends according to the incorporation probability (P_t). P_t denotes the probability to take out a gene from a host individual. In addition, each virus has *infrate_i* for the virus infection.

$$infrate_{i, t+1} = \begin{cases} (1+\alpha) \cdot infrate_{i, t} & \text{if } fitvirus_i > 0 \\ (1-\alpha) \cdot infrate_{i, t} & \text{if } fitvirus_i \leq 0 \end{cases} \qquad (3)$$

where α (>0) is coefficient. When *fitvirus_i* is high, *infrate_i* becomes high. The increase of *infrate_i* accelerates the increase of effective schemata by virus infection. Furthermore, each virus has a life force as follows:

$$life_{i, t+1} = r \times life_{i, t} + fitvisus_i \qquad (4)$$

where *t* and *r* mean the generation and the life reduction rate, respectively. If $life_{i,t+1}$ takes a negative value, the virus individual takes out a new substring with the incorporation operator from the randomly selected host individual. The VE-GA is based on a steady-state model [20] and its procedure is as follows:

```
        Initialization
                repeat
                        Selection
                        Crossover
                        Mutation
                        Virus _infection
                        Replacement
                until Termination _condition = True
        end.
```

Initialization randomly generates an initial host population, and then a virus individual is generated as a substring of a host individual according to the incorporation probability. The initial length of each virus individual is determined by P_t. Consequently, the virus randomly takes out each gene according to P_t. 'Delete least fitness' is used as the selection scheme, which eliminates the worst host individual [20]. Virus infection operator is introduced into GA as new searching operators. New individuals generated by virus infections are generated as children. After virus infections, if the fitness is improved compared with its parent, then the generated child is replaced with its parent. Consequently, the successfully infected host individuals survive into the next generation. This indicates the virus infection operator can be regarded as a local hill-climbing operator.

4 Fuzzy Manufacturing Scheduling Problem

Fuzzy operations research has been applied to solve difficult optimization problems [8,26,27]. In the previous work concerning fuzzy manufacturing problems, processing time, due date, maximal delay, and others are fuzzified, and these kinds of problems are researched as fuzzy constraints and fuzzy multi-criteria problems. In this chapter, we use fuzzy theory to represent ambiguous transportation time of the conveyor module [35].

4.1 Fuzzy Flow Shop Scheduling Problem

The scheduling module has the machining time on each machining center, but the transportation time is received from the conveyor module. However, the transportation time is not complete, since conveyor units decide the actual transportation time according to the planned schedule, as mentioned before. Consequently, the scheduling module must decide a schedule based on the received incomplete information including transportation time estimated by the conveyor module. We therefore use the fuzzy theory to represent the transportation time between machining centers. Each transportation time differs due to different material and product, and the scheduling module receives only the average, minimum and maximum of estimated transportation time. Consequently, we apply a triangular fuzzy number based on these values as shown in Figure 9. In Figure 9, f_c, f_l and f_u denote the values corresponding to the 1.0-level set, the lower and upper bounds of α-level set of fuzzy number F, respectively.

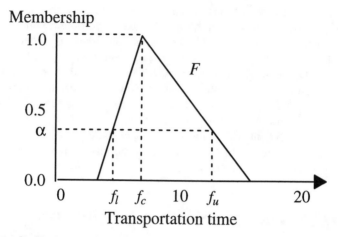

Figure 9: Transportation time represented by triangular fuzzy number F

The objective is to order the given jobs for minimizing the makespan which is defined as consuming time until completion of all jobs. Let t_i be a completion time of job i. The completion time is based on the processing time, transportation time and waiting time. The makespan T is generally defined as follows:

$$T = \max\{t_1, t_2, \cdots, t_n\}$$

(5)

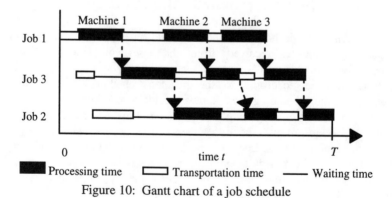

Figure 10: Gantt chart of a job schedule

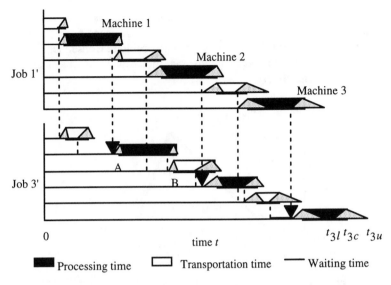

Figure 11: Gantt chart of job 1 with fuzzy transportation time

We present one example of scheduling three jobs on three machines (Figure 10). The order of this schedule is 1 -> 3 -> 2. In this case, the job 1 is processed without waiting time. The jobs 2 and 3 are processed after the processing of the preceding job. However, this example doesn't consider fuzzy transportation time. Figure 11 shows the Gantt chart with fuzzy transportation time of job 1' and job 3'. Each transportation time of all jobs is fuzzified. The fuzziness of transportation time increases as conveyer units transport the bucket of job 1', though the fuzziness does not increase in the machine processing (see Figure 11). Next, we consider the fuzziness concerning job 3'. In job 3', there are two types of inheritances of fuzzy time. In 'A' of the Figure 11, job 3' is waiting for processing job 1' in the machine 1, and job 3' inherits the fuzziness of job 1'. On the other hand, in 'B' of the Figure 11, job 3' is not waiting for transporting of job 1', since the required conveyor unit is free. Consequently, job 3' directly inherits the fuzziness of job 3'. Actually, the calculation of the fuzzy time is based on the maximum operator of the preceding job and current job, and the shape of the triangular fuzzy number sometimes changes into the non-triangular fuzzy number [8].

Figure 12 shows an example of maximum operator of $F1$ and $F2$. In this example, the fuzzy time of the preceding job is $F1$ and the fuzzy time of the current job is $F2$. Consequently, the maximum operator determines the shape of fuzzy number according to the later jobs against time. However, this maximum operator makes the fuzzy flow shop scheduling problem very complex and the calculation of makespan takes much time. Therefore, the maximum operation is approximated by using f_c, f_l and f_u (Figure 13). This maximum operator is defined as follows:

$$\max 2(F_1, F_2) = \{\max(f_{1l}, f_{2l}), \max(f_{1c}, f_{2c}), \max(f_{1u}, f_{2u})\} \tag{6}$$

where triangular fuzzy number i is $F_i = (f_{il}, f_{ic}, f_{iu})$. Consequently, the makespan must be defined as T_c, T_l and T_u which are calculated by using f_c, f_l and f_u, respectively. This is approximately applied for solving this scheduling problem. Consequently, T_c, T_l and T_u can be approximately regarded as the average makespan, minimal makespan and maximal makespan, respectively.

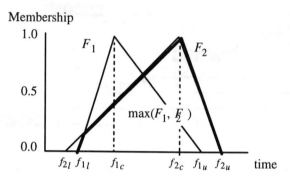

Figure 12: Maximum operator of triangular fuzzy numbers $F1$ and $F2$

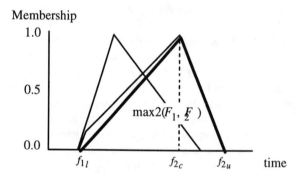

Figure 13: Maximum operator of triangular fuzzy numbers $F1$ and $F2$

4.2 Application to Fuzzy Flow Shop Scheduling Problem

This subsection shows the application of the VE-GA to the fuzzy flow shop scheduling problem. The fuzzy flow shop scheduling problem formulated in the previous subsection can be defined as a permutation problem. The genotype of candidate solutions is defined as the positive number between 1 and the number of jobs. Here, the overlapping of the same number on the candidate solution is forbidden. Next, we consider genetic operators. The cycle crossover (CX) and partially matched crossover (PMX) [12] are used as crossover operators. Figure 14 shows examples of these crossovers in the case of five jobs. First, the CX chooses a starting gene ('1' of P1 in Figure 14 (a)), not a crossing site. Second, the CX chooses the gene '4' of the locus 2 of P2, and next finds the gene '4' on the string of P1. Thus the CX repeats this symbolic processing until returning to the first chosen gene, and the CX makes a closed round of substrings between two individuals. Finally, the CX exchanges the remaining substrings. On the other hand, the PMX chooses two break-points (Figure 14 (b)). Next, the PMX replaces '3' with '2', and '5' with '4' on P1 to exchange the chosen substrings without overlapping. This symbolic processing is repeated until no overlapping occurs. Finally, the remaining genes are copied from the parents. These crossover operators are used for global search. Next, we consider mutation operators for the local search. A simple mutation operator exchanges two randomly selected genes (exchanging mutation) (Figure 15 (a)). Furthermore, a shift operator is also used for solving the flow shop scheduling problem. The shift operator cuts a randomly selected substring and inserts the substring into other locus on the candidate solution (Figure 15 (b)). The shift operator has often been applied for solving scheduling problems as local search.

| P1: | 3 1 2 4 5 | | P1: | 3 1 | 2 4 | 5 |
| P2: | 2 4 3 5 1 | | P2: | 2 4 | 3 5 | 1 |

⇓   ⇓ Break-points

| O1: | * 1 * 4 * | | O1: | 2 * 3 5 4 |
| O2: | * 4 * * * | | O2: | 3 5 2 4 * |

⇓   ⇓

| O1: | 2 1 3 4 5 | | O1: | 2 1 3 5 4 |
| O2: | 3 4 2 5 1 | | O2: | 3 5 2 4 1 |

Figure 14: Crossover operator for permutation

Next, we consider virus infection operators. As mentioned before, the virus infection operators are reverse transcription and incorporation. Figure 16 shows an example of reverse transcription operator which overwrites the virus' string on a host individual like the PMX. The incorporation takes out a substring from a host individual. The fitness function is based on the makespan defined in the previous section as follows,

$$fitness = w_1 T_l + w_2 T_c + w_3 T_u \qquad (7)$$

where w_1, w_2 and w_3 are weight coefficients. This is a multi-objective function based on the makespan calculated by approximated fuzzy transportation time. Next, we show the parameters concerning the VE-GA. The host population size and virus population size are 100 and 10, respectively. Crossover probability, mutation (shift) probability per gene and initial/maximal virus infection rates are 0.8, 0.01, 0.01 and 0.1, respectively. The numbers of jobs and machines are 30 and 10, respectively. Each machining time and fuzzy transportation time are given. Furthermore, we assume α is zero in this simulation. Consequently, f_c, f_l and f_u are the values corresponding to the 1.0-level set, the lower and upper bounds of fuzzy number F, respectively.

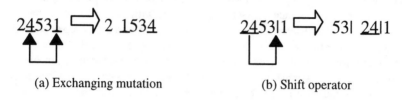

(a) Exchanging mutation   (b) Shift operator

Figure 15: Mutation operators for permutation problems

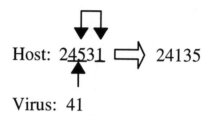

Figure 16: A reverse transcription for permutation problems

In this section, we compare simulation results of the fuzzy flow shop scheduling problem for the following cases,

- Case 1: $(w_1, w_2, w_3) = ($ 1.0,   0,   0)
- Case 2: $(w_1, w_2, w_3) = ($ 0,   1.0,   0)
- Case 3: $(w_1, w_2, w_3) = ($ 0.2,   0.5,   0.3)

Figure 17 shows the comparison of simulation results of the SSGA and VE-GA. This simulation result shows that the VE-GA outperforms the SSGA. The reason would be that the VE-GA generates effective sub-schedules and combines them by reverse transcription. Figure 18 shows simulation results of Case 3 by the VE-GA. Each makespan in this figure means the average of 30 trials of simulations. Each makespan decreases with the increase of the evaluation times. Table 1 shows the makespans obtained by the VE-GA and the actual makespans. The actual makespan is calculated by using the conveyor units based on the best schedule of each case. Though T_l and T_c of Case 3 are inferior to the other best values, the actual makespan is superior to others.

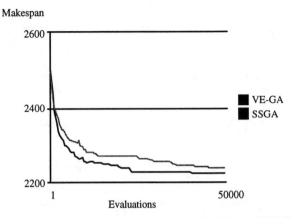

Figure 17: Comparison result of SSGA and VE-GA

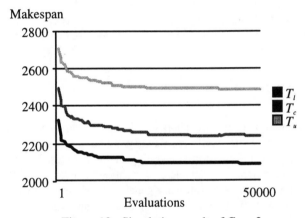

Figure 18: Simulation result of Case 3

Table 1: Simulation results of Case 1, 2 and 3

	Makespan by VEGA			Actual makespan
	T_l	T_c	T_u	
Case 1	2082	2320	2562	2305
Case 2	2101	2220	2534	2252
Case 3	2093	2245	2491	2238

Next, we discuss other cases by changing simulation parameters. We alter the simulation parameters concerning jobs and machines, while we use the weight coefficients of the previous cases.

- Case 4: $(w_1, w_2, w_3) = (0.2, 0.5, 0.3)$ for 20 jobs on 10 machines
- Case 5: $(w_1, w_2, w_3) = (0.2, 0.5, 0.3)$ for 50 jobs on 10 machines

Table 2 shows the simulation results of case 4 and 5. The obtained makespan T_c is similar to the actual makespan. From these simulation results, the scheduling module can obtain an effective schedule by fuzzifying transportation time. This indicates that the fuzzified information is effective when a module has incomplete information.

Table 2: Simulation results of case 4 and 5

	Makespan by VEGA			Actual makespan
	T_l	T_c	T_u	
Case 4	1472	1576.4	1763.4	1578
Case 5	3060.2	3327.2	3648.2	3315

5 Summary

This chapter presented a fuzzy flow shop scheduling problem in the self-organizing manufacturing systems. In the self-organizing manufacturing system, each module does not have complete information concerning other modules. We therefore apply fuzzy theory to represent incomplete information concerning other modules. Furthermore, we apply a virus-evolutionary genetic algorithm to the fuzzy flow shop scheduling problem with fuzzy transportation time as an example. The simulation results indicate that the fuzzified information is effective when a module has incomplete information. However, the performance of each module is dependent on the representation of fuzzy number.

On the other hand, we have solved tool location problems [7] and path planning problems. In the future, we intend to integrate these optimization problems on the self-organizing manufacturing systems.

References

[1] Thamgiah, S. R., Vinayagamoorthy, R., Gubbi, A. V. (1993), Vehicle Routing with Time Deadlines using Genetic and Local Algorithm, *Proc. of The Fifth International Conference on Genetic Algorithms*, pp.506-513.

[2] Pu, P., Hughes, J. (1994), Integrating AGV Schedules in a Scheduling System for a Flexible Manufacturing Environment, *Proc. of IEEE International Conference on Robotics and Automation*, pp.3149-3154.

[3] Macchiaroli, R., Riemma, S. (1994), Clustering Methods for Production Planning and Scheduling in a Flexible Manufacturing System, *Proc. of IEEE International Conference on Robotics and Automation*, pp.3155-3160.

[4] Kim, G.H., Lee, C.S.G. (1995), Genetic Reinforcement Learning Approach to the Machine Scheduling Problem, *Proc. of The International Conference on Robotic and Automation*, Vol.1, pp.196-201.

[5] Wang, J., Luh, P.B. (1995), Optimization-Based Scheduling of a Machining Center, *Proc. of The International Conference on Robotic and Automation*, Vol.1, pp.502-507.

[6] Starke, J., Kubota, N., Fukuda, T., (1995), Combinatorial Optimization with Higher Order Neural Networks - Cost Oriented Competing Processes in Flexible Manufacturing System, *Proc. of The International Conference on Neural Network*, pp.2658-2663.

[7] Kubota, N., Fukuda, T., Shimojima, K. (1996), Virus-Evolutionary Genetic Algorithm for A Self-Organizing Manufacturing System, *Computer & Industrial Engineering Journal*, Vol.30, No.4, pp.1015-1026.

[8] Ishibuchi, H., Murata, T., Lee, K.H. (1996), Formulation of Fuzzy Flowshop Scheduling Problems with Fuzzy Processing Time, *Proc. of The Fifth IEEE International Conference on Fuzzy Systems*, pp.199-205.

[9] Kartalopoulos, S.V. (1996), *Understanding Neural Networks and Fuzzy Logic*, IEEE Press.

[10] Kubota, N., Shimojima, K., Fukuda, T. (1996), The Role of Virus Infection in A Virus-Evolutionary Genetic Algorithm, *Journal of Applied Mathematics and Computer Science*, Vol.6, No.3, pp.415-429.

[11] Holland, J.H. (1975), *Adaptation in Natural and Artificial Systems*, University of Michigan Press.

[12] Goldberg, D.E. (1989), *Genetic Algorithm in Search, Optimization, and Machine Learning*, Addison Wesley.

[13] Fogel, D.B. (1995), *Evolutionary Computation*, IEEE Press.

[14] Russell, S.J., Norvig, P. (1995), Artificial Intelligence, Prentice-Hall, Inc.

[15] Anderson, J. A., Rosenfeld, E. (1988), *Neurocomputing - Foundations of Research*, The MIT Press.

[16] Zurada, J. M., Marks II, R. J., Robinson, C. J. (1994), *Computational Intelligence - Imitating Life*, IEEE Press.

[17] Palaniswami, M., Attikiouzel, Y., Marks II, R.J., Fogel, D., Fukuda, T. (1995), *Computational Intelligence - A Dynamic System Perspective*, IEEE Press.

[18] Zadeh, L. A. (1965), Fuzzy Sets, Information and Control, Vol.8, pp.338-353.

[19] Langton, C.G. (1995), *Artificial Life -An Overview*, The MIT Press.

[20] Syswerda, G. (1991), A Study of Reproduction in Generational and Steady-State Genetic Algorithms, *Foundations of Genetic Algorithms*, Morgan Kaufmann 94/101.

[21] Ridley, M. (1993), *Evolution*, Blackwell Scientific Publications.

[22] Anderson, N. (1970), Evolutionary Significance of Virus Infection, *Nature*, Vol.227, pp.1346-1347.

[23] Nakahara, H., Sagawa, T. (1989), *Virus Theory of Evolution*, Tairyusha (in Japanese).

[24] Primrose, S.B., Dimmock, N.J. (1980), *Introduction to Modern Virology*, Blackwell Scientific Publications.

[25] Kubota, N., Fukuda, T., Arai, F., Shimojima, K. (1994), Genetic Algorithm with Age Structure and Its Application to Self-Organizing Manufacturing System, *Proc. of The IEEE Symposium on Emerging Technologies and Factory Automation*, pp.472-477.

[26] Inuiguchi, M., Sakawa, M. (1996), Portfolio Selection under Independent Possibilistic Information, *Proc. of The Fifth IEEE International Conference on Fuzzy Systems*, pp.187-193.

[27] Wang, H.G., Rooda, J.E., Haan, J.F. (1996), Solve Scheduling Problems with a Fuzzy Approach, *Proc. of The Fifth IEEE International Conference on Fuzzy Systems*, 194/198.

[28] Jang, J.-S.R., Sun, C.-T., Mizutani, E. (1997), *Neuro-Fuzzy and Soft Computing*, New Jersey: Prentice-Hall, Inc.

[29] Cleveland, G. A., Smith, S. F. (1989), Using Genetic Algorithms to Scheduling Flow Shop Releases, *Proc. of The Third International Conference on Genetic Algorithms*, pp.160-169.

[30] Holsapple, C., Jacob, V., et al. (1993), A Genetics-Based Hybrid Scheduler for Generating Static Schedules in Flexible Manufacturing Contexts, *The IEEE Trans. on System, Man, and Cybernetics*, Vol.23, No.4, pp.953-972.

[31] Rahmani, A. T., Ono, N. (1993), A Genetic Algorithm for Channel Routing Problem, *Proc. of The Fifth International Conference on Genetic Algorithms*, 494/498.

[32] Shimojima, K., Kubota, N., Fukuda, T. (1996), RBF Fuzzy Controller with Virus-Evolutionary Genetic Algorithm, *Proc. of The International Conference on Neural Networks*, pp.1040-1043.

[33] Herrera, F., Vergegay, J.L. Edited (1996), Studies in Fuzziness, Vol.8, *Genetic Algorithms and Soft Computing*, Physica-Verlag, A Springer-Verlag Company.

[34] Ecker, J., Kupferschmid, M. (1988), *Introduction to Operations Research*, New York: John Wiley & Sons Inc.

[35] Kubota, N., Arakawa, T., Fukuda, T., et al. (1997), Fuzzy Manufacturing Scheduling by Virus-Evolutionary Genetic Algorithm in Self-Organizing Manufacturing System, *Proc. of The Sixth IEEE International Conference on Fuzzy Systems*, pp.1283-1288.

Chapter 8:

Intelligent Telecommunication Technologies

INTELLIGENT TELECOMMUNICATION TECHNOLOGIES

Gary Weiss, John Eddy, Sholom Weiss
Network & Computing Services
AT&T Labs
AT&T Corporation
U.S.A.

Telecommunication networks are extremely complex systems requiring high reliability and availability. The effective management of these networks is a critical, but complex, task. To help with this problem, the telecommunications industry has heavily invested in intelligent technologies. This chapter describes intelligent technologies and applications used within the telecommunications industry. Section 1 describes expert systems and data mining technologies. Section 2 describes several intelligent telecommunication applications and the intelligent technologies they employ. The next two sections provide detailed descriptions of representative modern telecommunication applications. Section 3 describes the ANSWER expert system, which monitors and maintains all of the 4ESS switching elements in the AT&T network. This system is noteworthy for the fact that it combines object and rule-based technologies, to gain advantages from each. Section 4 describes the use of data mining to predict extremely rare telecommunication equipment failures. This telecommunication application, and several others described earlier in the chapter, highlight the increasing use of data mining technology in the telecommunications industry to *automatically* acquire useful knowledge from the large quantities of data which are routinely available.

1 Intelligent Technologies

For many years the telecommunication industry has relied on intelligent solutions to help manage telecommunication networks. Building such applications involved acquiring valuable telecommunication knowledge from human experts and then applying this knowledge, typically by embedding it in an expert system. This knowledge acquisition process is so time-consuming that it is referred to as the "knowledge acquisition bottleneck". Data mining techniques are now being applied to industrial applications to break this bottleneck, by replacing the manual knowledge acquisition process with automated knowledge discovery. Telecommunication networks, which routinely generate tremendous amounts of data, are ideal candidates for data mining [1]. This section will describe expert system and data mining technologies and how they are evolving to solve complex industrial problems.

1.1 Expert Systems

Expert systems are programs which represent and apply factual knowledge of specific areas of expertise to solve problems [2]. Expert systems have been applied extensively within the telecommunications industry, but not without problems. Early expert systems required a knowledge engineer to acquire knowledge from the domain experts and encode this knowledge in a rule-based expert system. These rules were very "ad-hoc" and as the number of rules increased, the expert system became more difficult to understand and modify. The 4ESS-ES expert system, which is described later in this chapter, is an example of such a "first generation" expert system. Second generation expert systems attempted to solve these problems by using stronger methods, such as model-based and functional reasoning. Model-based reasoning is of interest to the telecommunications industry since model-based approaches can represent the structure and behavior of the telecommunication network components declaratively and then reason from first principles. While these expert systems seem preferable to first generation systems, they have not seen the same level of commercial success. In the field of telecommunications, this is because it is often too difficult to specify a behavioral or functional model at a sufficiently high level to make the model practical and yet have it be useful.

The design of telecommunication expert systems needs to recognize that virtually all telecommunication equipment incorporates self-diagnostic capabilities and hence it is not necessary to fully model the telecommunications network [3]. However, this does not mean that we should return to the previous approach of writing ad-hoc rules to reason based on the results of the self-diagnostic tests. Section 3 describes a hybrid approach which uses "affective" relations and object-oriented technology to define an abstract non-behavioral model for modeling devices. Another related approach, described in this chapter, is to use data mining to automatically build a causal, or Bayesian, network to explain a telecommunication network's behavior.

1.2 Knowledge Discovery and Data Mining

1.2.1 Overview

Knowledge discovery is a field which has emerged from various disciplines, including artificial intelligence, machine learning, statistics and databases. The knowledge discovery process involves identifying valid, novel, potentially useful and ultimately understandable patterns in data [4]. Data mining, the most researched topic in this process, involves finding interesting patterns in the data via data analysis and discovery algorithms. The knowledge discovery process, which has been described in detail in several recent papers [4, 5], is comprised of the following steps:

1. *data preparation:* selecting, cleaning and preprocessing the data (e.g., filling in missing values) and transforming it so that it is suitable for data mining

2. *data mining:* finding patterns in the data

3. *interpretation and evaluation*: interpreting and evaluating the patterns produced by data mining

A key motivation for knowledge discovery is that it can replace or minimize the need for the time-consuming process of manually acquiring knowledge from a domain expert. Knowledge discovery is especially attractive to the telecommunications industry since:

- Telecommunication networks are typically too complex to build complete simulation models

- Huge quantities of data are routinely available

- Domain experts often are not aware of subtle patterns in data and hence automated knowledge discovery can acquire new, previously unknown, knowledge

Many of the applications in this chapter utilize knowledge discovery. The step in the knowledge discovery process which typically requires the most work for telecommunications applications is the transformation step, which involves identifying useful features to represent the data. This step is complicated by the fact that telecommunication networks produce *sequences* of alarms, where it is not the individual alarms which are of importance but the behavior over time of the network. Since most data mining methods do not directly operate on temporal sequences, these sequences must be transformed so that these methods can be used. The Scout application in Section 2.1.4 and the forecasting application in Section 4 both take this approach. An alternative approach is to develop a data mining method which can reason about temporal relationships. Such a system, the telecommunication network alarm sequence analyzer, is described in Section 2.1.3.

1.2.2 Data Mining

Data mining finds interesting patterns in data. It is an example of inductive learning, since it is based on generalizing from past instances. A typical data mining application from the telecommunications industry is to predict the failure of a network component based on past alarm history. Data mining can be used to solve many tasks, including the following:

- *classification:* learning to map an example into one of several classes

- *clustering*: partitioning examples into categories which are not predefined

- *dependency modeling*: finding a model that explains dependencies between variables

- *sequential and temporal pattern detection*: discovering sequential or temporal patterns between/among examples

These tasks can be associated with real telecommunication problems. All of the applications described in this chapter can be considered classification tasks (e.g., is a network element faulty or not). The Trouble Locator and APRI systems, described in Section 2.1.2 and 2.2.1, respectively, build dependency models. The TASA application described in Section 2.1.3, and to a lesser degree the forecasting application described in Section 4, are both examples of temporal pattern detection. NYNEX has used clustering to target the most lucrative direct mail markets and to tailor sales messages to produce the maximum impact.

There are many data mining methods for solving the various data mining tasks. These methods vary in several ways, including: the time they require for learning, their tolerance of noise, the expected format of the data and the concepts they are capable of expressing. Rule induction and Bayesian, or causal, networks are two data mining methods used extensively within the telecommunications industry and by applications described in this chapter. Rule induction systems generate rule sets capable of classifying new examples, while Bayesian networks learn probabilistic concepts to account for the observed data. Both rule induction systems and Bayesian networks are particularly appropriate for telecommunication applications. Rule induction systems are appropriate because rules are easy to understand and can easily be incorporated into existing rule-based expert systems. The Swap-1 rule induction system [6] is used by two applications in this chapter. Bayesian networks are also appropriate since many telecommunication problems, such as isolating a faulty hardware component, are best handled probabilistically, due to a lack of complete simulation models. Many other data mining methods, such as decision trees and neural networks, can also be used to solve data mining tasks.

2 Intelligent Applications

This section describes several representative intelligent telecommunication applications and the intelligent techniques they employ. A more comprehensive listing, but with only a brief description of each, can be found in [7].

2.1 Network Management Applications

Network management applications, which involve the monitoring, diagnosis, and maintenance of telecommunication networks, are the most important applications in the telecommunication industry. Five such applications are described in this section.

2.1.1 Max & Opti-Max: Locating Problems in the Local Loop

The Max (Maintenance administrator expert) system [8], developed by NYNEX, diagnoses customer reported telephone problems in the local loop, the final segment of the telephone network that connects the customer to a central office. Max is a rule-based expert system which diagnoses problems based on results of an electrical test on the customer's phone line, specific knowledge of the customer's phone line and general equipment knowledge. Max determines where the trouble lies and selects the type of technician to solve the problem. Max was deployed in 1990 and has been able to reduce the number of incorrect technician dispatches over previous methods. One problem with Max is that its performance is affected by the local characteristics of each site and thus numerous rule parameters must be tuned to optimize its performance. This tuning process is time consuming and for this reason a system called Opti-Max [9] was created to automatically tune these parameters to appropriate values. Opti-Max takes as input a set of training examples, each of which includes a problem description and a diagnosis assigned by an expert, and then uses a hill-climbing search to find a set of parameter values which perform well on these examples. Opti-Max performs a type of automated knowledge discovery.

2.1.2 Trouble Locator: Locating Cable Network Troubles

Pacific Bell has an intelligent system which determines the location of troubles in a local telephone cable network [10]. This system uses data generated by a nightly automated test to help narrow down potential cables or network equipment which may be faulty; however, the test results are not sufficient to determine the exact cause. The Trouble Locator uses a Bayesian network and Bayesian inference [11] to solve this problem. The system begins by generating a local plant topology graph and then from this generates a Bayesian network, where each node in the network contains state information (belief of failure) of a plant component. This network also takes into account historical information about the components and the data from the overnight test. The belief of failure is then propagated throughout the network until equilibrium is reached, at which point a ranked list of faulty components can be generated. This system is used by preventative maintenance analysts as a decision support system.

2.1.3 TASA: Finding Frequently Occurring Alarm Episodes

The Telecommunication Network Alarm Sequence Analyzer (TASA) [12] is a system for extracting knowledge about the behavior of the network from a database of telecommunication network alarms. The goal of this system is to locate regularities in the alarm sequences in order to filter redundant alarms, locate problems in the network and predict future faults. TASA operates in two phases. In the first phase, specialized algorithms are used to find rules that describe frequently occurring alarm episodes from the sequential alarm data [13]. An episode describes a set of alarm sequences over a given time period and this set can include alarm sequences in which the specific order of alarms does not matter. An example rule describing an alarm episode is: *if alarms of types A and B occur within 5 seconds, then an alarm of type C occurs within 60 seconds with probability 0.7.* In the second phase, collections of episodes are interactively manipulated by the user so that *interesting* episodes from the original set can be found.   TASA supports this process by providing operations to prune uninteresting episodes, order the set of episodes and group similar episodes.   Pruning and ordering of the rules is accomplished by specifying the values of various attributes of the rules (e.g., the types or severities of the alarms or the confidence or frequency of such rules).   TASA has been tested with telecommunication alarm data and interesting rules have been found and incorporated into existing alarm handling systems.

2.1.4 Scout: Identifying Network Faults via Data Mining

AT&T's Scout system proactively identifies recurring transient faults [14]. It operates by mining historical telecommunication data using machine learning and correlation techniques. In one approach, Scout identifies patterns of chronic problems directly from the data by examining the network behavior over periods of days and weeks. To do this, features which summarize time-varying historical data are extracted from the data so that standard machine learning algorithms can be used (i.e., algorithms which are not capable of explicit temporal reasoning). This featurization is accomplished by using two fixed consecutive time windows, W_1 and W_2. The objective is to use the measurements from W_1 to predict problems in W_2. One way of summarizing these measurements is to count the number of times each feature occurs within the window. Scout then used Swap-1 [6] to learn rules that predict recurring transient faults.

Another version of Scout uses a topological map of the network in order to improve its performance. The addition of this topological knowledge allows Scout to learn using time intervals of minutes and hours instead of days and weeks—something which is extremely important if acute failures are to be predicted. This knowledge also allows Scout to effectively identify problems with the same root cause. Scout has been deployed in AT&T's Network Service Centers since 1992 and has successfully increased technician productivity by identifying root cause problems and recurring transient problems.

2.1.5 4ESS-ES: Network Management for 4ESS Switches

Most of the switching capacity for domestic long distance traffic in the AT&T network is provided by 4ESS switches.   Until very recently, the 4ESS-ES (4ESS Expert System) was responsible for managing these switches: for monitoring them, running diagnostic tests and filtering alarms. The 4ESS-ES is a first generation rule-based expert system, implemented in 1990 using C5, a C version of the popular OPS-5 [15] rule-based language. It consists mainly of shallow ad-hoc rules acquired over a period of many years from domain experts and suffers the same problems as most first generation systems—it is difficult to modify and maintain.   This system was redesigned and re-implemented in 1996 using a hybrid, object-oriented, rule-based paradigm, which is described in detail in Section 3.

2.2 Other Intelligent Applications

In addition to network management applications, the telecommunication industry has developed many other types of intelligent applications, including: marketing applications, product configuration applications, help-desk applications and fraud detection/security applications.   Since these applications are not unique to the telecommunication industry, only a single application will be described.

2.2.1 APRI: Predicting Uncollectible Debt

The telecommunications industry incurs billions of dollars of uncollectible debt each year.   The Advanced Pattern Recognition and Identification (APRI) system was developed by AT&T's Consumer Laboratory to predict the probability of uncollectible debt based on historical data, including data of past uncollectibles [16]. The output of APRI is fed into a decision support system which can take a variety of actions, including blocking a call from being completed.   APRI automatically constructs Bayesian network models for classification problems using extremely large databases. Bayesian networks were chosen for this problem due to the inherently probabilistic nature of the prediction problem and due to the highly unequal misclassification costs (i.e., the cost of mistakenly labeling an account as uncollectible vs. mistakenly labeling it as collectible) and skewed class distributions.

3 ANSWER: A Hybrid Approach to Network Management

This section describes ANSWER (Automatic Network Surveillance with Expert Rules), the operation support system responsible for maintaining the 4ESS switches in the AT&T long distance network. This system replaces the 4ESS-ES, the "first generation" expert system described in Section 2.1.5. ANSWER is noteworthy for the fact that it utilizes both rule-based *and* object-oriented technologies, by employing a rule-based extension to the C++ object-oriented programming language. The inclusion of object oriented technology facilitated the design and implementation of ANSWER by providing a principled way to model the 4ESS as a hierarchical collection of devices.

This section is organized as follows. Section 3.1 provides a functional overview of ANSWER. Section 3.2 describes the object model used by ANSWER to model the 4ESS switch. Section 3.3 provides a brief description of R++, the rule-based extension to C++ which was used to implement the expert system component of ANSWER. Section 3.4 discusses the types of reasoning performed by ANSWER and illustrates this with several examples. Finally, Section 3.5 summarizes the significance and contributions of the approach taken by ANSWER.

3.1 Functional Overview

Surveillance technicians at AT&T's two network control centers use ANSWER to help them monitor and maintain the 4ESS switches, which handle the majority of calls in the AT&T long distance network. Their goal, and the goal of ANSWER, is to minimize the number of service affecting incidents and the number of blocked or lost calls. ANSWER helps to achieve this goal by observing thousands of 4ESS alarm messages and notifying technicians of conditions which are serious and most likely will require human intervention.

ANSWER is a complete telecommunications operation support system and includes many components. The central and most important component is the knowledge base, which is responsible for all of ANSWER's intelligent behavior. The basic input/output functionality of ANSWER, from the perspective of its knowledge base, is shown in Figure 1.

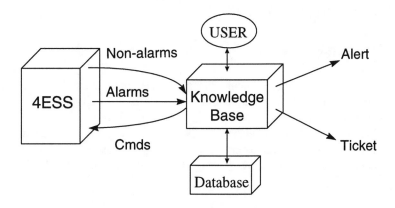

Figure 1: Functional View of ANSWER

The key inputs to the knowledge base are alarm and non-alarm messages from the 4ESS switches. Alarm messages provide information about anomalous conditions which occur on a specific device within the 4ESS, while non-alarm messages provide status information or the results of diagnostics previously requested by the knowledge base. The key outputs of the knowledge base are commands to the 4ESS (e.g., to request diagnostics to be run) and notifications to the technicians of problems which require further attention. These notifications come in the form of alerts and tickets. Alerts are sent to the surveillance technicians at the network control centers, who then decide what action to take. They may either ignore the alert, defer processing of the alert pending additional information, or manually create a "work order" ticket and dispatch it to the on-site work force. Members of the on-site work force are located at each 4ESS switch and can make physical equipment repairs such as replacing a faulty circuit pack. In cases where the need for physical human intervention is clear, the knowledge base may autonomously create the ticket and directly dispatch it to the on-site work force, bypassing the centralized surveillance technicians.

The main task of the knowledge base is to decide when to generate an alert or ticket. These notifications are not generated for each alarm received by the knowledge base, and hence one of the key functions of the knowledge base is to perform *alarm filtering*. For example, in many cases an alert or ticket is only generated if a threshold number of alarms is exceeded within a specified period of time. The knowledge base is just one part of ANSWER. In addition to the inputs and outputs just described, the knowledge base is also connected to a database and to users, via a graphical user interface. The database is used by ANSWER to provide persistent storage of alarms, alerts and other information, some of which is placed there by the knowledge base and some of which is placed there by other parts of the system. Users can also interact with the knowledge base via the graphical user interface to retrieve information and to set various options to customize the behavior of the knowledge base.

3.2 The Object Model

3.2.1 Overview

One of the key advantages and distinguishing characteristics of ANSWER's knowledge base is that, in addition to using rule-based programming, it also uses object-oriented technology—a technology now in widespread use in industrial applications. For object oriented technology to be useful in this context, there must be a way for the knowledge base to model the 4ESS as a collection of objects. Such an object model is shown in Figure 2 using Rumbaugh's Object Modeling Technique [17].

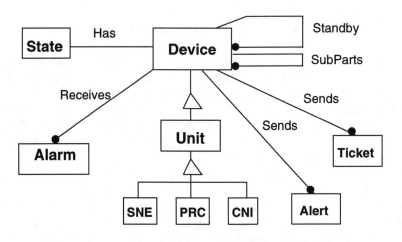

Figure 2: The 4ESS Object Model

The 4ESS is readily viewed as a collection of devices and consequently *device* is the central object in the 4ESS object model. The object model is described by the following:

- subparts: a one-to-many relation on device that allows any device (including the 4ESS itself) to be viewed as a hierarchical collection of devices

- standby: a one-to-many relation on device that specifies the devices able to take over for a device if it fails

- state: the state of a device (in-service, out-of-service, etc.) and the time it entered that state

- alarm: each device has an ordered list of alarms, which contains the alarms generated by the 4ESS on behalf of the device

- alert and ticket: these objects are associated with a device and are created when the knowledge base decides the device may require human intervention

In addition, Figure 2 specifies an inheritance hierarchy for the device class. Device is intended to represent a relatively abstract object. The device class has a subclass named Unit which represents a generic 4ESS device. Finally, the unit class has many subclasses, of which only three are shown in the figure. These subclasses represent either a very specific 4ESS hardware component (e.g., PRC represents the main processor) or a specific class of equipment that shares many common characteristics. Inheritance allows us to share and/or specialize device behavior, as appropriate. By having an object-oriented language integrated with a rule-based language, we can inherit not only methods and data members (i.e., functions and variables), but also rule-driven behavior. For example, ANSWER's PRC class only contains rules which specify behavior unique to processor devices—generic device behavior is inherited from the unit and devices classes.

3.2.2 The Device Model and Model Instantiation

Devices are the key object in our model and therefore it is important to understand how these objects are used, and in particular, how they are created. A key requirement for our model is that it be *dynamically* built from the information sent to it from the 4ESS. There are two reasons for this requirement: flexibility and efficiency. The flexibility of a dynamic model arises from the fact that no up-front configuration information is required—which is essential since each 4ESS switch is unique and components are continually added and removed. The second advantage of a dynamic model is that it permits us to model only the components which have abnormal activity, thereby reducing the size of the model and thus realizing time and space savings.

The knowledge base is driven primarily by two types of events: 4ESS alarms and one-second timer ticks. Each 4ESS alarm refers to a device by specifying up to three levels of device information (i.e., the 4ESS device hierarchy is at most 3 levels deep, excluding the 4ESS itself). At each level in the hierarchy, a device type is specified, along with an integer-valued device identifier, to ensure that each device within a 4ESS switch is unique. The timer ticks update the expert system's internal clock and drives all of its time-based behavior. A device model, which is a view of the devices in the object model at some instant in time, is shown in Figure 3. This figure will also be used to describe the device creation process.

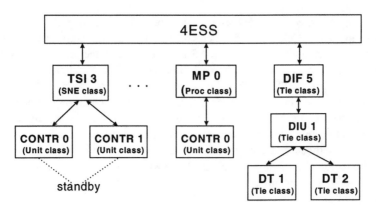

Figure 3: A Device Model

When the knowledge base receives an alarm and the device specified in the alarm doesn't already exist in the model, then it is created. The class of the device object is determined by a table lookup. For example, when a TSI:3 device is created, an object of class SNE is created. The model requires that all "ancestors" of this device (i.e., devices that contain this device) be present in the model, so if they do not already exist in the model then they are created. For example, when the knowledge base receives an alarm for the device "DIF:5 DIU:1 DT:2" it will first attempt to create the DT:2 object. However, if the DIF:5 or DIU:1 of which this DT:2 is a part do not already exist in the model, they will be created first. When devices are created, data driven rules check for "invariant" relations and create them in the model if appropriate. For example, if "TSI:3 CONTR:1" already exists in the model, then the creation of "TSI:3 CONTR:0" will cause a standby relation to be formed between these two objects. Device deletion is driven by timer events; a device is deleted if it is in the "in-service" state and has been in that state for a specified period of time.

3.3 R++: A Rule-Based Extension to C++

In order for ANSWER to make effective use of the 4ESS object model and still use rule-based inference to implement the "reasoning" in ANSWER, an implementation language was needed that supports both the object-oriented and rule-based programming paradigms and provides for the tight integration of rules and objects (e.g., so that rules can be triggered based on changes in the data members of an object). An evaluation of existing programming languages indicated that no satisfactory language was available, so R++, a rule-based extension to the C++ object oriented language, was developed.

R++ rules are considered another type of C++ member function and share the object-oriented properties of C++ member functions: inheritance, polymorphism and dynamic binding. R++ is implemented as a preprocessor which runs before the C++ compiler is invoked. Figure 4 shows the declaration of ANSWER's Device class. Note that each device's *sub_parts* and *standby* devices are specified by a set of device pointers. The optional *monitored* keyword in the class declaration identifies data members which may trigger rule evaluation. The declaration also includes the declaration of the link_standbys rule, which ensures that the standby relation is always kept up-to-date.

```
class Device {
protected:
    String                     type;        // type of device (e.g., TSI)
    int                        number;      // identifies device uniquely
    monitored State            *state;      // ptr. to device's state information
    monitored Alarm            *new_alarm;  // ptr to newest alarm received
    monitored Device           *part_of;    // points to device this is part of
    monitored Set_of_p<Device> sub_parts ;  // set of devices that are sub-parts
    monitored Set_of_p<Device> standby;     // pointer to set of standby devices

    rule link_standbys;
};
```

Figure 4: Declaration of Class "Device"

Rules have a special *if-then* syntax, where the if (antecedent) and then (consequent) parts are separated by an arrow ($\Rightarrow$). The rule in figure 5a can be translated as: *if there is a new alarm for this device and the state of a standby of this device is out-of-service, then send an alert.* R++ also provides the ability to write rules which operate on container classes, like sets and lists. Using an R++ feature called "branch binding", a rule can be applied to each element of the container (the at-sign "@" is the branch-binding operator). The rule in Figure 5b relies on the fact that there is a list called *Devices* that contains all of the devices in the model. For those not familiar with C++, the variable *this* always refers to the object itself—in the case of the rule in Figure 5b, the device on whom *link_standbys* is being performed. The antecedent of the rule in Figure 5b can be translated as: *for each device dev in the set Devices, check if dev is the standby of this device.* The consequent then updates the standby field of each device to reflect the new standby relationship.

```
// alert if get alarm and standby out of service   // link standby devices together
rule Device::alert_if_standby_out_service          rule Device::link_standbys
{                                                   {
    new_alarm &&                                        Device *dev @ Devices &&
    Device *stby = standby &&                           is_standby(dev)
    State *st = stby→state &&                       ⇒
    state→name == "out_of_service"                      this→add_standby(dev);
⇒                                                       dev→add_standby(this);
    send_alert("standby_oos, this, stby);           };
};
```
| (a) | (b) |

Figure 5: Two R++ Rules from ANSWER

The key difference between rules and ordinary C++ member functions is that changes to data members in the antecedent of the rule automatically cause the rule to be evaluated and, if the antecedent evaluates to TRUE, then the consequent is executed. Thus, rules are *data-driven*. In the example in Figure 5a, whenever a new alarm is received on a device or the state of one of its standby device changes, the rule will be automatically reevaluated. The key difference between R++ rules and rules in other rule-based languages is that R++ rules are *path-based*. This means that the antecedent of an R++ rule can only include data members which the class has access to— typically through a pointer reference. Even though R++ rules are therefore less expressive than rules in other languages (because they cannot reference arbitrary objects), this is an advantage because it ensures that R++ rules *respect the object model*. For those interested in a more in-depth understanding of R++, see [18].

3.4 Reasoning Model

The 4ESS object model provides a principled way of reasoning about the failures in the 4ESS switches. It implicitly contains information about the structure and behavior of the 4ESS. For example, if a standby relationship exists between two device objects, A and B, then device A's standby field will point to device B, and vice versa. Much of the reasoning in ANSWER is accomplished by using *affective relations*. Affective relations define a highly abstract non-behavioral representation for modeling devices and are named for the fact that one component affects another in a diagnostically important way [19, 20]. These relations are too weak to simulate device behavior, but serve to organize the domain knowledge in a coherent way; ad-hoc heuristics are replaced by a smaller set of general principles based on affective relations. Affective relations express aspects of the design at a level of abstraction that expert troubleshooters use to link symptoms to faults, and hence are easily acquired.

Two important affective relations used by ANSWER are the standby and sub-part relations. These relations are very general and can potentially apply to any device. Rules which maintain and use the standby relation were shown earlier in Figure 5. For example, the rule in Figure 5a shows how the standby relation is important for monitoring the state of the 4ESS, since this rule will cause a "warning" alert to be sent out when an alert comes in on a device whose standby is already out-of-service. The sub-part relation is very important for diagnosis, since it can be used to isolate faults. For example, ANSWER has a rule which says that if many of a device A's sub-parts fail, then the failure is most likely with device A.

It is worthwhile to compare the reasoning in ANSWER with that of its predecessor, the 4ESS-ES. In the 4ESS-ES, the reasoning was not based on affective relations, due to the lack of a general model of the 4ESS; instead, the reasoning in that system was based on many (overly) specialized ad-hoc rules. There were many cases where a single general rule was not quite adequate due to small differences in device behavior. The solution to this problem in the 4ESS-ES was to have a completely separate, nearly identical, rule for each device; the solution in ANSWER is to have a single general rule and specialize it using inheritance for the few devices which require special handling.

3.5 Discussion

ANSWER's hybrid approach of using rule-based and object-oriented technologies has proven to be highly effective. By providing an abstract device object with diagnostically motivated affective relations, a simple form of model-based reasoning was able to be applied to a domain normally too complex for such methods. Thus, this approach has led to a middle-ground between model-based reasoning and heuristic (ad-hoc) expert systems. The use of object oriented technology also provided a principled approach for designing, implementing and organizing the expert system, and is responsible for ANSWER being a more comprehensible and maintainable system than its predecessor, the 4ESS-ES. Another significant advantage of our approach is that by using a slight extension to a "mainstream" programming language for implementing the knowledge base, the entire ANSWER system could essentially be implemented using a single language. This permitted the tight integration of the knowledge base with the rest of ANSWER. In the 4ESS-ES, interface routines had to be written to allow the knowledge base's C5 code to communicate with the rest of the system. This prevented the C5 rules from being triggered by changes in other parts of the system, and this led to several artificial and sub-optimal architecture and design decisions.

ANSWER is fully deployed and is monitoring and maintaining all of AT&T's 4ESS switches. Additional operation support systems are now being implemented using R++ and the approach described in this section; in fact, some of the design and implementation work done for ANSWER is being reused on these new projects.

4 Forecasting Telecommunication Equipment Failures from Time Series Data

[jke1]The previous section described how combining object-oriented and rule-based technologies improved the development and maintainability of telecommunication-based expert systems. The example described in this section shows how data mining can improve the quality of the domain knowledge to be incorporated into such systems and also minimize the manual effort required to acquire this knowledge.

Reliability is a critical factor in the design of telecommunications networks. Errors may occur during the transmission of data over the network, but these errors can be detected and the data rerouted through alternate paths. The effect of the failure of a single component is limited due to the redundancy in modern large-scale telecommunications networks. The failure of a singular, major component, like an entire switch or a major component in a switch, is a very rare, but catastrophic event. In order to help diagnose and prevent problems before they occur, modern telecommunication equipment contains self-diagnostic testing capabilities. When any of these tests fail, an alarm message is sent to a centralized site, where it may be handled by a human or by an expert system (such as the ANSWER expert system described in the previous section). Many of these alarm messages are caused by temporary transient problems. The main objective of the data mining effort described in this section is to identify patterns of alarms that can help predict catastrophic equipment failures. These rare events may not be forecast with 100% accuracy, but their effect is so serious that identifying any increase in risk of failure is of great value.

We describe a general approach for transforming time-series data into the classical case-based representation. Standard machine learning classification methods, such as neural nets or decision trees, can then be applied to the transformed data. Predictive performance is maximized by varying a sampling period window and a prediction period window during the data transformation. We applied this technique to time-series data with 176 features over tens of thousands of cases, with the goal of forecasting a rare catastrophic failure that can occur over a massive communications network.

4.1 The Problem: Mining Time Series Data

Data mining techniques have been successfully applied to classification tasks. Many classification techniques have been researched over the past twenty years, resulting in many useful algorithms for finding predictive patterns in data. The data used in classification tasks are modeled in a standard case-based representation, where each case includes a set of feature variables and a single class variable. The prediction task is then to predict the class variable based on the feature variables. To take advantage of existing techniques, it is necessary to model the data using the case-based representation. Unfortunately, the data sets from many tasks are not naturally expressed in this standard format. Time series data, for example, are not naturally expressed in the standard case-based format and cannot be trivially converted into this format. Time series may contain one or more variables; the telecommunication alarm time series discussed later in this section contains several variables, but the simple time series presented in Figure 6 contains only a single variable.

TIME	MESSAGE
509	B
601	A
601	C
607	X
702	D
.	
.	
.	
952	A
953	C
953	X
967	B

Figure 6: Prototypical Time Series Data

In the time series in Figure 6 the number represents a time unit, perhaps seconds, and captures the ordering and positioning of each datum on a continuous time line. The message that occurred at that time is uniquely identified by a message letter (A, B, C, etc.). A general goal of our data-mining effort is to discover the pattern of alarms that identifies the pending arrival of some distinctive event. In our domain, the distinctive events are network and equipment faults, which themselves cause an alarm to be generated. Therefore, our goal is to identify a pattern of alarms that identify the pending arrival of the *target* alarm—the alarm to be predicted. In Figure 6 the target alarm is represented by the letter X. Our pattern of alarms can be thought of as the precondition of a rule, where the consequent of the rule is the prediction of the target event. A simple rule that might be induced from the data in Figure 6 is:

IF C occurs, *THEN* X occurs next.

For most real world time series and associated prediction problems, there are seldom such simple and obvious rules. Instead, a great deal of processing power, data modeling and machine learning are required to induce the rules. For these time series, not only do we not know what pattern of messages are strongly predictive of an event, we also do not know how far back in time to search for the predictive patterns. Similarly, we do not know how far into the future we can successfully predict the occurrence of the interesting event. A data-mining technique is needed that systematically varies window sizes in order to maximize the predictive performance of the rules uncovered by the classification method. The techniques that we describe have been applied to a very large database of time series data that represents alarm messages that are emitted by equipment in a large telecommunications network. There were 176 different message types with nearly one million separate messages. Our objective was to predict *extremely* rare, network critical failures.

4.1.1 Models for Representing Time Series Data

A standard model for representing data for classification tasks is shown in Figure 7. In this spreadsheet format, each row represents a single case. For each case, the columns represent the values of features, F_1 through F_n. The example data shown in the figure are numeric, but nominal or categorical features (such as true and false) are also possible. In fact, for our particular task of predicting network equipment failures, the features were categorical and included features such as the type of alarm and the name of the equipment reporting the problem. The final column in the figure, C, is special because it contains the class of the case—that is, the value the classification task is attempting to predict. While multiple values (such as, child, teen, adult, senior) or numeric ranges (such as, Age > 35) are possible, the class variable is usually binary (e.g., 1 indicates a fault will occur and a 0 that a fault will not occur).

	F_1	F_2	F_3	...	F_n	C
S_1	1	3	20	...	9	1
S_2	0	6	15	...	8	0
S_3	1	7	8	...	10	0
S_4	1	4	6	...	7	1
.	.	.	.	...	.	.
.	.	.	.	...	.	.
.	.	.	.	...	.	.
S_n	0	1	2	...	5	1

Figure 7: Standard Case-Based Format for a Classification Task

Our goal is to model time-series data using the standard classification format shown in Figure 7. One area of research that has successfully dealt with time ordered data is time series analysis. Figure 8 shows a typical time-series analysis problem involving unit sales data of a fictitious product. The figure shows that the unit sales for today is 56. It also shows the sales of the product in the previous 5 days, t-1 through t-5.

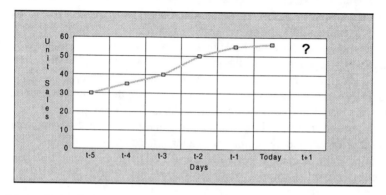

Figure 8: An Ordered Time Series of Unit Sales for a Fictitious Product

A time-series analysis of unit sales might attempt to predict the unit sales for tomorrow (time t+1) by looking at the prior unit sales. The following is a hypothetical equation for forecasting future sales:

$$S_{t+1} = (w * S_t) + \left((1-w) * \left(\left(\sum_{i=1}^{n} S_{t-i} \right) / n \right) \right)$$

Equation 1: A time-series analysis equation to forecast sales

The equation shows that tomorrow's unit sales is a weighted function of the current sales and the average of the previous days sales, where the weight is w and the number of previous days is n. This "linear" approach is the classical forecasting method. The classical time-series approach cannot be readily applied to certain complex data-mining tasks. In Figure 8, the measure of sales was a continuous variable, whereas we are interested in predicting a discrete, categorical, class variable—the event corresponding to a catastrophic failure of switching equipment. Furthermore, the features we use to make this prediction, the fields in the alarm messages, are also categorical. Classical time-series analysis requires numerical features. Also, time-series analysis has been most successful when the measured variables are univariate. In the sales example, there is only one measure, unit sales each day. In fact, what this equation suggests is that today's sales is a strong indicator of tomorrow's sales. It is a very different situation when the raw data are time-stamped messages that are used to forecast rare catastrophic events. Events are discrete, that is, they either occur or they do not. Also, these data involve many different variables.

It is fascinating to see how time-series analysis repeatedly uses the same data over and over to make predictions. Our approach borrows a few concepts from classical linear time-series analysis to learn rules that will forecast a future event. At any point in time, we look backward a fixed unit of time and observe the count of each message type. Then we look forward some other fixed unit of time and observe whether the crucial event occurred. As a simple example, suppose that there are only three types of messages: A, B and X messages and it is the X message we want to predict. As shown in Figure 9, it is possible to look back from any point in time and determine the frequency of A and B messages (and possibly X messages) and then look forward into the future to determine if any X message has occurred.

```
                    PAST          CURRENT        FUTURE
S₀  |--------A--------B----B-----------A-------|-----------------------X--------------|
              Monitor Window                    Prediction Window
```

Figure 9: Using the Past to Predict the Future

Each case is represented by a monitor window, M, and a prediction window, P. The monitor window contains the messages that are monitored in order to make a prediction about the future and the prediction window is scanned for the alarms that we are trying to predict (i.e., determines the class of the case).

Figure 10 demonstrates the process of generating cases from a time series by repeatedly shifting the window forward by one prediction window. The top of the figure shows the alarms on a continuous time line and below that are the separate cases, S_1 - S_n.

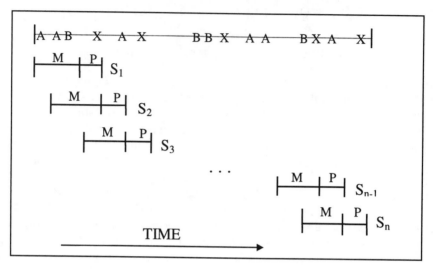

Figure 10: Samples of Monitor and Prediction Windows Across Time

From the time series we can now generate a case-based representation of the data. Each message type (A, B and X) corresponds to one of the features in Figure 7 and the value of each feature is the frequency count of that message in the monitor window. The value of the classification variable (the C of the last column in Figure 7) becomes either the frequency count of the target alarm in the prediction window or a 1 (or 0) to indicate the presence (or absence) of the target alarm in the prediction window. In this chapter we use the later encoding for the class variable, since we are only concerned with whether the target alarm occurs or not. The case-based representation of the time-series data in Figure 9 is shown in the first row of Figure 11 and the first three samples from Figure 10, S_1 - S_3, are shown in the following three lines. The entry for S_1 in Figure 11 indicates that there are two messages of type A and one message of type B within the monitor window, no X alarms within the monitor window and that the target message, X, does occur in the prediction window. This method of modeling time-series data is very general and can be applied to any data regardless of number of variables, window sizes and period of time.

	A	B	X	C
S_0	2	2	0	1
S_1	2	1	0	1
S_2	1	1	1	0
S_3	1	0	1	1

Figure 11: Case-Based Representation of Time-Series Data

4.1.2 Exploring Window Sizes

Selecting the monitor window size is difficult when predicting the occurrence of rare events in communication networks. The messages in this domain are tracked to the second. There is nothing in the domain that suggests how to help decide how far back into the past to look for a pattern of messages. The problem is to discover where in time the critical information lies that indicates an upcoming catastrophic event. Is it important to monitor the messages that occurred in the previous fifteen minutes? In the previous hour, day, week, or even month? Without some special understanding about this domain it is not possible to know a priori what size monitor window is appropriate. The data must be mined by exploring various sizes of the monitor window.

Similarly, there must be a fixed size for the prediction window of time for forecasting the predicted event. It is useless to merely say that sometime in the future the event we are looking for will occur. In many domains it is always the case that the event will eventually occur. It is necessary to say an event will occur in the next hour, the next day, or some other time unit. Again, it is necessary to mine the data by exploration to discover what prediction window works for a particular task. While a priori we do not know anything about the sizes of the windows that will help us forecast events, we do know some desirable characteristics of the window sizes. For the monitor window, we prefer that the window is small rather than large, since, for example, it is simpler to keep track of the messages from the previous fifteen minutes than from the previous hour. The prediction window requires more of a balancing act. Too short of a prediction window will lead to predictions which are not useful. For example, when predicting a failure in a telecommunication network, it is necessary to predict the failure far enough in advance so that there is enough time to repair or reroute around the failure before it occurs; however, if the prediction window is too large, then the predictions may be meaningless (e.g., predicting that a failure will occur sometime in the next two years is not typically a useful prediction). Given the amount of time that it takes to execute most learning algorithms on large amounts of data, it is impractical to explore all possible window sizes. Figure 12 describes a reasonable procedure for mining the data with a pre-selected list of window sizes.

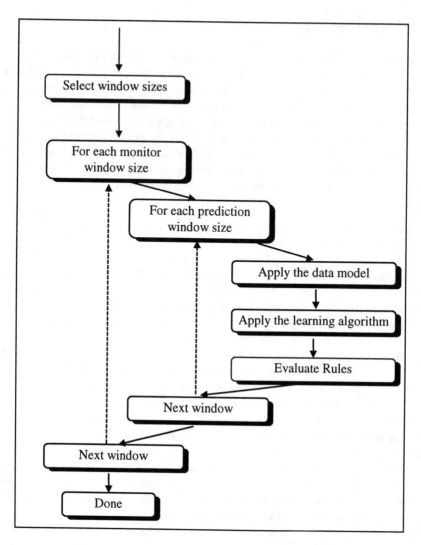

Figure 12: Algorithm for Data Mining with Various Window Sizes

4.1.3 Testing the Model on a Large Database

The massive AT&T communication network is made up of high-capacity communication links connected by telecommunication switches. The total number of switches is surprisingly small, fewer than 150, even though the network spans the entire continental United States. The complete failure of a switch is a potentially catastrophic event. AT&T uses many strategies to minimize the effects of a complete switch failure on network traffic. Network traffic can immediately and automatically be routed through other switches by sophisticated software that observes the network traffic flow as a whole. The rerouting occurs on excess network capacity that is specifically provided to handle any congestion problems. AT&T also has many years of experience in designing and building fault tolerant control software that is embedded in the switches. The result is that a catastrophic switch failure is extremely unlikely and its effects are handled by excess network capacity so loss of network call traffic is minimized. Nonetheless, while the failure of a switch is rare, when it does occur the consequences are serious. Ideally, it would be best to forecast the occurrence of a failure and correct it before it occurs or at least minimize its effects by rerouting the calls prior to the failure.

We studied a historical database that contains alarm messages of over 50 switches for a period of two months. Switches generate nearly 100,000 alarm messages a week. Our database was filtered to somewhat less than 1 million alarm messages with fewer than 50 failures. Furthermore, many of these failures were bunched in time, indicating that there was only a single failure. While the goal is to forecast a catastrophic event, the paucity of cases for the failure events would require extremely strong predictors to achieve high accuracy forecasts. An alternative strategy is to identify some patterns that are highly predictive, but forecast only a subset of the catastrophic events (i.e., to trade-off recall for higher precision). Experiments were performed with varying time periods for the monitor and prediction window. The SWAP-1 rule induction system was used and learned prediction rules of the form: "If A and B occur in the monitor period, then a failure will occur in the prediction period." The best results were achieved when the monitor and prediction windows were both set to 15 minutes. Not all failures could be predicted accurately, but two patterns were identified that occurred prior to failures but never prior to normal periods. These results indicate that further study is warranted. However, before a more comprehensive study can be undertaken, more data must be obtained. In our case the problem isn't so much the lack of data, but rather the scarcity of failures within the data.

5 Conclusion

This chapter has described several intelligent telecommunication technologies and applications. Two technologies were highlighted: expert system technology and data mining technology. Expert system technology is the more mature technology, with many commercial successes over the past two decades. This chapter's description of ANSWER shows how object technology—a technology which is enjoying great commercial success—can be integrated with rule-based technology to make it easier to develop and maintain an expert system.

Both rule-based expert system and data mining technologies help the telecommunications industry deal with the large quantities of available data. For example, the ANSWER expert system processes thousands of alarm messages daily and from these is able to diagnose equipment problems. In this case, the knowledge contained within the expert system was manually acquired from domain experts. Data mining technology, however, allows useful knowledge to be automatically acquired directly from the data. This was demonstrated by several of the applications in Section 2 and by the data mining application in Section 4, which is an attempt to supplement the manually acquired rules in ANSWER with rules automatically acquired via data mining. While it is unlikely that data mining will totally eliminate the need to acquire knowledge from human experts, data mining technology is making significant contributions to the telecommunications industry and we expect these contributions to accelerate as advances are made in this relatively new technology.

References

[1] Weiss, S., Indurkhya, N. (1998), *Predictive Data Mining: A Practical Guide*, Morgan Kaufmann, San Francisco.

[2] Hayes-Roth, F., Waterman, D., Lenat, D. eds. (1983), *Building Expert Systems*, Addison-Wesley, Reading. MA.

[3] Crawford, J., Dvorak, D., Litman, D., Mishra, A., Patel-Schneider, P. (1995), Device Representation and Reasoning with Affective Relations, *Proceedings of the Fourteenth International Conference on Artificial Intelligence* (IJCAI-95), pp. 1814-1820, Montreal, Quebec, Canada.

[4] Fayyad, U., Piatetsky-Shapiro, G., Smyth, P. (1996), From Data Mining to Knowledge Discovery: An Overview, *Advances in Knowledge Discovery and Data Mining*, Fayyad, U., Piatetsky-Shapiro, G., Smyth, P, Uthurusamy, R., eds., MIT Press, pp. 1-34.

[5] Brachman, R., Anand, T. (1996), The Process of Knowledge Discovery in Databases, *Advances in Knowledge Discovery and Data Mining*, Fayyad, U., Piatetsky-Shapiro, G., Smyth, P., Uthurusamy, R., eds., MIT Press, pp. 37-57.

[6] Weiss, S., Indurkhya, N. (1993), Optimized Rule Induction, *IEEE Expert*, Vol. 8, No. 6, pp. 61-69.

[7] Hedberg, S. (1996), AI's Impact in Telecommunications—Today and Tomorrow, *IEEE Expert*, Vol. 11, No, 1, Feb., pp. 6-9.

[8] Rabinowitz, H., Flamholz, J., Wolin, E., Euchner, J. (1991), NYNEX MAX: A Telephone Trouble Screening Expert, *Innovative Applications of Artificial Intelligence 3*, Smith, R. & Scott, C., eds., AAAI Press, Menlo Park, CA, pp. 213-230.

[9] Merz, C., Pazzani, M., Danyluk, A. (1996), Tuning Numeric Parameters to Troubleshoot a Telephone-Network Loop, *IEEE Expert*, Vol. 11, No. 1, Feb., pp. 44-49.

[10] Chen, C., Hollidge, T., Sharma, D. (1996), Localization of Troubles in Telephone Cable Networks, *Innovative Applications of Artificial Intelligence*, Vol. 2, AAAI Press, Menlo Park, CA, pp. 1461-1470.

[11] Pearl, J. (1988), *Probabilistic Reasoning in Intelligent Systems: Networks of Plausible Inference*, Morgan Kaufmann, San Francisco.

[12] Hatonen, K., Klemettinen, M., Mannila, H., Ronkainen, P., Toivonen, H. (1996), Knowledge Discovery from Telecommunication Network Alarm Databases, *Twelfth International Conference on Data Engineering* (ICDE'96), New Orleans, Louisiana.

[13] Mannila, H., Toivonen, H., Verkamo, A. (1995), Discovering Frequent Episodes in Sequences, *First International Conference on Knowledge Discovery and Data Mining (KDD '95)*, pp. 210-215, Montreal, Canada, AAAI Press.

[14] Sasisekharan, R., Seshadri, V., Weiss, S. (1996), Data Mining and Forecasting in Large-Scale Telecommunication Networks, *IEEE Expert*, Vol. 11, No. 1, Feb., pp. 37-43.

[15] Cooper, T., Wogrin, N. (1988), *Rule-Based Programming with OPS5*, Morgan Kaufmann, San Mateo, CA.

[16] Ezawa, K., Norton, S. (1996), Constructing Bayesian Networks to Predict Uncollectible Telecommunication Accounts, *IEEE Expert*, Vol. 11, No. 5, Oct., pp. 45-50.

[17] Rumbaugh, J., Blaha, M., Premerlani, W., Eddy, F. (1991), *Object-Modeling and Design*, Prentice Hall.

[18] R++ home page: http://www.research.att.com/sw/tools/r++.

[19] Singhal, A., Weiss, G. M., Ros, J. (1996), A Model Based Reasoning Approach to Network Monitoring, *Proceedings of the ACM Workshop on Databases for Active and Real Time Systems* (DART '96), Rockville, Maryland, pp. 41-44.

[20] Mishra, A., Ros, J., Singhal, A., Weiss, G., Litman, D., Patel-Schneider, P., Dvorak, D., Crawford, J. (1996), R++: Using Rules in Object-Oriented Designs, *Addendum Object-Oriented Programming Systems, Languages, and Applications* (OOPSLA).

Chapter 9:

Immune Network-Based Distributed Diagnostic System

IMMUNE NETWORK-BASED DISTRIBUTED DIAGNOSTIC SYSTEM

M. Kayama
Hitachi Research Laboratory
Hitachi Ltd.
Japan

In this chapter, the immune network-based distributed diagnosis system is introduced as a typical intelligent sensor diagnostic technique in control plants. Conventionally when some trouble occurs in a control plant, such as deterioration of control accuracy, it is not easy to know its causes or specify faulty signals or sensor outputs. However using this diagnosis technique, faulty signals can be detected by using the mechanism of a biological immune system, which finds foreign intruding matter by mutual recognition between antibodies. The diagnosis system is especially suited to identify faulty sensors, such as age deteriorated ones, for example, which have been difficult to detect only by checking each sensor output independently. Therefore our system is expected to contribute to advanced preventive maintenance for industrial systems.

After describing the biological immune system briefly, the Immune Network for the sensor diagnostic system is presented in detail. Namely, several diagnostic functions are reviewed and their diagnosis capability compared. Learning Vector Quantization (LVQ) is also discussed as a way to generate the Immune Network automatically with data obtained from actual plants. Finally the immune diagnosis system is applied to several industrial plants and their effectiveness is evaluated.

1   Introduction

Higher reliability is demanded as industrial plants become larger and more complex. For this, it is necessary to avoid fault occurrence by detecting fault symptoms promptly and to prevent fault propagation through proper specification of faulty parts when faults occur.

In this chapter, we present sensor diagnostic techniques and introduce a distributed diagnosis system using the Immune Network [1] - [4] to detect abnormal sensor outputs accurately in a control system which includes many sensors. First we discuss the Immune Network from the viewpoint of biological and engineering immune

0-8493-9803-7/99/$0.00+$.50
© 1999 by CRC Press LLC

systems. To apply it to various kinds of diagnoses, several diagnosis functions are reviewed briefly. Then techniques to implement the immune diagnosis system and improve its diagnosis capability are investigated. Namely to create the Immune Network automatically by training with data obtained from an actual plant, we propose it to combine with the Learning Vector Quantization (LVQ) [5]. The developed system has two execution modes, namely, its training mode, where the LVQ extracts a correlation between every two sensors from their outputs when they work properly, and its diagnosis mode, where the LVQ contributes to testing every two sensors using the extracted correlation, and the Immune Network contributes to determining faulty sensors by integrating the local testing results obtained from the LVQ. Two methods to improve diagnosis capability of the developed system are also discussed. First we propose to judge whether testing data satisfy the correlation or not by mutual consent of several of their neighbor quantization vectors. For this, fuzziness is introduced for each quantization vector to calculate its contribution for testing data and to obtain the mutual consent easily. The proposed method is expected to decrease the misrecognition where normal testing data are classified as abnormal ones. As the second method, adaptive optimization of a threshold of quantization vectors for the judgment is investigated to avoid a meaningless conclusion being introduced by the diagnosis theorem [6].

Finally the immune diagnosis system is applied to several industrial plants, including temperature sensor diagnosis of the reheating furnace plant of a hot strip mill line, sensor output diagnosis of a cement plant, and breakout prediction for a continuous casting process, and their effectiveness is evaluated.

2   The Immune Network

2.1   Biological Immune System

The biological immune system consists of enormous numbers of lymphocytes classified into B-lymphocytes and T-lymphocytes. B-lymphocytes are cells, which yield antibody from their surface. T-lymphocytes help to regulate the activity of B-cells in antibody production. The antibody specifically recognizes an antigen, which is foreign intruding matter from outside by using a lock and key relationship. Then the antibody suppresses the antigen activity.

It has been proposed that there are also lock and key relationships between antibodies to stimulate and suppress each other, as well as those between an antibody and an antigen [7]-[9]. According to the hypothesis, the biological immune system, which had been regarded as a cell level recognition system, can be considered to be a concurrent, parallel and global recognition network system. From this viewpoint, antibodies and antigens do not have to be distinguished in this system, which constructs a mutual interaction network for recognizing other antibodies and antigens as to whether they are foreign matter or not.

Figure 1 is a schematic illustration describing the hypothetical immune network of Jerne. Many B-cells are connected by stimulation and suppression relationships through antibodies in the recognition network. Epitope, which is a foreign matter, is also connected through an antigen. In the figure, idiotope 1 (Id1) of antibody 1 stimulates B-cell 2, which attaches antibody 2 to B-cell 2 surface, through paratope 2 (P2). Viewed from the standpoint of antibody 2, idiotope 1 of antibody 1 works simultaneously as an antigen. As a result, B-cell 1 with antibody 1 is suppressed by antibody 2, while antibody 3 stimulates antibody 1 since the idiotope 3 of antibody 3 works as an antigen when viewed from antibody 1. In this way, these stimulation and suppression chains among antibodies construct a large-scaled chain network which works as a self and a not-self recognition system.

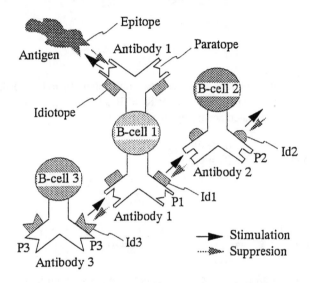

Figure 1. Jerne's idiotypic network hypothesis.

2.2 Structure of the Immune Network

The engineering immune network is an information processing method to which the biological immune network model represented in the previous section is applied. Figure 2 shows the Immune Network [1] - [3] proposed by Dr. Ishida and discussed in this chapter. Each unit corresponds to a sensor in the control system, where each unit tests other sensors as to whether their outputs are normal or not. So in the figure, u_1 tests u_2 and u_3, and u_2 tests u_3 and u_4, for example. T_{ij}, which is a weighted value of a synapse connecting units i and j, indicates the result that u_i tests u_j, as determined by equation (1).

$$T_{ij} = \left\{ \begin{array}{ll} 1 & (u_i \text{ judges the output of } u_j \text{ is correct}) \\ -1 & (u_i \text{ judges the output of } u_j \text{ is not correct}) \end{array} \right\} \quad (1)$$

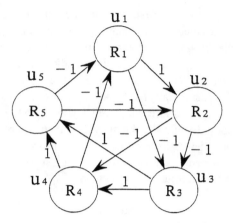

Figure 2. Immune Network.

R_i is reliability of unit i, namely, it is the maximum when $R_i = 1$, and the minimum when $R_i = 0$. To obtain the reliability vector $\mathbf{R} = (R_1, R_2, R_3 \ldots\ldots, R_n)$, u_i is selected randomly, and its R_i is updated according to equation (2):

$$R_i = \begin{cases} 1 & (D > 0) \\ \text{no change} & (D = 0) \\ 0 & (D < 0) \end{cases} \qquad (2)$$

$$D = \sum_{j=1\,(j \neq i)}^{n} T_{ji}R_j + \sum_{j=1\,(j \neq i)}^{n} T_{ij}R_j - (1/2) \sum_{e_{ij} \in \Omega_i} (T_{ij}+1) \qquad (3)$$

where Ω_i is the set of all tests done by u_i, e_{ij} is the synapse from u_i to u_j, and n is the number of units (number of sensors)

Equation (3) is a diagnosis function, where the first term on its right hand side is determined by integrating judgments of other units whether unit i is normal or not and its second term is decided by judgments of unit i for other units. When unit i judges normal units as abnormal ones or abnormal units as normal ones, the second term is smaller, which contributes to decreasing the D value. The equation (3) is the most primitive diagnosis function, which works for completed diagnosis and unsynchronized convergence execution. Other diagnosis functions, which have been proposed for incomplete or fuzzy diagnoses and synchronized convergence execution, are described in the next section. By repeating this execution, the reliability vector $\mathbf{R}$ converges to a certain value. Thus, faulty sensors can be specified by checking whether each R_i is 0 or 1.

Correspondence between the Immune Network and biological immune system, which is a mutual recognition network system as described in the previous section, can be considered as follows [1]-[3]. Unit u_i can be considered as B-cells yielding antibody, while their reliability R_i corresponds to their activity. $T_{ij} = 1$ means that B-cell i recognizes antibody of type j as a self-matter, while $T_{ij} = -1$ means that B-cell i recognizes antibody of type j, or antigen in the biological immune system, as foreign matter. In the biological immune systems, activity of antigen recognized as self-matter by other B-cells increases to the maximum, while activity of antigen recognized as foreign matter decreases, through mutual stimulation and suppression relationships. B-cells whose activity is decreased lose some of their ability to stimulate or suppress other B-cells. Through such mutual interactions, B-cells completely losing their activity cannot yield more antibody and are excluded from the living thing. The activity corresponds to reliability in the immune diagnostic system, where small activity units are specified as small reliability ones. Accordingly the signed graph described in Figure 2 was named the Immune Network.

2.3   Several Diagnosis Functions [3]

Before describing other diagnosis functions, equation (3) is modified to a synchronized equation and its convergence characteristics are discussed. The following dynamic equation can be defined, corresponding to equation (3).

$$\frac{dr_i(t)}{dt} = \sum_{j=1\,(j\ne 1)}^{n} T_{ji}^{*}\, R_j(t) - (1/2) \sum_{e_{ij} \in \Omega_i} (T_{ij} + 1) \tag{4}$$

where

$$R_i(t) = \frac{1}{1 + \exp\left(-r_i(t)\right)} \tag{5}$$

$$\tag{6}$$

From equation (4), there are competitive interactions between units, namely when T_{ij} is 1, $R_j = 1$ stimulates R_i to be 1, while when T_{ij} is -1, $R_j = 1$ suppresses it to be 0. The Liapnov function of equation (4) is represented by equation (7).

$$V(t) = -\sum_{i=1}^{n} \int_{0}^{r_i} \{(-1/2) \sum_{e_{ij} \in \Omega_i} (T_{ij} + 1)\}\, R_i'(y_i) dy_i$$

$$- (1/2) \sum_{i,j=1}^{n} T_{ij}^{*} R_i(t) R_j(t) \tag{7}$$

where

$$dV(t)/dt = -\sum_{i=1}^{n} R'_i(r_i) \{-(1/2) \sum_{e_{ij} \in \Omega_i} (T_{ij} + 1) + \sum_{j=1}^{n} T^*_{ij} R_j(t)\}^2$$

$$\leq 0 \tag{8}$$

Since a differential value of the Liapnov function is always smaller than 0, the energy of equation (4) decreases monotonously through the interactive execution between units. Therefore the convergence state of the Immune Network with the diagnosis function of equation (4) is proved to be a coherent diagnosis result based on testing results between units.

For diagnosis using equations (3) and (4), we assumed completeness of tests done by normal units, namely when R_i is 1, $T_{ij} = 1$ and $T_{ij} = -1$ mean $R_j = 1$ and -1, respectively. However the assumption is not always true in practical diagnoses, because tests between two units are not always complete. Tests done by inequality, for example, can possibly overlook an abnormal condition. The following diagnosis function is proposed for such incomplete diagnoses.

$$\frac{dr_i(t)}{dt} = \sum_{j=1 \, (j \neq i)}^{n} T^+_{ji} R_j(t) \tag{9}$$

$$T^+_{ij} = \begin{cases} T_{ij} + T_{ji} - 1 & \text{(Either } e_{ij} \text{ or } e_{ji} \text{ exists)} \\ 0 & \text{(Neither } e_{ij} \text{ nor } e_{ji} \text{ exists)} \end{cases} \tag{10}$$

In these two diagnosis functions, strict diagnosis conclusion, whereby each sensor is sure to be specified as to whether it is normal or abnormal, is given by the converged network. However, in some practical cases, when it is not certain which units are abnormal, it is not good to introduce fault occurrence of certain units arbitrarily. The following diagnosis functions have been proposed for allowing such fuzzy states for a diagnostic conclusion.

$$\frac{dr_i(t)}{dt} = \sum_{j=1 \, (j \neq i)}^{n} T^*_{ji} R_j(t) - (1/2) \sum_{e_{ij} \in \Omega_i} (T_{ij} + 1) - r_i(t) \tag{11}$$

$$\frac{dr_i(t)}{dt} = \sum_{j=1 \, (j \neq i)}^{n} T^+_{ji} R_j(t) - r_i(t) \tag{12}$$

By adding $- r_i(t)$ term to the right hand of equations (11) and (12), reliability of each unit retains its current value as calculated by the sum of other unit opinions without converging to its maximum or minimum value. The diagnoses by equations (4), (9), (11), and (12) have been named as complete test, incomplete test, fuzzy complete test, and fuzzy incomplete test models, respectively[3].

2.4 Determination of Synapse Values [10][11]

The first thing to be done for the diagnosis with the Immune Network is determination of T_{ij} for each synapse. To do this, we have to find sensor pairs correlated to each other in the control system, and represent their correlation by an equality or an inequality, for example. However, this is not so easy.

In this chapter, we investigate extraction of the correlation between every two sensors from training data collected from an actual plant during its normal working. As a suitable method to utilize time series data obtained from the plant continuously, the Learning Vector Quantization (LVQ) is introduced to extract the relationship between a pair of sensor outputs, where the correlation is accumulated as a set of quantization vectors in each quantization vector space.

Figure 3 describes the architecture of the proposed diagnosis system consisting of the LVQ and the Immune Network [10]-[12]. The developed system has two execution modes, namely, training and diagnosis modes. In the training mode, for training datum X_t, which is a set of sensor outputs from the plant, the Q_J which maximizes the value of $|X_t - Q_j|$ is extracted from $Q_1 - Q_j - Q_m$, where Q_j is the j-th quantization vector among m quantization vectors in total, and Q_J is updated by the following equation:

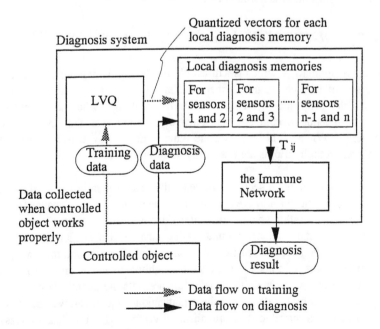

Figure 3. Architecture of the diagnosis system combining the immune network and LVQ.

$$Q^*_J = Q_J + \alpha \cdot (X_t - Q_j) \qquad\qquad (13)$$

where Q^*_J is an updated quantization vector and α is a training coefficient.

The above equation is calculated continuously for each quantization vector space to obtain converged quantization vectors, which are stored in the local diagnosis memories. From these executions, the correlation between each sensor pair during the normal working of the plant is extracted. This correlation is represented by the coordinates of the quantization vectors in each quantization vector space.

In the diagnosis mode, testing results T_{ij} are determined in each quantization vector space, depending on the degree of similarity between diagnosis data and data obtained from the normal working plant. Namely, according to whether the following d^2 calculated for Q_J, which has the minimum distance from the diagnosis data among Q_1 - Q_j - Q_m in the local diagnosis memory, is smaller than a certain value θ or not, each T_{ij} of the Immune Network is determined.

$$d^2 = (1/r) \cdot (X_t - Q_j)^2 \qquad\qquad (14)$$

The r is the dimension of the quantization vector, which is two or more, if necessary, as described in [10][11]. The Immune Network collects T_{ij} from all local diagnosis memories, performs the execution described in the previous section, and indicates whether each sensor output is normal or not.

2.5   Improvement of Diagnosis Capability [12]

Determining the optimal θ, which is a threshold for distinguishing whether testing data are normal or not in each diagnosis memory, is important for improving diagnosis capability of the proposed system. Generally speaking, when θ is small, the diagnosis system tends to conclude that a sensor is faulty even though every sensor works properly. When θ is large, on the other hand, the system can detect faulty sensors only when their outputs are drastically abnormal.

As mentioned in the previous section, conventional testing data in the local diagnosis memory are judged whether they are normal or not dependent on the distance from their nearest neighbor quantization vector. However since each test for classification is done by only one quantization vector, normal testing data located sufficiently inside the normal region are often recognized as abnormal ones. To overcome this, we present the judgment by mutual consent of several neighbor quantization vectors. One approach is to introduce a probability density function into the quantization vectors and to classify testing data by the density of the quantization vectors. However, for simple execution, fuzziness is introduced for quantization vectors. Testing data are classified by the integrated contributions of several quantization vectors as shown below. We define the following diagnosis function.

$$J_f = \sum_{i=1}^{m} g(i) \tag{15}$$

The g(i) is a fuzzy function shown in Figure 4, which is represented by equation (16).

$$g(i) = \begin{cases} 1 & (d_i^2 < \theta) \\ (\theta + \varepsilon - d_i^2)/\varepsilon & (\theta \leq d_i^2 < \theta + \varepsilon) \\ 0 & (\theta + \varepsilon \leq d_i^2) \end{cases} \tag{16}$$

$$d_i^2 = |X_t - Q_i|^2 \tag{17}$$

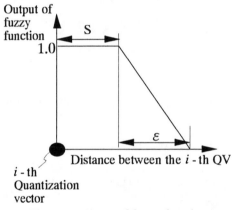

Figure 4. Shape of fuzzy function.

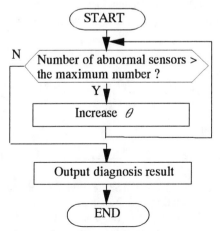

Figure 5. Algorithm for increasing θ adaptively.

where m is the number of quantization vectors, θ is the threshold of the quantization vectors, and ε is the gradient of the fuzzy function. When J_f calculated for a testing datum is larger than a certain value J_{th}, the datum is classified as normal. Since more quantization vectors usually exist near a testing datum inside the normal region, even though the distance from the nearest one is rather large, this method can decrease misclassification where normal testing data are classified as abnormal ones.

Additionally, to obtain more reliable diagnosis, θ is modified adaptively when diagnosing under real time conditions. As shown in Figure 5, when the number of abnormal sensors is larger than the maximum number defined by the diagnosis theorem [6], θ is continuously increased until the number of sensors is equal to it. Since a meaningless diagnostic conclusion is transformed to a meaningful one by this real time execution, the diagnosis reliability can be improved.

3   Application of the Immune Network To System Diagnosis Problems

3.1   Sensor Diagnosis of Reheating Furnace Plant

3.1.1   Simulation Conditions

First we simulate the capability of the system combining the Immune Network and the LVQ using the diagnosis provided by temperature sensors for a reheating furnace plant of a hot strip mill line. Figure 6 is a schematic illustration of the reheating furnace plant consisting of four heating rooms. Conventionally, temperature sensors are checked manually for their accuracy, after the reheating furnace has stopped operation, which is very time and cost consuming. It is desirable to check their accuracy automatically under working conditions.

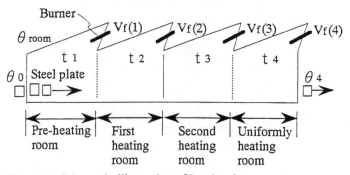

Figure 6. Schematic illustration of heating furnace plant.

To simplify the simulation, temperature of each heating room is assumed to be uniform. The Immune Network is constructed with four units corresponding to four temperature sensors. Since each temperature sensor is included in a feedback control loop for each heating room, where actuating values are energy magnitudes of burners $V_t(1) - V_t(4)$, and control values are $t_1 - t_4$, even when the sensor outputs are abnormal, the energy magnitudes of the burners are changed to make $t_1 - t_4$ agree with their set values. Therefore, we cannot detect abnormal sensors only by checking their outputs. To overcome this, as reported in our published papers [10][12], we consider closed correlations consisting of sensor outputs and other correlative state variables, such as the amount of energy being consumed by each burner, and we define all sensor outputs and state variables as axes of each quantization vector space.

We consider that input steel temperature θ_0, output steel temperature θ_4, room temperature θ_{room}, and energy amounts being consumed in the burners $V_t(1) - V_t(4)$ are other measurable state variables. By using them, four closed correlations consisting of $(t_1, t_2, V_t(1), V_t(2), \theta_0, \theta_{room})$, $(t_2, t_3, V_t(2), V_t(3), \theta_{room})$, $(t_3, t_4, V_t(3), V_t(4), \theta_{room})$, and $(t_4, t_1, V_t(1), V_t(2), V_t(3), V_t(4), \theta_0, \theta_4, \theta_{room})$ can be introduced from the energy flow balance of each heating room. On the assumption that θ_0, θ_4, θ_{room} and $V_t(1) - V_t(4)$ are reliable enough, the result that t_1 and t_2 test each other is

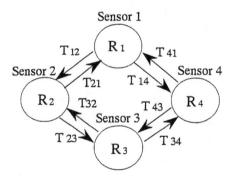

Figure 7. Immune network for diagnosing temperature sensor outputs of a reheating furnace plant.

Table 1. Simulation conditions.

Parameters	Values
Kind of steel	Carbon steel
Thickness of plate	0.2 m
θ_{room}	$0 - 30°C$
θ_0	$0 - 30°C$ (Cold charge) $400 - 550°C$ (Hot charge)
θ_4	$1000 - 1200°C$

obtained from the first closed correlation. In the same way, testing results of t_2 and t_3, t_3 and t_4, and t_4 and t_1 are given by the three other closed correlations. Figure 7 shows the Immune Network used for the temperature sensors diagnosis, including 4 units and 8 synapses, where T_{ij} is equal to T_{ji}.

Data for the simulation are collected with the heating furnace simulator developed previously [13]. Normal data used for training (training data) consist of 1344 sets, where several working conditions, such as θ_0, θ_4, and θ_{room}, are different, while normal data for diagnosis (normal diagnosis data) consist of 47 sets. In the same way, abnormal data used for diagnosis (abnormal diagnosis data) consist of 134 sets for each sensor and its output error value. Four output errors of 5, 10, 15, and 20°C are assumed for abnormal diagnosis data. Table 1 lists simulation conditions.

3.1.2 Simulation Results and Discussion

First, an example of the antibody reaction in vector quantization spaces (local diagnosis memories) is introduced. In the Immune network described in Figure 7, according to the diagnosis theorem [6], the maximum number of abnormal sensors which can be specified concurrently is one. Thus, we assume the occurrence of a single sensor fault without taking account of concurrent faults. In this simulation, each d^2 of equation (14) calculated in the corresponding vector quantization space, which is the distance between

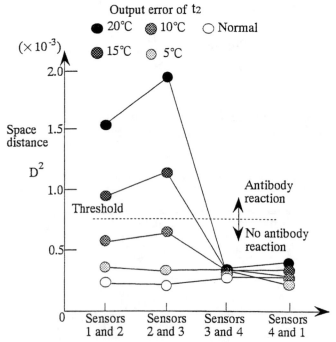

Figure 8. Antibody reaction in vector quantization spaces.

the diagnosis datum and its nearest neighbor quantization vector, indicates the extent of the immune body reaction. Figure 8 shows d^2 in vector quantization spaces, which have 40 quantization vectors, calculated by averaging 134 abnormal data, when sensor 2 has an output error.

In the figure, when a sensor fault occurs, d^2 of the two sensor pairs corresponding to the faulty sensor increases by the amount of its output error. The suitable threshold θ can be easily determined for their output error larger than 10°C. Figure 9 shows convergence behavior of the Immune Network, when the correct T_{ij} is set for each synapse of the Immune network under the suitable θ. Since this network is small, there is no convergence problem. Starting from the initial R=(1, 1, 1, 1), which indicates all sensors are normal, it converges to (1, 0, 1, 1), which concludes that the output of sensor 2 is abnormal. From this simulation, our system can specify the faulty sensor whose output error is larger than 10°C, when it is possible to collect various test data under faulty conditions.

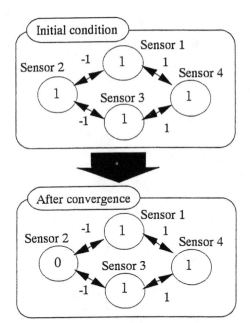

Figure 9. Convergence of the Immune Network.

In real control systems, we cannot expect to have various test data after the occurrence of a fault in the sensor. Usually, our diagnosis has to be concluded with a small number of data sets from specific plant conditions. Thus, we need to discuss the diagnosis capability of the system for this case. In Figure 10, the diagnosis rates $F_1(\Delta t)$ and F_2 are plotted against θ without introducing fuzzy quantization vectors, when abnormal output values of sensor 2 are changed from 0 to 20°C. $F_1(\Delta t)$ indicates the probability that the diagnosis system can specify an abnormal sensor when it has a Δt output error, while F_2 indicates the probability that it does not show the occurrence of a faulty sensor when every sensor output is normal. $F_1(\Delta t)$ and F_2 are between 0 and 1, and the larger values correspond to the improved diagnosis capability. The θ in the figure is normalized by the average distance between the training data and their nearest quantization vectors in each quantization vector space. As shown in Figure 10, $F_1(\Delta t)$

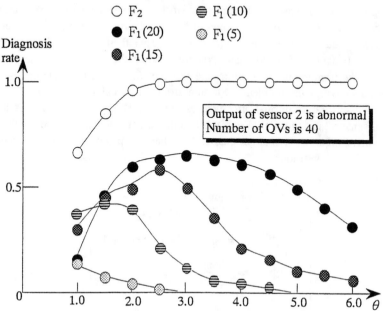

Figure 10. Relationship between θ and diagnosis rate.

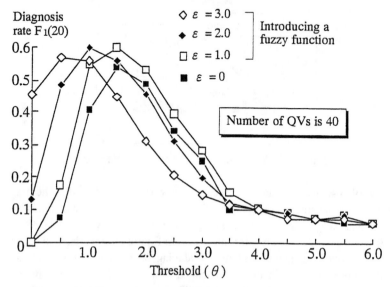

Figure 11. Diagnosis rates with various fuzzy functions.
(Sensor 4 has 20°C output error.)

varies with θ, which has a different optimal θ depending on Δt. The θ has to be more than 2.5 to obtain $F_2 = 1.0$ and to avoid diagnosis failure when every sensor output is normal; however, in this case, $F_1(\Delta t)$ is rather small when Δt is less than 10 °C.

Then, we discuss the diagnosis rates evaluated with the method proposed in section 2.5. Figure 11 shows the diagnosis rate with various fuzzy functions. J_{th} is 1.0 in this simulation. Generally the diagnosis rate F_1 is improved by introducing a fuzzy function without deteriorating F_2, though the result for F_2 is not described because of space limitation. When $\varepsilon = 1.0$, for example, a higher diagnosis rate is obtained for all θ values. Behavior of the diagnosis rate of this method is smoother for θ compared with the conventional method. Therefore it is not necessary to determine θ strictly in this method, which shortens the time needed for tuning θ.

Figure 12 shows the diagnosis rate plotted against the number of quantization vectors after θ and ε are tuned. The fuzzy function is found to work effectively to obtain a better diagnosis rate. Introducing adaptive optimization of θ under a real time condition, with 40 quantization vectors, the diagnosis rates are improved from 0.58 to 0.74 and from 0.29 to 0.40 for 20 °C and 10 °C output errors of T_4, respectively. By introducing fuzzy quantization vectors and adding the adaptive increase of θ, much better diagnosis rates can be obtained for both cases than for the maximum ones in Figure 11, which demonstrates the effectiveness of our algorithm.

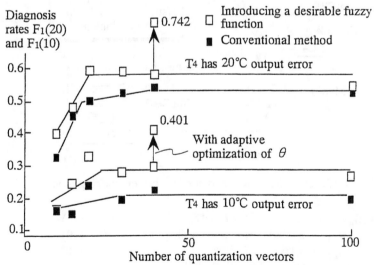

Figure 12. Diagnosis rates plotted against the number of quantization vectors. (θ and ε are tuned desirably.)

3.2   Sensor Diagnosis of Cement Process [3]

3.2.1   Diagnosis Network for Detecting Faulty Sensors

The preheating tower used in the cement manufacturing process shown in Figure 13 includes many sensors. We present the diagnosis of these sensors detecting output temperature of cyclones of the preheating tower. Since these sensors detect correlative values, the network consisting of many local tests between two sensors can be constructed by checking whether each correlation is satisfied under the normal condition or not. The following inequalities for local tests are extracted from the preheating tower by energy balances and some knowledge from experts.

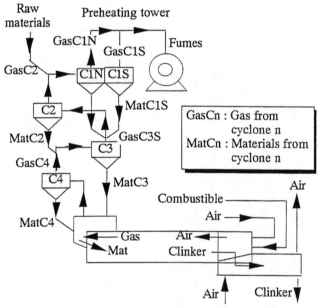

Figure 13. The schematic diagram of the cement making process.

$$A_{1n} < T_{GasCn} - T_{GasCn+1} < A_{2n}, \quad n = 1N, 1S, 2, 3 \tag{18}$$
$$A_{3n} < T_{MatCn+1} - T_{MatCn} < A_{4n}, \quad n = 1N, 1S, 2, 3 \tag{19}$$
$$T_{GasCn} > T_{MatCn}, \quad n = 1N, 1S, 2, 3, 4 \tag{20}$$
$$T_{GasCn} < T_{MatCn} + A_{5n}, \quad n = 1N, 1S, 2, 3, 4 \tag{21}$$
$$abs(T_{GasC1n} - T_{GasC1S}) < A_6 \tag{22}$$
$$abs(T_{MatC1n} - T_{MatC1S}) < A_7 \tag{23}$$

When $T_{GasCn} > T_{MatCn}$ is not satisfied, we can conclude that either T_{GasCn} or T_{MatCn} give the incorrect output, which means two sensors, T_{GasCn} and T_{MatCn} are testing each other.

By collecting these testing relations, the diagnosis network of Figure 14 can be obtained.

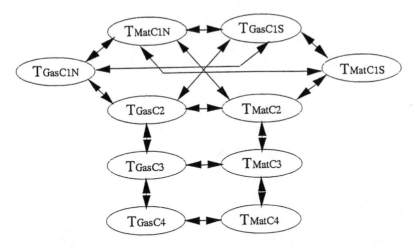

Figure 14. The Immune Network of the cement making process.

3.2.2   Simulation results

In this section, four immune diagnosis models which have different diagnosis functions, as described in the section 2.3, are evaluated through the following various cases of simulation.

(1) There is one faulty sensor

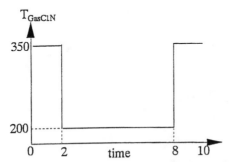

Figure 15. Sensor values of the T_{GasC1N}.

In this case, the faulty sensor can be specified by any one of the four models. When T_{GasC1N} is faulty between times 2 and 8 as shown in Figure 15 and other sensors are normal, for example, the reliability of sensor T_{GasC1N} is obtained as illustrated in Figure 16. When sensor outputs are varied concurrently under a real time condition, the correct diagnosis result is obtained because local testing results are calculated with relative correlations.

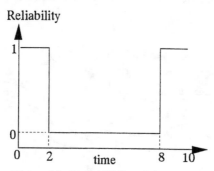

Figure 16. Reliabilities of the T_{GasC1N} obtained by the Immune Network.

(2) Some sensor outputs are doubtful

Consider the output of T_{GasC1N} is varied in Figure 17. When T_{GasC1N} is larger than 320 and smaller than 340, only the local testing result between T_{GasC1N} and T_{MatC1N} is incorrect. It is evident that one of the two sensors is faulty, however, it is impossible

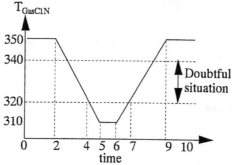

Figure 17. Sensor values of the T_{GasC1N}.

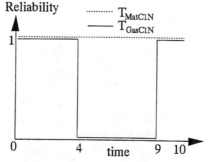

Figure 18. Reliabilities of the T_{GasC1N} obtained by the Immune Network with complete test model.

to specify which sensor is abnormal logically. Figures 18 - 21 represent the reliabilities of both sensors obtained by the complete test, incomplete test, fuzzy complete test, and fuzzy incomplete test models. According to Figure 18, the complete test model presents meaningful results, namely, deciding the output of T_{MatC1N} is abnormal. Figure 19 indicates that the incomplete test model introduces an improper diagnosis result. According to Figures 20 and 21, the fuzzy complete test and fuzzy incomplete test models give similar conclusions, where the doubtful state is obtained when it is not evident which sensor is abnormal. The fuzzy incomplete test model introduces a safer conclusion, which has less reliability than the fuzzy complete test model.

The complete test model is sensitive to whether the sensor outputs are normal or not, where each unit of them converges to 0 or 1 immediately. By contrast, the fuzzy incomplete test model can introduce the doubtful conclusion, where reliability is near 0.5, corresponding to the judgment that it is not evident whether some sensor outputs are normal or not.

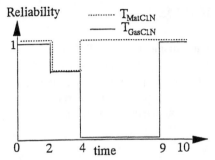

Figure 19. Reliabilities of the T_{GasC1N} obtained by the Immune Network with incomplete test model.

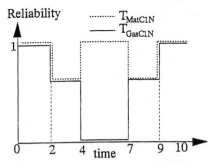

Figure 20. Reliabilities of the T_{GasC1N} obtained by the Immune Network with fuzzy complete test model.

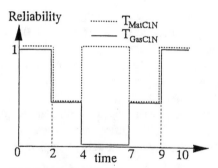

Figure 21. Reliabilities of the T_{GasC1N} obtained by the Immune Network with fuzzy incomplete test model.

3.3   Breakout Prediction System

3.3.1   Continuous Casting and Breakout

In this section, the immune diagnosis is applied to the breakout prediction system. Figure 22 illustrates a continuous casting system [14]. Molten steel supplied from the smelting pot through the tundish is poured into the mold and then pulled out from its bottom when cooled, while being hardened continuously. In the mold, the inside of the steel is still molten; however, its outside is a hardened crust called a shell. When the

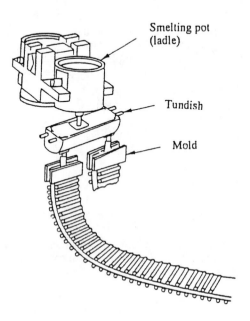

Figure 22.   Schematic illustration of continuous casting machine [14].

shell breaks for various reasons such as abnormal cooling in the mold, the inside molten steel will leak out. Breakout is an abnormal leakage, which causes extensive burning of the facilities and a long shutdown of the continuous caster. If the system can predict its occurrence in advance, breakout can be prevented by slowing down the steel pullout speed adequately.

Figure 23 describes the mechanism of the breakout occurrence schematically. The shell sticks the mold near its top side for some reason. When the sticking force exceeds the yield strength of the shell, the shell is torn as shown in Figure 23 (a). In Figure 23 (b), the shell repeatedly solidifies and tears, which causes the shell rupture to propagate downward and transversely at a speed lower than the casting speed. When the shell rupture leaves an unhealed region at the bottom end of the mold, breakout occurs as described in Figure 23 (c).

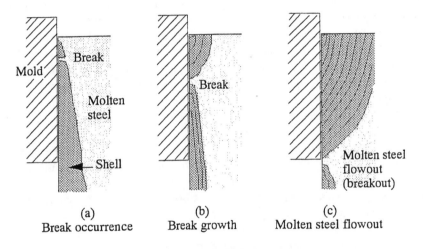

(a)   (b)   (c)
Break occurrence   Break growth   Molten steel flowout

Figure 23. Mechanism of breakout occurrence [14].

3.3.2   Breakout prediction system

A symptom of breakout is reflected by temperature behavior from a thermal couple measuring mold temperature every second. When the shell breaks, molten steel directly heats the mold to raise the temperature. Figure 24 is a typical temperature pattern corresponding to a breakout occurrence; namely it increases to the peak value, then decreases. Therefore in the conventional method, the occurrence of breakout is predicted by matching a detected temperature pattern and the typical breakout patterns [14]. However, other factors, such as a large oscillation of the molten surface in the mold and unbalanced powder thrown into the top of the mold to get smooth contact between molten steel and the mold wall, may produce similar temperature patterns.

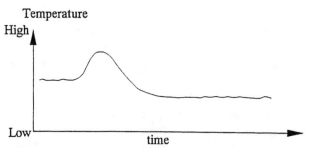

Figure 24. Typical thermal pattern before breakout.

The Immune Network for the breakout prediction system distinguishes between the breakout symptom and the similar temperature behavior caused by other factors. Before the diagnosis, the structure of the Immune Network is determined by connecting neighbor thermal couples, corresponding to units of the Immune Network. In the diagnosis, synapse values are updated every sampling time depending on the result for testing whether the correlation between every pair of units connected by the synapse is larger than a certain value under a real time condition. When it is larger, the synapse is updated to 1, which means the testing result is normal. When it is smaller, the synapse is -1 indicating that the testing result is abnormal. Integrating local diagnosis results with the selected diagnosis function, the Immune Network can conclude whether there are abnormal thermal couples or not, i.e., thermal couples with unusual output viewed from other neighbor ones. The immune diagnosis can classify the abnormal temperature behaviors into those caused by local or global factors. When they are caused by a local fault corresponding to a symptom of breakout, the specific thermal couple can be specified as an abnormal one by the Immune Network. Such a specific result may not be obtained, when they are caused by global troubles such as the large oscillation of the molten surface and unbalanced powder as mentioned above.

Table 2 indicates the prediction result using the data obtained from the actual plant. The breakout prediction system raises an alarm, after it detects the breakout symptom. In the table, prediction ratio R_p and hit ratio R_h are determined by the following equations. A better breakout prediction system has a large R_p and R_h.

$$R_p = (N_h)/(N_s) \qquad\qquad\qquad (25)$$

$$R_h = (N_h)/(N_p) \qquad\qquad\qquad (26)$$

Where N_h : number of correct alarms
N_s : number of occurrences of breakout symptom
N_p : number of alarms

Table 2. Evaluation of breakout prediction system.

	Fundamental prediction system	With immune diagnosis
Number of symptoms of breakout	8	
Number of alarms	26	19
Number of correct alarms	7	8
R_p	88%	100%
R_h	27%	42%

By adding the immune diagnosis to the conventional breakout prediction system, the number of false alarms can be reduced by excluding abnormal temperature behavior caused by other factors, which contributes to the improvement of the breakout prediction system.

3.4 Merits and Demerits of the Immune Diagnosis

The merits and demerits of the diagnosis system based on the Immune Network are summarized in this section. Basic merits are derived from the fact that the immune diagnosis is a distributed diagnosis system using relative knowledge. When additional components or sensors are installed in the system, it is easier to add corresponding units and synapses to the network without modifying the current network. Also partial changes of the network do not propagate to other parts of it. Therefore a very flexible and maintainable diagnosis system can be constructed. Another merit is that central processing is unnecessary for determining which sensors are abnormal based on their collected data. Completely distributed self-diagnosis for each sensor is possible by the Immune Network, if each sensor has a simple ability for detecting other sensor outputs and performing logic execution.

There are some demerits in the immune diagnosis. First other information besides fault occurrence can not be obtained by the Immune Network. To overcome this, combining it with an expert system, such as rule processing or artificial neural networks, seems to be effective and will have to be investigated further. The second demerit is that it is hard to extract correlations used for diagnosis and to determine threshold values for distinguishing whether the correlations are satisfied or not. A promising approach to solving this problem is the introduction of training methods for automatically extracting correlations or knowledge from data obtained from the plant. The learning vector quantization method described in this chapter is a helpful training method for it.

4   Conclusions

In this chapter, we have presented the distributed diagnosis system based on the biological immune system. Abnormal sensors, such as age-deteriorated ones, which have been difficult to detect only by checking output of each sensor independently, can be verified with this method.   We expect the system to contribute to advanced preventive maintenance for industrial plants.   Thus, a complete decenterized autonomous diagnosis system can be realized, where each sub-system observes outputs of other sub-systems, diagnoses its output by itself and give the alarm spontaneously when its output is judged to be abnormal. The self-diagnosis system presented in this chapter has many potential applications in contemporary large-scaled distributed industrial systems.

References and Further Reading

[1]   Ishida, Y. and Mizessyn, F. (1992), Learning Algorithm on an Immune Network Model: Application to Sensor Diagnosis,   *Proceedings of International Joint Conference on Neural Networks* '92, I, pp. 33-38

[2]   Ishida, Y. (1992), Autonomous Decentralized Diagnostic Algorithm forDistributed Diagnosis Models: Immune Network Model, *Trans. of Institute of Electronics, Information and Communication Engineers D-II* , J75, pp. 646-651 (in Japanese)

[3]   Ishida, Y. and Mizessyn, F. (1994), Sensor Diagnosis of Process Plants by an Immune-Based Model, *Trans. of Institute of Systems, Control and Information Engineers*, Vol. 4, No. 1, pp. 1-8 (in Japanese)

[4]   Ishiguro, A.,   Kondo, T., Watanabe, Y. and Uchikawa, Y. (1995),   An Immunological Approach to Behavior Control of Autonomous Mobile Robots - Construction of Immune Networks through Learning, *Proceedings of International Workshop on Soft Computing in Industry* '96, pp. 263-267

[5]   Kohonen, T. (1982), Associative Memory - A System Theoretical Approach, *Springer Verlag*

[6]   Preparata, F. P. et al. (1967),   On the Connection Assignment Problem of Diagnosable Systems, *IEEE Trans. of Electronic Computers*, EC - 16, pp. 848

[7]   Jerne, N. K. (1973), The Immune System, *Scientific American*, Vol. 229, No. 1, pp. 52-60

[8]   Jerne, N. K. (1984),   Idiotypic Networks and Other Preconceived Ideas, *Immunological Rev.*, Vol. 79, pp. 5-24

[9] Farmer, J. D., Packard, N. H. and Perelson, A. S. (1986), The immune system, adaptation, and machine learning, *Physica*, 22D, pp. 187-204

[10] Kayama, M., Sugita, Y. and Morooka, Y. (1995), Sensor Diagnosis System Combining Immune Network and Learning Vector Quantization, *Trans. of Institute of Electrical Engineers*, Vol. 115-D, pp. 859-866 (in Japanese)

[11] Kayama, M., Sugita, Y., Morooka, Y. and Fukuoka, S. (1995), Distributed Diagnosis System Combining the Immune Network and Learning Vector Quantization, *IEEE 21st International Conference on Industrial Electronics, Control, and Instrumentation '95*, pp. 1531-1536

[12] Kayama, M., Sugita, Y., Morooka, Y. and Fukuoka, S. (1996), Improving Capability of the Distributed Diagnosis System Combining the Immune Network and Learning Vector Quantization, *Proceedings of International Workshop on Soft Computing in Industry '96*, pp. 257-262

[13] Kayama, M., Sugita, Y., Morooka, Y. and Saito, Y. (1995), Adjusting Neural Networks for Accurate Control Model Tuning, *Proceedings of the International Joint Conference of the 4th International Conference on Fuzzy Systems and the 2nd International Fuzzy Engineering Symposium*, pp. 1995-2000

[14] Tanaka, T., Endo, H., Kamada, N., Naito, S. and Kominami, H. (1991), Trouble Forecasting System by Multi-Neural Networks, *Artificial Neural Networks*, T. Kohonen et al. (Editors), Vol. 1, pp. 835-840

Chapter 10:

Current and Future Applications of Intelligent Techniques in the Electric Power Industry

CURRENT AND FUTURE APPLICATIONS OF INTELLIGENT TECHNIQUES IN THE ELECTRIC POWER INDUSTRY

A. Martin Wildberger
Strategic Science and Technology
Electric Power Research Institute, Palo Alto, California
U.S.A.

Abstract: The Electric Power Research Institute (EPRI), on behalf of its member companies and their customers, has applied intelligent techniques, such as neural networks, fuzzy logic and genetic algorithms, to many of the control and optimization tasks inherent in the generation, delivery, and use of electric power. EPRI is also engaged in research directed toward performance verification and automated design of these intelligent systems in order to overcome critical barriers to their more widespread use, especially in safety related engineering applications. Other current research and development emphasizes the use of multiple, adaptive and evolving intelligent agents to model the power grid, the economics of power markets, and the changes in the power industry under deregulation.

1   Introduction

The Electric Power Research Institute (EPRI) was formed in 1973 to apply advanced science and technology for the benefit of the electric utilities, which were its original founding members, and of their customers. EPRI's research and development now covers a wide range of technologies emphasizing the generation, delivery, and use of electricity, but including many other aspects of energy and the environment. EPRI is a not-for-profit corporation funded through voluntary contributions by over 800 members and affiliates worldwide. This chapter describes some of EPRI's recent and continuing research and development projects that apply intelligent techniques to engineering systems. Most of these projects also involve theory, since advances in theoretical understanding are often necessary in order to address critical barriers faced in practical applications.

Projects reviewed briefly in this chapter include:

- power system planning and operations improvement through (1) short-term load forecasting by neural networks, (2) unit commitment optimization by genetic algorithms, and (3) inter-area scheduling by fuzzy neural networks.
- a group of projects co-sponsored with the United States National Science Foundation in the area of intelligent control systems.
- other intelligent control systems projects, employing neural networks and fuzzy logic in a variety of power system, power plant and environmental controls.
- successful use of genetic algorithms (1) to test an expert system for improving the performance of fossil-fueled power plants, and (2) to design and optimize neural networks in a variety of contexts such as: heat-rate improvement of nuclear plant operation, reduction of NO_x emission from combustion, as well as forecasting building energy requirements for economic operation under real-time pricing of power.
- research into ways to reduce the opacity and better guarantee the performance of neural networks in order to make their use feasible in safety-related applications, and to guarantee the stability and robustness of fuzzy logic control systems in order to broaden their range of practical industrial applications.
- exploration of ways to use autonomous evolving agents as a modeling technique for the electric power market and ultimately for the industry itself as it moves toward deregulation and increased competition.
- preliminary investigation of multiple adaptive agents as a modeling method for real-time, distributed control of the electric power grid.

2   Power Generation Scheduling

The day-to-day operation of the electric power system includes a variety of essential planning tasks. These include economic scheduling of generating capacity, fuel purchases, power transactions, and short-term maintenance, as well as security analysis. All of these require accurate estimates, at multiple planning horizons, of power load demand, of the actual costs of generation and of prospective forward prices of purchased power. These estimates then feed computer programs that use various mathematical models to generate optimal plans with due allowance for uncertainties and for the effect of sequential decisions made between the time of the analysis and the actual implementation of the plans.   Recent research has demonstrated the benefit of intelligent techniques for expediting the optimization process. Neural networks, in particular, are now in routine use for power load demand forecasting.

2.1   Short-Term Load Forecasting

The accuracy of short-term hourly load forecasts has a significant impact on the efficient operation of any electric utility. Traditional short-term load forecasting methods include regression analysis, time series approximation, and similar-day look up. These tools are cumbersome to maintain and do not provide sufficient accuracy, especially under weather conditions that change rapidly. The demand for electric power depends strongly on the weather and on the local human response to that weather. Both are highly non-linear processes. Their behavior also differs across different geographic areas depending on such factors as the kinds of industrial and commercial facilities, the styles of building construction and their ages.

Under EPRI sponsorship, Southern Methodist University, working with the local utility, TU Electric, has developed an artificial neural network-based short-term load forecaster (ANNSTLF) that is now implemented at more than 20 utilities of various sizes and geographic locations. [1] Several of them are using it on line in an adaptive mode. Since load forecast accuracy is highly dependent on temperature forecasts, a separate neural net-based temperature forecaster was also developed.

The basic model in ANNSTLF is customized to each particular utility's area through a training process that requires three years of historical load and weather data. Daily operation of the forecaster requires three sets of input data: the previous day's actual loads, the previous day's actual weather parameters, and forecast weather parameters out to the forecast horizon. All updating is done automatically. The mean absolute percentage error for the ANNSTLF model ranges from 2-4%, depending on utility size and the nature of the loads.

2.2   Unit Commitment Optimization

The problem of planning which power generating units to use in order to supply consumer demands and to allow some reserve for contingencies is known as the "Unit Commitment Problem." This is a highly constrained mixed-integer programming problem of the class known as "portfolio" or "knapsack." Most software used by most electric utilities for this purpose employs Lagrangian multipliers solved numerically. Dynamic programming is also used by a few power system control centers. Both methods are slow, not particularly adapted to having their speed increased by parallel computing, and very sensitive to initial conditions.

M. H. Hassoun of Wayne State University used global optimization by genetic algorithms, along with parallel local solutions by coupled gradient neural networks, to solve the unit commitment problem. This EPRI project provided the proof of concept for a faster, global optimization technique that may eventually save considerable money for electric utilities. [2] Used in this context, genetic algorithms have an additional advantage. They provide multiple, suboptimal solutions not much worse than the true optimum. Between the time the planning software is run and the time that the "Dispatcher" (the operator of the power system) must actually perform an "economic dispatch" of power, a significant change in the power system topology may have occurred due to equipment failure, weather, or even an unexpected increase/decrease in customer demand. One or more of the originally suboptimal solutions may fit within the new constraints, and be able to be used by the Dispatcher while the planning software is being run again. Furthermore, the genetic algorithm can be expected to converge very rapidly when it is restarted using the previous set of suboptimal trial solutions along with the new fitness criteria.

2.3   Inter-Area Transfer Optimization

In another completed project, S. M. Shahidehpour, at the Illinois Institute of Technology, applied neural networks and fuzzy logic to the broader, multi-area, optimal power generation scheduling problem in order to help power system operators determine the optimum power flows between various areas and minimize the cost of operation of an interconnected power network.   In this study, operating constraints were presented as heuristic rules in the system, and artificial neural networks were used at pre-processor and post-processor stages.   These results were enhanced by a fuzzy set to represent various possibilities for unit states and load forecast uncertainties.   This use of intelligent techniques in the multi-area generation scheduling is intended to supplement the dynamic programming method of unit commitment.   Proof-of-concept testing has demonstrated that this combined approach can cost-effectively schedule generation for both single and multiarea power system simulations.   To schedule a sample interconnected four-area system with 26 power plants per area, the fuzzy approach required 3.3 minutes when run on a PC-based neural network emulation, versus more than 40 minutes for conventional dynamic programming analysis on the same machine.   A final report has been published. [3]

3   Joint Intelligent Control Projects With NSF

From 1992 through 1995 EPRI co-sponsored with the National Science Foundation (NSF) a group of twenty-one projects which addressed various techniques for intelligent and adaptive control, and were about evenly divided among applications to Nuclear Power, Electric Power Systems, and Fossil Power Plants.   Some approaches to intelligent control that have been investigated by the joint EPRI/NSF projects include:
*   Supervisory Planning: with the plan either pre-stored, generated in real-time by automated reasoning, or learned from human examples.
*   Qualitative Modeling: using expert systems, either rule-based or frame-based, and either completely or incompletely deterministic (for instance, using fuzzy logic).
*   Computational Intelligence & Machine Learning: using neural networks, genetic algorithms, and other evolutionary or reinforcement learning methods, sometimes combined with mathematical optimization techniques.

Among their research goals has been:
*   methods for learning and adaptation in heterogeneous systems
*   methods for reasoning and planning

- analysis of interaction of multiple agents, both human and machine
- techniques for transformation of data into knowledge
- methods for rule generation and modification
- automatic knowledge interpretation
- techniques for development of qualitative and quantitative models
- methods for autonomous process operation
- intelligent sensors and actuators
- tools and techniques for intelligent control system verification and validation

The remainder of this section briefly describes several representative examples of the technology and applications investigated.

The use of Flexible AC Transmission Systems (FACTS), and other high-power, active control devices, throughout power delivery systems promises significant increases in the performance, efficiency, and capacity of existing networks. These solid-state electronic devices, analogous to integrated circuits but operational at multi-megawatt power levels, can convert electricity to a wide range of voltages, numbers of phases and frequencies with minimal electrical loss and component wear. They enable control and tuning of all power circuits for maximum performance and cost-effectiveness, promising enhanced energy efficiency and flexible value-added service offerings from electricity providers. [4] However, to realize these benefits, new control techniques are required. In a project at the University of Wisconsin, Madison, William Sethares developed methods, based on a energy function approach, to coordinate the activities of the numerous dispersed controllers that would be involved in such applications, and to optimize the exchange of information between them. He also explored the use of the genetic algorithm to help set up high-level "goals" (such as load management) for the FACTS devices to accomplish. He employed interval mathematical methods in order to deal with the structural uncertainty caused by power system disruptions in a formal and rapid manner without excessive conservatism.

Asok Ray, at Penn State, University Park Campus, pursued investigations aimed at predicting impending failures and extending service life (at the expense of some reduction in dynamic performance). This research extended system theoretic and intelligent techniques to include models of the properties of materials with the goal of increasing reliability, availability, component durability and maintainability of steam-electric power plants.

Also at Penn State, University Park Campus, Robert M. Edwards, building on previous work in neural network, fuzzy logic, optimal, and robust control on the Penn State TRIGA reactor, developed a multi-variable control capability for that reactor using control rod motion & coolant flow. His approach is to use learning systems-based intelligent re-configurable control in the expectation of achieving good temperature performance over the full power range. The system was demonstrated on a hybrid simulation/reactor demonstration and showed good performance under a broad range of conditions.

Panos Antsaklis, at the University of Notre Dame, investigated methods for obtaining effective DES (discrete event systems) plant models from sequences of observed events. His approach uses optimal designs of state space partitions to define the observed events and uses query-based inductive inference procedures to identify the plant's effective DES dynamics. The emphasis in this project was on methods exhibiting relatively low computational and sample complexity.

At the University of California, Santa Barbara, Alan J. Laub and his colleagues used fuzzy forms of tunable non-linear approximants in an adaptive feedback control loop for decentralized process control. Their approach has been to formalize set-partitioned dynamical systems in a mathematical framework so as to simplify analysis and to capture relevant concepts. This system incorporates partitioned observers, as well as transitional and interior controllers into an overall numerical-logical feedback loop.

David D. Yao, at Columbia University, has been engaged in research to integrate stochastic and combinatorial aspects of discrete systems by using greedy algorithms for optimization, and by imposing a monotone structure for supervisory control using token-based realizations of individual distributed controls. His approach has possible applications to production and transportation systems as well as to electric power systems.

In a project specifically directed toward automatic generation control (AGC), Roger L. King, at Mississippi State University, used a combination of symbolic artificial intelligence and neural networks to enhance moment-to-moment balancing of generation with load within a given control area by intelligently evaluating uncertainties associated with changing power conditions. This project developed, for load forecasting, an intelligent architecture that can monitor and reason about dynamic changes in the load and generation facilities. The resulting integrated AGC control system was tested with data supplied by the Alabama Power Company.

In a project at the University of Texas at Arlington, Frank L. Lewis, Kai Liu, and others completed several controls applications in power system load frequency control and AGC, including a fuzzy logic AGC controller. They are now exploring the fundamentals and the optimization of multiloop frameworks for intelligent control based on fuzzy logic, neural networks (NNs), and knowledge-based systems. [5]

Multiloop frameworks incorporate both nested and interacting control loops, embodying the idea that an intelligent controller should do what an ideal expert human operator would do, i.e., assess the current state of a system, apply the resulting knowledge to achieve an immediate performance improvement by manipulating only a few of the controllable parameters, and continuously repeat the process. Typically, NNs or other artificial intelligence techniques are employed to decide what to control and either conventional quantitative approaches or fuzzy logic methods are used to determine how to control it. In terms of a feedback control model, the limited goal-setting approach of the heuristic component provides an outer control loop around the inner feedback loop; this second loop selectively modifies the standard with which the inner loop compares its own output in order to generate the error that drives its actual control operations.

To date, the research team has derived a rigorous multiloop framework for intelligent control, as well as strict proofs indicating design criteria for NN and fuzzy controllers guaranteeing tracking behavior and bounded internal signals. They have also developed novel tuning algorithms making NNs in multiloop systems robust and tolerant of random disturbances or changes in system configuration. Moreover, these algorithms provide stability during NN training, eliminating the need for off-line learning.

4   Other Intelligent Control Projects

Control and optimization continue to be the most promising applications of intelligent techniques in the power industry. The following are a sampling of recent and current research projects supported by EPRI in these areas.

EPRI, in partnership with Southern Company Services and Radian Corporation in the USA and with PowerGen in the UK, has developed a family of intelligent boiler combustion control tools. These use various forms of neural networks including radial basis functions. Their primary purpose has been the reduction of atmospheric pollution, but they also serve to optimize combustion in general through heat rate improvement. [6]

Since the 1990 Clean Air Act Amendments and subsequent implementing regulations, electric utilities in the United States have been required to reduce NO_x emissions and maintain these low levels. Some 6000 USA non-utility boilers are also affected by this legislation. Generic NO_x Control Intelligent Systems (GNOCIS) can improve performance in all these units after training with each unit's historical data. Different versions of GNOCIS can provide plant operational support ranging from "open loop" advice to the operator during steady state boiler operation, to "closed loop" automation by sending optimum setpoints via the plant's digital distributed control system to the control devices for dampers, pulverizers, etc. GNOCIS was first tested in plants operated by Georgia Power in the US and by PowerGen in the UK. It is now being installed in many other plants.

In a project that includes both new technique exploration and the development of new theory, Bernard Widrow and his students at Stanford University have been advancing the capabilities of neural networks for increasingly complex control problems beginning with two generators linked by a tie-line and feeding two independent, time-varying loads. Voltage and frequency control were considered independently, but voltage and frequency controllers were combined within the same model system. Theoretical work was developed to show the equivalence between two important algorithms used in the adaptation of neural network controllers, namely real-time backpropagation and backpropagation-through-time, and to provide an easy method for deriving new adaptation algorithms. Based on this theoretical work, stabilization circuits are now being developed that will allow an extension of the operational range of the controllers. Other applications of neural networks in this project have included a void fraction correlation for nuclear reactors and work in non-linear filtering for identification and prediction. [7]

During startup of a large steam turbine, few key heat-up variables are measurable. Operators must rely on empirical rules and observations such as "temperature is rising" to guide the startup, and automation is impractical using conventional tools. Consequently, very conservative turbine ramp-up rates are employed that are not fuel efficient and may subject components to more thermal stress than is necessary. Because fuzzy analysis can handle the vague, approximate information and the heuristic rules associated with turbine startup, EPRI supported General Electric Co. in research that applied fuzzy logic to this problem. This effort aims to optimize turbine startup by utilizing expert knowledge in a fuzzy logic approach coupled with traditional model-predictive controls. Automated control will also allow the startup procedure to be linked to the load dispatch center for more efficient generating unit dispatch. This research has resulted in a formal patent application.

A project at M. I. T. under the direction of Annaruda Annaswamy is specifically directed to the development of adaptive controllers that can deliver high performance for systems that function in uncertain environments. The researchers are testing judicious combinations of adaptive strategies and neural network configurations to discern the systems' interactions with the environment, provide feedback information about key variables, and generate appropriate commands using on-board computational devices. Current emphasis is on incorporating gain-scheduling controllers in the neural network models for the adaptive control of linear time-varying systems. [8] Their designs for non-linear control of heat exchange have recently been tested successfully at EPRI's Instrumentation and Control Center, located in the Tennessee Valley Authority's Kingston Power Plant.

5   Testing An Expert System With A Genetic Algorithm

There is, at present, neither a firm theory nor a set of "engineering handbook" procedures to guide the design of any adaptive system, whether it is trained (like a neural network) or evolved (like a genetic algorithm), and whether or not it is permitted to continue adapting on-line while it is in actual service. Most of these systems continue to be built almost entirely by trial and error, with some guidance from the designer's prior experience. This approach to design, as well as the nature of adaptability itself, makes it extremely difficult either to guarantee the performance of an untried design or even to validate it by testing after it is implemented.

The most promising approach to automating the validation of adaptive control systems after their implementation may be a purely pragmatic one that, itself, uses adaptive techniques. Originally suggested by John Grefenstette [9] of the Naval Research Laboratory (NRL), this approach to validating an adaptive system employs a genetic algorithm (GA) that serves as a "devil's advocate" by attempting to make the adaptive control system fail. This method requires a validated simulation of the "plant" (the underlying system to be controlled) as well as the adaptive controller to be tested. The need for a valid simulation of the plant may seem merely to move the problem of validation down one level. However, as long as the plant, without its controller, is not self-adaptive, representing it by a validated model and simulation is possible with well known technology. The individual population members of the "devil's advocate" GA represent possible operating conditions for the plant and its environment as well as possible plant failure modes (if the adaptive control system is expected to overcome these also). The fitness function for the GA encourages the evolution of population members that cause unsatisfactory performance by the control system. The successful evolution of one or more such individuals demonstrates that the adaptive control system is inadequate in its handling of the particular situation represented by each such individual. Either the control system must be improved or that particular combination of circumstances must be prevented from occurring by a separate safety device or other defensive mechanism.

Clearly, this approach has the potential to uncover all the modes of failure in the adaptive control system, but does not provide absolute assurance if, after many generations of evolution, no more instances of unsatisfactory control occur. As is well known, testing only reveals "bugs," not the absence of them. Some subsequent generation of the algorithm might yet overpower the controller. However, subject to compactness of the parameter space, after a sufficient number of generations have passed, the most successful individuals in each successive generation represent bounds within which the adaptive controller performs satisfactorily. If guaranteed performance is required to be unbounded in one or more dimensions, this pragmatic approach fails, and proofs using formal logic, such as those described in Section 7, would be needed to ensure the adaptive system's unbounded correctness.

A recent EPRI project tested the use of genetic algorithms to validate a rule-based expert system. [10,11] In any practical application, validation is critical to expert system success. Most fielded expert systems are validated by testing whether the expert system provides appropriate conclusions for specific cases. Since exhaustive testing of all rule combinations is not computationally feasible in any real-world expert system, cases where the system provides inappropriate conclusions are easily missed. This project was conducted jointly by EPRI, NRL, New York Electric & Gas (NYSEG), and DHR Technologies. The Fossil Thermal Performance Advisor (FTPA) is an expert system developed by personnel at DHR for NYSEG. It provides the operator of a coal-fired steam power plant with recommendations for improving the performance of the plant. The FTPA is currently in operation in several plants, and some early installations have been running continually for over five years. NRL provided the GA software. NYSEG furnished the FTPA along with data from one of their plants, and, under the leadership of Edward Roache, personnel from DHR Technologies programmed the required modifications to the FTPA as well as additional bridging software. DHR also provided a neural network model of an actual power plant, in lieu of a more conventional plant simulation based on a causal model.

The individual population members of the GA were designed to represent possible operating conditions for the plant and its environment. Its fitness function encouraged the evolution of population members that produced unsatisfactory performance by the plant but were either inadequately diagnosed by the expert system or caused the expert system to recommend actions which actually decreased plant performance. Besides errors purposely inserted for test purposes, the GA successfully exposed an error in the expert system which had not previously been detected by designers or operators over three years of actual use.

This successful proof-of-concept test suggests that genetic algorithms may be useful not only for the initial validation of a symbolic artificial intelligence "expert system," but also for adapting that system to changes in the configuration of the plant or for customizing it for other plants that are only basically similar to the one for which it was originally designed. Customization typically requires almost as many engineering man-hours as designing the original expert system, and it is a critical barrier to the greater use of symbolic artificial intelligence in industry. Even if an accurate simulation is not available for the new plant, the original expert system could be installed there and a genetic algorithm used to "tune" it to the new plant over some period of actual operation.

6   Genetic Synthesis & Optimization Of Neural Networks

A key shortcoming of the current state of neural network technology is the lack of any effective design methodology. Neural network technology is becoming widely accepted in various industries, including the electricity enterprise. Numerous operating applications have demonstrated significant performance improvements over prior methods. But current approaches to developing neural network applications are a critical barrier to realizing the full potential of this technology. Optimizing neural network applications is a formidable design task requiring myriad choices in the number of neurons and layers, their interconnections, and the training algorithm to be employed as well as all its parameters.

EPRI has been sponsoring research by Tariq Samad and Steven A. Harp at Honeywell Technology Center in the use of genetic algorithms to synthesize and optimize the design of neural networks. Initial investigation was directed at validating the approach by optimizing an already trained neural network developed manually in a realistic application of heat rate modeling performed for the Tennessee Valley

Authority (TVA) by Robert Uhrig at the University of Tennessee. The same data sets, from two different units at the TVA's Sequoyah Nuclear Power Plant, were used for network training and testing. Appropriate criteria for optimization were determined to include accuracy (e.g., low error prediction of plant gross heat rate), learning speed, and network simplicity (e.g., low number and density of connections). Neural network design experiments and evaluations began with a review of various network designs appropriate for the thermodynamic modeling application. Experiments were conducted that showed the genetically optimized networks had a significant performance improvement over manually developed networks. This research also demonstrated that the choice of input variables is critical in neural network applications. The genetic algorithm's ability to simultaneously optimize input selections, along with network structures and learning parameters, was vital to its accurate modeling. Another result was that genetic optimization need not be limited to evolving individual trained networks. Neural network architectures can be designed for classes of applications and then later trained on specific data for different applications within a given class. [12, 13]

Experiments on three additional applications have been completed: engine NO_x emissions, ozone levels in New York City, and building energy requirements for economic operation under real-time pricing of electric power in a competitive market. In this last case, the genetic algorithm was used to design and optimize a neural network model using data from the Marriott Marquis Hotel in New York City. The data included two years of hourly loads, rates, weather information, etc. obtained earlier in a joint EPRI and Consolidated Edison Real-Time Pricing (RTP) experiment. All three cases resulted in the automatic production of models competitive with the best neural networks and conventional non-linear statistical models developed for these problems by the exercise of considerable statistical expertise and manual adjustment.

Demonstration software has been developed that runs under Microsoft Windows on a PC. The software features an easy-to-use graphical interface and incorporates tutorial material on neural networks, genetic algorithms, and the neurogenetic design technique. The problems mentioned above are included along with optimized network models for them. The software also contains a neural network specification and training facility, allowing users to test and compare their own hand-crafted designs with the genetically optimized ones.

7 Quality Assurance for Intelligent Techniques

The automatic verification of software developed using conventional methods of computing is feasible, although it is expensive and often impractical for large, complex systems -- the very ones for which it is most needed. On the other hand, similar feasibility is not at all clear if the software to be verified is also capable of self-adaptation on-line: that is, the software can learn to modify its behavior from the experience it obtains while actually operating. Except for some very specialized cases, the global correctness of adaptive software cannot presently be proved by formal methods. The more intelligence that is programmed into a system and the more adaptable it is made, the more difficult it is to prove that the system will never perform incorrectly. Indeed, if enough intelligence can be programmed into an automated system, it will become difficult even to judge whether its response to specific cases is appropriate. Its decisions may represent an improvement over those of its designers.

Nevertheless, EPRI has been supporting research directed toward formal methods of verification in the specific areas of neural networks and fuzzy logic control systems.

7.1   Making Neural Networks More Transparent

Although combining a neural network with a causal model, as in neuro-fuzzy control, helps to provide both general performance boundaries and a convincing explanation for the network's output, the inherent opacity of neural networks' internal operations still makes it difficult to prove their correctness by formal logic alone. [14] By the opacity of neural networks is meant that it has not been possible to derive any clear logical relationship between their interior configuration and their external behavior except in a few special cases. [15,16] One such example [17] extracts classification algorithms from trained neural networks by relating separation hyperplanes to the neuronal weights, but the procedure used, while systematic, includes heuristic elements.

In the case of some neural networks having only Boolean inputs and outputs, formal, logical relations have been able to be derived and associated with the network structure and weights. [18, 19, 20] The investigators, primarily Hassoun and Sethi at Wayne State University, have been able to extract diagnostic rules for systemic lupus in the medical domain and thinning rules for OCR processing in the document imaging domain. With EPRI support, an attempt has been made to extend this approach from networks having binary inputs to those with multilevel discrete inputs and thence to continuous inputs. The aim has been to develop generic tools for analyzing and synthesizing neural networks that yield a symbolic representation of the numerical weights of a neural network in familiar forms such as production rules, decision trees, and Boolean relations.

So far, these investigations have resulted in the development of a backtracking tree search procedure for weight interpretation of neurons with binary inputs. Using this procedure, a better understanding of the feedforward neural networks can be achieved and the equivalent decision making rules can be extracted. Search algorithms employing threshold and multi-valued logic are being tested with a variety of different feedforward network architectures.

Another goal of the project is to exploit the correspondence between sequential machines and recurrent neural networks to formulate new methods of analysis and transparent design for multilayer recurrent neural systems, with application to associative neural memory, rule-based systems, and modular design theory.

7.2 A Differential Geometry View of Rough-Fuzzy Control

Although fuzzy, and fuzzy-neural, controllers have met with considerable success, there are still many questions to be answered before their design can be made systematic rather than heuristic. There are a lack of provable design criteria that would guarantee, or narrowly bound, the stability, robustness and optimality of the resulting system. Although testing can demonstrate the robustness and the bounded behavior of most fuzzy systems after their construction, even this cannot be done for fuzzy systems that are actually adaptive (self-learning) while in use. [21, 22]

Classical control theory generally starts by developing a mathematical model of the "plant" to be controlled. This is commonly called the identification problem and the model is typically expressed as a set of differential equations. The solution of this plant model then becomes a model for a controller. For optimal control, the solution must take into account performance: constraints, goals, error bounds, etc. For robust control, the plant model may also have to be enhanced by the inclusion of exogenous factors representing its (assumed uncontrollable) environment. If the plant model is causal (rather than statistical) and based on physical principles, verification using formal methods is possible during the design phase. Validation is also straightforward because the behavior of the uncontrolled plant is known explicitly and testing the controller at plant operating extremes is usually adequate.

In effect, fuzzy logic control is a methodology for constructing the controller directly using only a vague approximation of the plant to be controlled. Fuzzy logic control focuses on plants whose models are difficult or impossible to derive either because the plant itself is not well understood or because it is so complex that any explicit model would be impractical to solve in a reasonable time.

However, it is also possible to model the controller directly by using the theory of differential manifolds. [23] Finding the "correct" set of linguistic rules is essential to the successful design of a fuzzy logic controller. Alternative sets, expressing alternative models, may be obtained from the procedural knowledge of human experts and/or from naive and qualitative partial models of the plant. By combining all these alternative models into a rough set [24], they can be shown to form an inverse limit system. [25] If the "best" components from each alternative model are selected and integrated consistently, i.e., if the inverse limit can be exhibited, these control functions form a "substantial neighborhood" of an integral manifold that is the geometric representation of a solution of the plant model. It should be possible to perform this integration of the alternative control models automatically, using evolutionary computing.

Stability can then be addressed by investigating the behavior of the solutions lying in a neighborhood of the one particular solution, the integral manifold derived by this approach. In differential geometry, such a neighborhood of an integral submanifold is often called a tubular neighborhood (because in three-space it resembles a tube surrounding the integral submanifold). Using some additional geometric information, such a tubular neighborhood might be constructed as the closure of the "substantial neighborhood" as derived above and considered as a "substantial subset" of the tubular neighborhood. Stability would then be achieved by setting bounds on the membership functions of the fuzzy sets that would keep the controller within that manifold.

At least two serious problems may prevent this approach from being successful in a particular case. The subsystem models will not converge unless they are compatible enough to form an inverse limit system, and discontinuities may force model decomposition resulting in multiple manifolds. The first problem might arise in practical cases where the opinions of human experts were logically contradictory. The second might occur in cases where the actual plant dynamics include phase changes or other jump discontinuities.

EPRI has initiated a project to investigate this approach in detail. The principal investigator is T. Y. Lin of San Jose State University, working with additional researchers from other institutions, primarily Lotfi Zadeh and others at the University of California, Berkeley. At this time, an existence proof has been developed that guarantees such a system can always be made stable and robust, but a constructive proof that would provide an algorithmic procedure with guaranteed convergence in a finite number of steps has not yet been obtained.

8   Modeling the Electric Enterprise

The current world-wide trend toward free competition in electric power raises issues, not yet being faced in the United States or in many other nations that are moving toward greater competition in electric power, as to whether such an open, competitive market can be fair and profitable to all participants while continuing to guarantee to the ultimate consumer of power, at the best possible price, secure, reliable electric service, of whatever quality that particular consumer requires. How to control a heterogeneous, widely dispersed, yet globally interconnected system is a serious technological problem in any case. Most plans for management of the transmission network, supporting the competitive buying and selling of electric power, call for some form of centralized administrative agency, called an "Independent System Operator" (ISO), that will have the responsibility and authority to ensure the secure transmission of power and to administer the allocation among participants of the cost that security entails.

EPRI is developing a multiple, intelligent agents-based model and simulation to serve as a "scenario-free" testbed for "what if" studies and computer experiments to study the largely unknown effects from deregulation, unbundling and competition, without requiring any *a priori* assumptions about global scenarios that involve assumed political agendas. Its major constraints will be the laws of physics and the cost or availability of possible technological and economic solutions. Political accommodations and corporate restructuring will appear as global emergent behavior from these locally fixed agents cooperating and/or competing among themselves. This view, of course, has considerable similarity to the mathematical theory of games of strategy, but, unlike the generalized games solved by von Neumann or Nash, these are repeated games with non-zero sum payoffs. [26] Information theoretic considerations are pertinent and these may, in turn, be represented by entropy in the state or phase space in which the system operates.

Early work in this area has emphasized modeling free market forces and competitive strategies as limited only by the physics of electricity and the topology of the grid. Ultimately, the complete model and computer simulation will test how different policies might affect the participants, how much central authority is required, or desirable, and whether free economic cooperation and competition can, by itself, optimize the efficiency and security of network operation for the mutual benefit of all.

8.1   Simulating The Electric Power Market

Experiments with real people engaging in artificial economic systems have shown considerable deviations of actual behavior from theory. To gather more information quickly, researchers have been developing computer simulations by applying various forms of evolutionary algorithms to the modeling of economic systems, especially those embodying financial or commodity markets. [27] Most of these models treat the participants in the economic system as relatively autonomous agents representing individuals or institutions whose strategies can change and evolve as they engage both in competitive and in cooperative behavior so as to survive and prevail in a basically competitive environment. Evolutionary algorithms provide a convenient way to model the bounded rationality of real human beings as contrasted with the perfect rationality assumed by neo-classical economic theory. Studying economic systems using discrete event simulations with multiple adaptive agents makes it easy to include effects of imperfect information as well as the costs and benefits of information. The market, or other economic system, can be started in any prescribed state and the researcher can observe whether equilibrium (or any other hypothesized state) will actually evolve from the actions of the agents. Various strategies and regulations can be prescribed or be allowed to evolve, and the effects of new strategies or regulations can be immediately ascertained.

Commodity markets are a form of Dutch auction in which each prospective seller sets a high price, and reduces it gradually until some buyer accepts the sale at that price. Meanwhile, each prospective buyer sets a low price and gradually raises it until some prospective seller agrees to sell at that price. In simulated auction markets, many intelligent and adaptive agents buy and sell, each with whatever physical and economic constraints the modeler wishes to impose. The simulation provides a general framework but allows behavior to emerge by actual or simulated human interaction with the simulations as with an artificial world. The market and the strategies of the agents evolve in a series of computer experiments which explore the various possible configurations that the market can take subject to different degrees and kinds of cooperation, competition and regulation. Results may include development of conditions for Nash equilibria, strategies that "clear the market", mutually beneficial strategies, the implications of differential information, and the likelihood of "chaos" developing. John Miller, of Carnegie-Mellon University and the Santa Fe Institute (SFI), along with others associated with SFI, has been exploring adaptive models of auction markets. They have run over 66 million auctions on machines. [27]

Bulk electric power has, in the past, been traded between separate electric utilities through bilateral bargaining agreements. With the advent of deregulation and competition in the power industry, "power pool" arrangements that resemble Dutch auction commodity markets are now being set up both by institutions and by private parties. One example is the New York State Power Pool. However, there are significant differences that must be addressed in modeling the electric power market as compared with other commodity markets. Electricity has the shortest shelf-life of any manufactured product. Its perishability is partly compensated by the ability to transport it at almost the speed of light. But the infrastructure required for that transportation is made up of local parts that have limited capacities, and the viability of the whole system depends in an extremely complex way on the performance of each of those parts. In brokering electric power, the locations of the buyer and seller (load and generation) have a significant effect on the price because the cost of delivery depends on all the other deliveries that are being made at that instant.

Software developed under EPRI sponsorship by Gerald Sheblé at Iowa State University [28], and available via the Internet for non-profit use [29], is based on a form of genetic algorithm. It permits the user to observe the changes in strategies used by agent-traders in a bulk power market as they learn from repeated "play" which strategies, theirs and other traders, are the most successful. Each "play" consists of one Dutch style auction where buyers (distributors) raise their bids and sellers (generators) lower their offering prices until the market "clears."

In this project, a fixed schedule for power generation was assumed to exist over a short time horizon. The utility's primary concern in optimization under these conditions is the loading of equipment and the allocation of contracts. The demonstration software, running under Windows on a Pentium PC, uses linear approximations for actual power system operational constraint, but evaluates the interchange bids fast enough to simulate real-time auctioning.

8.2   Risk-Based Contingency Analysis

Planning for the avoidance of system failures, and recovery from those that cannot be avoided, is called "contingency analysis" by the electric utilities. These failures are most often caused by natural forces such as lightning strikes, but may also result from material fatigue or human error. Contingency analysis is typically handled by starting with the actual power flows in the network, removing one component at a time (with replacement) and adding generation as necessary to guarantee uninterrupted operation should that component fail. In the competitive business environment resulting from deregulation, contracts for the delivery of power, formed bilaterally or through an open market, may not all be able to be accommodated by the transmission grid capacity, especially if secure operation must be guaranteed despite component failure.

In a project started in 1996, V. C. Ramesh at the Illinois Institute of Technology is investigating a multiple agent approach to performing risk-based contingency analysis. Two sets of agents are involved, operating orthogonally to each other. In one set, each agent represents a contract between one seller and one buyer of power. The grid is expected to simultaneously transmit the power flows implied by all of them. In the other set, each agent represents one potential major equipment failure, such as a power pole struck by lightning or a transformer explosion. Based on the contracted flows of power in the network, and the probability of the failure each agent represents, the agent for each particular contingency calculates the probable cost of the additional power required to maintain all contracted interchanges after that particular failure. The result is a family of Pareto optimal curves which represent those configurations of the network that provide for security against all the represented contingencies at various degrees of risk. This part of the programming is presently operating under Windows NT on a Pentium PC. The code is written in the form of JAVA applications for ease in transfer to a multiple processor computer system, as would be required for real-time operation. When the second set of agents, each representing a contract, is complete, the resultant Pareto surfaces will represent the trade-off, at various degrees of risk, between the loss resulting from denying a contract versus the loss resulting from accepting it and failing to fulfill it because of some contingency.

8.3   Evolving the New Electric Enterprise

Following the initial efforts toward economic market modeling which were described in Section 8.1, the next step in the development of a comprehensive, high-fidelity, scenario-free modeling and optimization tool began in January, 1997, at Honeywell Technology Center. This project is intended to produce a meaningful first prototype implementation in one year. The first version of this tool will treat several aspects of the operation of the electric power industry in a simplified manner, but it will nevertheless be of immediate benefit to EPRI members for gaining strategic insights into the electricity marketplace. Two specific applications will be implemented in the tool. Candidates include: real-time pricing, co-generation, retail wheeling, and the effects of new technological developments. The base functionality of the tool and the selected applications will be implemented in a PC Windows platform and will feature a graphical user interface designed to be familiar to utility personnel. To the extent practicable, file input/output formats will be adopted that are in common use today, such as the PSS/E data format for transmission networks, so that EPRI members and other users will be able to tailor the applications for their own organizations. The tool is using object-oriented technology, along with a suitably abstract agent model definition, in order to facilitate future enhancements.

This prototype version of the model includes base-classes of the following entities:

G: Generation unit agents
T: Transmission system agents
L: Load agents
C: Corporate agents

The design and implementation of these agents is sufficiently generic as not to limit how users may extend the system by specializing these classes or by defining new ones to allow for different kinds of generation, transmission, load, and corporate agents. It is intended to gradually extend this model and simulation to include all four of the applications mentioned above as well as the effects of trading in futures, options and various derivatives. Further enhancements will emphasize greater fidelity in modeling the implication for each transaction of the resulting power flow (stability, security, etc.) on the existing network.

When complete, this model of the power system, and of the industry, could be used repeatedly for "what if" studies and computer experiments intended to provide insight into the evolution of the entire electric power industry under various forms of exogenous constraints. As these artificial agents evolve in a series of experiments, this simulation should expose the various possible configurations that the market and the industry could take, subject to different degrees and kinds of cooperation, competition and regulation. Possible results will be the development of conditions for equilibria, strategies or regulations that destabilize the market, mutually beneficial strategies, the implications of differential information, and the conditions under which chaotic behavior might develop. Individual companies may use it to examine the potential of entering into new partnerships or attempting to exploit new market segments. In addition, it will serve as a practical way to estimate the benefits of implementing any proposed new technology or making hypothetical changes to existing equipment and operating practices.

9   Distributed Control Of The Electric Power Grid

Following from, and elaborating on, the physical constraints being modeled as part of the economic simulations described in Section 8, EPRI is pursuing a conceptual design for real-time, distributed control of the power system of the next century by intelligent agents operating locally with minimal supervisory control. The design integrates modeling, computation, sensing and control to meet the goals of efficiency and security in a geographically distributed system, subject to unavoidable natural disasters, and operated by partly competing and partly cooperating business organizations.

The computational model underlying this distributed control system will employ multiple intelligent agents to represent individual components of the grid - generators, transformers, buses - as if they were intelligent robots ("softbots"), cooperating and sometimes competing to keep the whole system operating in the most efficient manner despite whatever contingencies might befall it.

Each isolatable component of the electric power grid will be represented by an agent of limited intelligence which seeks to ensure its own survival while optimizing its performance in the context of the other agents. For instance, a single bus will strive to stay within its voltage and power flow limits while still operating in the context of the voltages and flows imposed on it by the combination of other agents representing generators, loads, transformers, etc. All lines, and most other components, have safety and capacity restrictions which are relatively "soft." High and low voltage limits, for instance, may not be exceeded by specified percentages for more than specified time periods. Maximum thermal limits, expressed in megavolt-amperes (MVA), are also set in percentage-time, but, ultimately, most over-stressed components would melt and overhead lines would sag until they caused a short circuit to the earth.

Any specific class of component may have additional survival constraints which may not be exceeded and, if exceeded, may require replacement or off-line maintenance. For instance, the chemical state of the oil bath in a large transformer must stay within specified limits for safe operation. Its state may be tested periodically by taking samples, or instrumentation may be installed for continuous monitoring. The cost-benefit of this instrumentation for each transformer is an example of the management information the distributed model and simulation will provide.

More complex components, such as a generating plant or a substation, will be analyzed using object-oriented methods to model them as class and object hierarchies of simpler components. In addition to being a natural way to implement multi-agent simulations, object oriented programming is also a convenient technology for building libraries of reusable software and, in this case, will facilitate the exchange of agent (component) descriptions and potential improvements among EPRI's members and all interested researchers in the electric power community. These agents and subagents, represented as semi-autonomous "active objects," can be made to evolve by using a combination of genetic algorithms and genetic programming. In this context, classes are treated as an analogy of biological genotypes and the objects instantiated from them as an analogy of their phenotypes.

Class attributes, which may stand for characteristics, capabilities, limitations or strategies possessed by potential agents, can be selected and recombined when instantiating objects to form different individuals by the operations typical of genetic algorithms, such as crossover and mutation. The physics of each component will determine its allowable strategies and behaviors. Existing instrumentation and control capabilities will be augmented in computer experiments with hypothetical capabilities which could be made optional in order to evaluate their benefit and the actual way in which their use might evolve. The operational parts of each class, its services or methods, may also be evolved through genetic programming using similar techniques. Success or "fitness" in this context combines the agent's own survival with meeting the global security and efficiency goals.

A recent project has produced an Integrated Knowledge Framework (IKF) that describes the management and operational functions at a generic, coal-fired, steam power plant. [30, 31] This framework identifies the data, information and knowledge required for the important functions typically performed at a fossil power plant, as well as the flow of that data, information and knowledge between the function that generates it and those that use it. The project was conducted by a team of utility, EPRI, and equipment vendor personnel led by the author. The resultant, object-oriented model contains 422 classes, interconnected through three different types of relations. While not solely developed as a design for distributed agent control and containing many classes which would not be appropriate for instantiation as active objects, this model defines, at an abstract level, all the structure needed to model the generation aspects of electric power with intelligent agents.

9.1   Issues: Time, Credit, Communication

A major issue in the design of agents is the interplay of short and long term evolution to provide real-time adaptation to events that can only be anticipated in a very general way, viz., lighting strikes. In the longer time frame, the softbots must learn new strategies and/or modify old ones in such a way that they can become better able to handle real-time control. Their long term fitness should be based mainly on the evolution of strategies for cooperation, methods for raising the sum of the game for all players. [32, 33] However, their strategies for short term operation must adapt in real-time and may create temporary conflicts in real-time control, which must also be resolved in that same time frame. To reduce conflicts in the short term requires "look ahead" for real-time resolution. The strategies for where and how to "look" must have evolved over the long term. This is complicated in the electric power system case by the occurrence of non-ergodic effects. The state of the network after a failure, for instance, does not always allow a determination of the root cause of the problem. An analysis of the sequence of events may be necessary. While recovery from the degraded state may not hinge on knowing the root cause, efficient recovery and future prevention would.

Credit assignment is not particularly difficult when the situation provides immediate reward and/or precise information about the effects of actions taken. [34] However, in the present case, the large number of parallel decisions and actions make it difficult to determine in real-time the exact benefits to the overall system of each individual's behavior. The present plan is to address this by taking advantage of the large number of individual components of each class that are found in the network. For purposes of long term evolution, they are treated as members of the same species so that combinations of strategies that were beneficial for real-time operation tend to be preserved and spread over the components of that same type.

Since individual agents are expected to collaborate and, indeed, are "in it together" as far as successful operation of the whole grid is concerned, it would appear necessary that they all have complete information about each other's state, actions and even decisions to take actions. However, this degree of detailed communication is not practical because of the combination of elapsed time and bandwidth that would be required. Therefore, it is assumed that each individual agent, in its own context, will contain a very rudimentary model (representation) of the entire system, which will also be subject to the long term evolution process. Only information about exceptions will be transmitted intentionally and explicitly over communication channels set up for that purpose. Even the frequency of these exception messages can be reduced by employing "tags" [34] that might include unused capacity, reaction (ramp-up) time, etc. communicated as standing messages that remain valid until revised. However, the electric power grid itself provides some virtually instantaneous information about its own state that is available locally to each component through instrumentation that would be required in any case. Local voltage, current and frequency will not provide all the necessary information but they can produce a first order approximation on which exception reporting can then be based.

9.2 Bridging Continuous and Discrete Models

Individual agent-based models are most commonly and conveniently realized as discrete event simulations. However, the electric power system is conventionally modeled with continuous differential equations. Of course, these equations are typically solved by some discrete numerical technique, but it is still necessary for the new model being developed to provide a common ground and smooth transition between discrete and continuous approaches to the same phenomena.

In a project, started in 1994 at San Jose State University, Rudy Rucker and his students are developing techniques for using cellular automata (CA) to model certain aspects of the power grid. [35] The long term goal is to perfect a distributed-computation simulation of the global behavior of a circuit (viz., stability) based on the local behavior of the individual components, and to test this approach by examining possible CA representations of power quality (harmonics, load induced transients, etc.) where cells might represent individual loads (viz., appliances) within a building.

A cellular-automaton implementation of partial differential equations has been developed, including: the heat equation, the wave equation (or telegrapher's equation), the damped driven oscillator, the damped driven oscillator coupled with the wave equation, and the Fermi-Pasta-Ulam non-linear soliton wave. These simulations have never before been implemented as pure cellular automata. The CA implementation makes it possible to rapidly explore alternate parameter settings, to breed and mutate parameter settings, and to view space-time diagrams of the simulation in real time. The latest release, CAPOW 5.0 (Cellular Automata Power Simulator, Version 5), has been made available as freeware, for non-profit use only, and posted on the Internet. [36] This 32 bit, Windows 95, or Windows NT program includes the necessary support files that allow a user to define rules by writing small C++ code modules and compiling them into *.DLL files.

Research is continuing on how best to use this software for real world problems, as well as on extending these techniques to branching networks and to higher-dimensional systems. This modeling approach, while it makes use of computations carried out by local rules on a spatially extended lattice, does not include any explicit intelligence or agency in the individual cells. However, genetic algorithms have been used to guide the evolution of CA, [37] and that possibility will be explored.

9.3 Neural Network For Operator Interface Simplification

Even with complete automation, the dispatcher of electric power must be kept aware of the information required to supervise the network by setting goals and intervening as necessary. Bernard Widrow and his students at Stanford University are beginning to derive a practical way to use a neural network as an interface between the dispatcher and the real power system. They are developing a new reward/punishment algorithm for neural network learning: "learning-with-a-critic," which can be used for fast training of a neural network under any performance criterion. Trained on-line by this method, the network would provide a model system of reduced complexity but of sufficient richness to make full use of the dispatcher's experience and knowledge. Under the supervision of the dispatcher, it would process the vast number of detailed control actions that must take place in precisely the correct order required for safe transitions between system states.

10   Summary

The Electric Power Research Institute (EPRI) has applied neural networks, fuzzy logic and genetic algorithms for control and optimization of electric power generation, delivery, and use. EPRI has also been attempting to develop performance verification and automated design methods for intelligent and adaptive systems so that they can be readily used in engineering applications where reliability and safety are paramount. Most of EPRI's current research into intelligent techniques is directed at the use of multiple, adaptive, intelligent agents to model and simulate the control of the power grid, the economics of power markets, and the evolution of the power industry under deregulation.

11 References

[1]   Electric Power Research Institute (1995), *Hourly Load Forecasting Using Artificial Neural Networks*, Technical Report, TR-105278, EPRI Dist. Ctr., Pleasant Hill, CA (Sep.).

[2]   Electric Power Research Institute (1994), *Optimization of the Unit Commitment Problem by a Coupled Gradient Network and by a Genetic Algorithm*, Technical Report, TR-103697, EPRI Dist. Ctr., Pleasant Hill, CA (May).

[3]   Electric Power Research Institute (1994), *Applications of Artificial Neural Networks in Multi-Area Generation Scheduling With Fuzzy Data*, Technical Report, TR-104219, EPRI Dist. Ctr., Pleasant Hill, CA (Jul.)

[4]   Electric Power Research Institute (1996), *High-Power Electronics Advanced Technology Program*. Brochure, BR-1006800, EPRI Dist. Ctr., Pleasant Hill, CA.

[5]   Liu, K., R.R. Shoults and F.L. Lewis (1994), Load-Frequency Control (LFC) Via Fuzzy Logic. *Mission Earth: Modeling and Simulation for a Sustainable Future, Proceedings of the 1995 Western Multiconference* (Las Vegas, Nevada, Jan. 15-18), Society for Computer Simulation, San Diego, CA, USA, pp. 35-45.

[6]   Electric Power Research Institute (1996), *Proceedings: 1996 Heat Rate Improvement Conference*, Technical Report, TR-106529, EPRI Dist. Ctr., Pleasant Hill, CA (May).

[7]   Electric Power Research Institute (1995), *Development of Neural Network Controllers for Power Industry Applications: Volumes 1 & 2*, Technical Report, TR-106533-V1/2, EPRI Dist. Ctr., Pleasant Hill, CA (Nov.).

[8]   Annaswamy, A.M. (1994), Recursive Parameter Estimation Using Theta-Adaptive Neural Networks, *Mission Earth: Modeling and Simulation for a Sustainable Future, Proceedings of the 1995 Western Multiconference*, (Las Vegas, Nevada, Jan. 15-18), Society for Computer Simulation, San Diego, CA, USA, pp. 7-14.

[9]   Grefenstette, J.J. ed. (1987), *Genetic Algorithms and Their Applications: Proceedings of the Second International Conference on Genetic Algorithms*. (Cambridge, MA, July 1987) Lawrence Erlbaum, Hillsdale, NJ.

[10]   Roache, E.A., K.A. Hickok, K.F. Loje, M.W. Hunt and J.J. Grefenstette (1995), Genetic Algorithms for Expert System Validation, ° *Mission Earth: Modeling and Simulation for a Sustainable Future, Proceedings of the 1995*

Western Multiconference, (Las Vegas, Nevada, Jan. 15-18), Society for Computer Simulation, San Diego, CA, pp. 45-51.

[11] Electric Power Research Institute (1996), *Genetic Algorithm Testbed for Expert System Testing,* Technical Report, TR-106004, EPRI Dist. Ctr., Pleasant Hill, CA (Jan.).

[12] Electric Power Research Institute (1994), *Genetic Optimization of Neural Network Architecture,* Technical Report, TR-104074, EPRI Dist. Ctr., Pleasant Hill, CA (Mar.).

[13] Harp, S.A., and T. Samad (1994), Genetic Algorithms and Neural Networks for Optimized Modeling and Control, *Mission Earth: Modeling and Simulation for a Sustainable Future, Proceedings of the 1995 Western Multiconference* (Las Vegas, Nevada, Jan. 15-18), Society for Computer Simulation, San Diego, CA, pp. 14-23.

[14] Wildberger, A.M. (1994), Alleviating the Opacity of Neural Nets. *Proceedings of IEEE International Conference on Neural Networks,* (Orlando, FL, June 26-July 2), Vol. IV, pp. 2373-2376.

[15] Minsky, M. (1991), Logical versus Analogical or Symbolic versus Connectionist or Neat versus Scruffy, *AI Magazine,* Vol. 12, pp. 34 - 51.

[16] Wildberger, A.M. and K.A. Hickok (1989), Introduction to Neural Networks, In *Advances in AI and Simulation,* R. Uttamsingh and A.M. Wildberger, eds., Society for Computer Simulation, San Diego, CA, pp. 227-232.

[17] Abe, S., M. Kayama, H. Takenaga, and T. Kitamura (1993), Extracting Algorithms from Pattern Classification Networks, *Neural Networks* 6, no. 5, pp. 729-735.

[18] Hassoun, M. and P. Watta (1991), Exact Associative Neural Memory Dynamics Utilizing Boolean Matrices, *IEEE Trans. Neural Networks,* Vol. 2, pp. 437-448

[19] Sethi, I.K. and J.H. Yoo (1992), SIR: Simultaneous Induction of Rules Using Neural Networks, *Proc. Int'l Joint Conf. Neural Networks,* Baltimore, Vol. 1, pp. 359-364.

[20] Sethi, I.K., J.H. Yoo, and C. Brickman (1993), Extraction of Diagnostic Rules Using Neural Networks, *Proc. Sixth Annual IEEE Computer-Based Medical Systems Symposium* (Ann Arbor, June), pp. 217-222.

[21] Electric Power Research Institute (1994), *Fuzzy Logic,* Technical Brief, TB-103725, EPRI Dist. Ctr., Pleasant Hill, CA (Jan.).

[22] Wildberger, A.M. (1995), The Hard Part of Soft Computing, *Soft Computing: Rough Sets, Fuzzy Logic, Neural Networks, Uncertainty Management, Knowledge Discovery,* T.Y. Lin and A.M. Wildberger, eds., Society for Computer Simulation, San Diego, CA, pp. 236-239.

[23]   Eilenberg, S. and N. Steenrod (1952), *Foundations of Algebraic Topology*, Princeton University Press, Princeton, NJ.

[24]   Pawlak, Z. (1982), Rough Sets, *International Journal of Computer and Information Sciences*, Vol. 11, pp. 341-356.

[25]   Lin, T.Y. (1994), Fuzzy Logic Controller and Rough Logic, *Soft Computing: Rough Sets, Fuzzy Logic, Neural Network, Uncertainty Management and Knowledge Discovery*, Society for Computer Simulation, San Diego, CA, pp. 125-129.

[26]   Nash, J.F. (1953), Two-Person Cooperative Games, *Econometrica*, 21, pp. 128-140.

[27]   Friedman, D. and J. Rust, eds. (1993), *The Double Auction Market*, Addison Wesley, Reading, MA.

[28]   Electric Power Research Institute (1997), *Computer Simulation of Adaptive Agents for an Electric Power Auction*, Technical Report, TR106975, EPRI Dist. Ctr., Pleasant Hill, CA.

[29]   Sheblé, G. (gsheble@iastate.edu) (1997), MARKET.ZIP, from Web site, http://vulcan.ee.iastate.edu/~sheble/download.html.

[30]   Electric Power Research Institute (1996), *Integrated Knowledge Framework (IKF) for Coal-Fired Power Plants*, Technical Report, TR-106211-V1/2/3, EPRI Dist. Ctr., Pleasant Hill, CA (Mar.).

[31]   Wildberger, A.M. (1997), Object-Oriented, Integrated Knowledge Framework for Electric Power Plants, *Proceedings of Object-Oriented Simulation Conference (OOS'97)*, Society for Computer Simulation, San Diego, CA, pp. 3-10.

[32]   Axelrod, R. (1994), *The Evolution of Cooperation*, Basic Books, New York City, NY.

[33]   Brams, S.T. and W. Mattli (1993), Theory of Moves: Overview and Examples, *Conflict Management and Peace Science*, 12(2), pp. 1-29.

[34]   Holland, J.H. (1993), *The Effect of Labels (Tags) on Social Interactions*, Technical Report, SFI 93-10-064, Santa Fe Institute, Santa Fe, NM.

[35]   Electric Power Research Institute (1994), *Evolutionary Computing*, Technical Brief, TB-104097, EPRI Dist. Ctr., Pleasant Hill, CA (Jun.).

[36]   Rucker, R. (rucker@jupiter.sjsu.edu) (1997), CAPOW5.ZIP, from WEB site, http://www.mathcs.sjsu.edu/capow/.

[37]   Crutchfield, J.P. and Mitchell, M. (1994), *The Evolution of Emergent Computation*, Technical Report, SFI 94-03-012, Santa Fe Institute, Santa Fe, NM.

INDEX